Contents

page		
10	**① Preliminaries**	
12		• Foreword *Howard Mandel*
18		• Acknowledgments *Daniela Veronesi*
22		• About This Book *Daniela Veronesi*
24		• Editor's Notes *Daniela Veronesi*
28		• On Conduction: My Experience with Butch Morris *J.A. Deane*
30		• An Exceptional Reciprocity *Allan Graubard*
32	**② The Art of Conduction** *Lawrence D. "Butch" Morris*	
33		• Conduction Definition
34		• The "Extra Dimension"
38		• Comprehending Conduction
40	**③ Introduction to the Conduction Lexicon** *Lawrence D. "Butch" Morris*	
42		• Directives
43		• The Conductor
45		• The Instrumentalist
46		• The Ensemble
47		• Practice and Performance
48	**④ The Conduction Lexicon** *Lawrence D. "Butch" Morris*	
50		• Classification of Directives
52		• The Process of Conduction: Basic Parameters
54 – 157		• Conduction Directives
		- Directive Activation
		- Directive Endings
		- Dynamics
		- Articulation
		- Repeats
		- Time-Tempo-Pulse/Rhythm
		- Tempo Modifications
		- Tonality/Pitch
		- Evolutionary Transformations
		- Events
		- Effects/Instrument-Specific Directives
		- Score-Related Directives

page	158	⑤ Personal Notes *Lawrence D. "Butch" Morris*
	160	• An Interview with "Butch" Morris
	162	• Notes and Sketches
	172	• In Conversation

	174	⑥ How to use the Conduction Lexicon *Daniela Veronesi and J.A. Deane*
	176	• Suggested Teaching Order *J.A. Deane*
	178	• Exercises *J.A. Deane and Daniela Veronesi*
	180	• Types of Downbeats *Daniela Veronesi*

	182	⑦ "Butch" Morris and the Evolution of Conduction® *Daniela Veronesi*
	184	• A Biography
	187	• A Name, a Lexicon, a Practice: Some Notes on the Evolution of Conduction

	190	⑧ Conduction Chronology and Discography
	192	• Conduction Chronology
	214	• Conduction Discography

| | 218 | Contributors |

Preliminaries 1

Foreword

Howard Mandel

Humans play with sound. It's one of the unique, and defining activities of our species. The possibilities of what comes from such play are infinite, but any notable result is a balanced integration of imaginative freedom and skilled control.

Those precepts underlie the music of Lawrence Douglas "Butch" Morris (1947-2013), especially his lexicon of hand directives – signs and gestures devised and refined for creative, compositional utilization in group improvisations, the practice of which Morris called Conduction®. That lexicon is the heart of this book, *The Art of Conduction*, Morris's meticulously planned and detailed instructional legacy.

Conduction emerges from what seems to be a basic need of people who want to make up music as they go; improvising, rather than laboring to reproduce what someone else has written. The dream of improvisers – the very *ideal* of improvisation, imagined ever since the emergence in 1958 of iconic iconoclast Ornette Coleman and even back to the days of Buddy Bolden as within the grasp of jazz musicians – is that beautiful, rich, multipart music can be created whole cloth, spontaneously, by suitably attuned individuals with no or very little preparation.

Yet in reality meaningful group improvisation is only possible if the whole cloth's constituent threads are indeed woven together, typically on a loom of tradition or some other agreed upon framework. It's all a question of organization: whether or how improvisers systematize themselves. Some principle must serve to unite individuals toward collective goals, and this is what Morris offers with Conduction – which preserves, as well, the freedom of the collective's every individual.

The cultures of Africa, Persia and Asia that historically excelled at improvisational music did so on the basis of rules for tonality, scales or modes and rhythmic patterns dictated (or generated) by age-old customs. In addition, the music was most often monophonic – a single melodic line. Conductors were not required. Tradition conveyed through oral instruction was itself the conductor of the way the music would be played. Individuals were free to create, within fixed – however capacious – guidelines.

In contrast, Western musical culture led to the development of written scores that inscribed the explicit instructions of individual composers regarding pitch, duration, attack, and structure, almost exclusively within the confines of a devoutly embraced harmonic universe. That universe was often depicted as having multitude parts and contrasting or even conflicting

 Preliminaries

dimensions. Conductors acted as the midwives or mediators for those composers, interlocutors meant to help ensembles realize their scores' commands in large part by focusing on the composition's facets, mindful as the composer himself.

Inevitably, necessarily and irrepressibly, conductors add their own interpretations to compositions. They may recast the compositions dramatically, but they don't commonly face an ensemble or an audience without a composition or equivalent elements of theme, sonic resources and duration to start with, intending to conjure sonatas much less symphonies as they go by using whatever notes selected in the moment by the musicians themselves.

That's what Morris did, simultaneously broadening a conductor's compositional responsibilities and giving overt determination of musical content to ensembles' constituent members.

"Music notation is symbolic of music, just like writing is symbolic of speech," Morris once told an interviewer on National Public Radio (NPR). "What I wanted to do and why I started doing this in the first place is I realized there is a great divide between what is notated and what is created. I wanted to understand what that divide was."

Over the course of thirty-five years Morris delved deeply into the question, and eventually found a path toward bridging the gap. He devised and refined a silent vocabulary that can be readily understood by anyone on earth with eyes and ears. He construed a universally accessible symbolic language rooted in the ancient practice of chironomy – hand movements – that can be transformed into sound. He came to understand that he had in Conduction a didactic tool, of use in widening and deepening the musicianship of any who seriously took it up.

Morris's accomplishments have already been presented worldwide; see the Conduction Chronology of some two-hundred concerts held from Brooklyn to Buenos Aires, Istanbul to Tokyo. Now that you hold *The Art of Conduction* in your hands, you may soon be able to employ the discipline and enjoy the benefits of Conduction, too.

To start with: As music precedes speech, physical gestures precede writing, so in the name of immediacy as well as universality Morris chose the conductors' medium for transmitting information. The section titled "Directives" (Chapter 3) details Morris's static hand/baton signs, designed to indicate entrances and endings, among other actions, and moving hand/arm gestures to (in his words) "visually express or demonstrate sonic ideas."

Nothing in Conduction denotes or implies a musician's individual contribution to the collective sound. Indeed, throughout *The Art of Conduction* Morris repeatedly encourages players to express themselves originally, within an atmosphere of mutual support or teamwork. As J.A. Deane, one of Morris's closest collaborators who has become among the most experienced and incisive practitioners of Conduction, writes: "An energetic feedback loop develops between the symbolic (conductor) and the sonic (ensemble); and through this energetic exchange, a musical form emerges *on its own*." So saying, Deane asserts that Conduction actually does enable the improvisers' ideal, allowing individuals who've mastered the lexicon to work together to summon up never-before-imagined musical complexity without predetermination, in real time.

Of course, Morris has not been alone in looking for answers to eduring musical challenges. For the past century and a half or so Western modernists have subjected all artistic conventions to first principle critiques, proposing several genuinely radical, highly conceptualized alternatives to long-established premises. At the same time, consumers of Western popular culture have ever more fervently embraced music they like whether anyone authoritative or credentialed considers it "good" or not. The crowd seems to favor obvious energies and life-like emotions.

In this context, jazz musicians – and Morris was avowedly a jazz musician – evolved to become the most daring present-day contingent of professional composing performers or improvising interpreters. Jazz musicians are congenitally or ideologically driven to make music new, believing music must both gratify musicians and contain some accessible appeal to the listening public.

Such appeal, Morris suggests here in his essay "The Extra Dimension," relies on "the essence of swing." Elsewhere in this book he declares that the opportunity for improvisers to improvise and for interpreters to interpret *the same material* is what makes Conduction possible. So, according to Morris, inherent momentum and the option of return are fundamental to its viability. Such assertions were not born of sudden epiphanies; Morris thought about his methodology long and hard before arriving at his conclusions.

His musical journey had its twists and turns. He played trumpet as a teenager, first influenced by Dizzy Gillespie and Clifford Brown, later by Don Cherry and Booker Little. Upon hearing Gil Evans's orchestral arrangements of *Porgy and Bess* featuring Miles Davis, Morris set himself to learning whatever other instruments he could find. His experiences jamming around Los Angeles, transcribing arrangements for a recording studio and eventually practicing music in the cab of the ambulance he drove as a soldier in Vietnam all shaped his ambitions. After discharge from military service, Morris gained communitarian perspective making music with Horace Tapscott's Pan-Afrikan Peoples Arkestra in Watts, and soon thereafter in Oakland, where he attended workshops convened by drummer Charles Moffett.

"Charles would lead his ensemble rehearsals with no music," Morris is quoted as saying in an article in *DownBeat* magazine. "He would just conduct, with a relatively undeveloped vocabulary of gestures. I knew it could be taken further." In the same piece, Morris recalled a conversation he'd had with a college professor of conducting. "I asked my teacher, 'How to you get the orchestra to go back to letter B?' and she said, 'You don't do that.' That's when I knew I had a profession."

His emergence as a jazz conductor dates to the debut of saxophonist David Murray's Big Band in New York in 1978. At the time, the bandleaders Gil Evans and Sun Ra – both of whom Morris was familiar with – used improvisatory cues during their large ensemble sprawling sets, rather as Count Basie's 1930s Kansas City Orchestra employed "head arrangements."

However, both Evans and Ra had band books filled with at least sketches of parts and charts. Both bandleaders fronted ensembles whose members worked with them often and knew their ways. Both were keyboardists, able to quickly voice and launch a familiar theme, signify soloists (who had considerable latitude to sculpt their own statements) and wave in diverse motifs or sections. The freewheeling aesthetic of the era suited both Evans's and Ra's tastes. Both their ensembles tended to be wild and expansive, exciting if likely to veer out of control.

Morris's conducting of "Duet for Big Band," a sixteen-minute track on Murray's 1984 album *Live at Sweet Basil, vol. 1* (Black Saint), provides a glimpse of how he employed his nascent lexicon of directives within such nominally "jazz" spheres (Evans's orchestra had a weekly gig at Sweet Basil, and Ra's Arkestra played there, too). At first, tubaist Bob Stewart puffs four notes to the bar in time with bassist Fred Hopkins and drummer Billy Higgins hitting his snare drum's rim. Imagine them following Morris's downbeat. Then the bass slips out from under the tuba; envision Morris's right arm crooked over his head, his hand slightly clasped so his forefinger protrudes, flicking a pulse that slows the beat and calls for sounds from Hopkins's bass or Stewart's tuba in unpredictable alternation.

It's as if Morris is trying to catch one or the other off guard. But next he draws a syncopated rhythm from these player's staggered notes, and that catchy figure pulls in the entire band, an eleven-tet whose individuals swirl around each other as in early jazz polyphonic style. They are not anarchic, though – throughout Morris manages dynamic crescendos and diminuendos, and summons a variety of repeated motifs – riffs – from single or partnered instruments.

"I'm a jazz musician," Morris said on NPR. "I know what I am. Whether the music you think I'm playing or professing is jazz or not is kind of not my problem, you know what I mean?" Few fans in 1984 would have argued that what Morris did with Murray wasn't jazz, but they might not have so classified Morris's official Conduction no. 1: *Current Trends in Racism in Modern America*.

That piece was forged against the backdrop of efforts to reform group improvisation attempted by such East Village composer-performers as John Zorn and Elliott Sharp, who lived across the street from Morris and with whom he occasionally collaborated. Zorn, who used elaborate board games to jump-start open-ended musicians' interactions, and Sharp, who experimented in his compositions with algorithms and aleatory elements, were informed by jazz but didn't self-identify with its lineage. No matter: Morris, secure in his personal roots, was free of genre bias and ready to follow musical ideas wherever they might lead.

When downtown music fans flocked to the Kitchen, a performance loft in Manhattan's Soho district, on the cold night of February 1, 1985, to hear Morris's *Current Trends,* no one knew what to expect. As he later wrote in liner notes to the 10-CD album *Testament*: *A Conduction Collection* (New World Records, 1995), he was searching for a manner in which to "further develop

THE ART OF CONDUCTION

an ensemble music of collective imagination – not in any way to downplay a soloist, but to have the ensemble featured at all times." His doctrine was that "collective improvisation must have a prime focus, and the use of notation alone [is] not enough for the contemporary improviser." From that basis he had arrived at the concept and term "conduction," to signify both "conducted improvisation" and "the physical aspect of communication and heat."

Both those phrases can be related not only to Morris's musical concept, but also to current trends in racism in modern America today, in 2017, just as in 1985. Is it an exaggeration or misapprehension to perceive "trends" in day-to-day relations among Americans acting on some level with considerations of race as amounting to the aggregation of the improvised behavior of each such American? Or that each individual's race-related responses are channeled, guided, *conducted* by social policies and historical forces? To acknowledge that physical aspects of "communication and heat" have fueled attitudes and assumptions regarding "race" since the founding of America and probably long before is to agree that the topic Morris chose for Conduction no. 1 was a perfect reflection of his musical initiative.

In Conduction no. 1, as in American race relations, individuals' actions matter, but are typically subsumed into a larger ensemble sound, a field of social projections. Particular individual and group reactions may be requested and sequenced but are not completely controlled and may possibly not be successfully executed. Those who live in the present, whether musicians or simply citizens, do what they can and what they will. To believe one can exert total control over an outpouring of music or advance of history is to be delusional and/or tyrannical.

Morris understood all this, and in consequence shored up the cooperative aspects of Conduction to mitigate individual musicians' "mistakes," and guard against conductors' tendencies toward self-centered control. It is one of the outstanding hallmarks of Conduction that its creator envisioned it to be an "act of communion, a place where all musicians from any background could navigate and give of themselves in an earnest engagement of mind." Over the course of his career, Morris was able to successfully introduce not only jazz-related ensembles and new music groups, but also classical symphony orchestras, virtuosi of the indigenous musics of Turkey and Japan, spoken word artists and combinations of all of the above to Conduction. To master Morris's lexicon of directives requires patient study, but even a cursory glance at the directives as Morris demonstrates them in the drawings here will stir readers to consider the deepest elements of sound production, projection and expression, from which music is born.

Here there are no staffs to read, no keys to know, no meters to count, but instead a stimulating new mind-set to absorb and adopt. Morris hoped Conduction would be a practice freely shared and widely adopted for its value as an instrument of musical investigation and experimentation, so *The Art of Conduction* is meant to be a workbook, presenting the set of signals by which musicians can communicate and create together clearly enough for quick implementation. Morris insisted that Conduction was more than a style

or genre, a game, a system for the extrapolation of motifs or a process by which musicians could impose their wills on each other. He conceived Conduction so that humans across all boundaries and borders could play music with each other more fluidly, fluently and with more compelling interaction than ever before.

It is up to the students and practitioners of Conduction to make that happen, and already many have. Direct associates of Morris, such as Deane, Greg Tate and Wayne Horvitz, have become adept at applying his directives to their performances. Other musicians who had tangential contact with Morris or perhaps had only heard of his work have begun to employ something like chironomy, if not Conduction itself, in Morris's wake. There are other large improvising ensembles now, conducted more or less spontaneously by estimable Walter Thompson, Adam Rudolph and Karl Berger, each of whom has developed his own processes, but Conduction as Morris formulated and outlined it offers insights and guidelines beyond what others have done to date.

Someday that may change. As Morris knew, the possibilities resulting from a balanced integration of imaginative freedom and skilled control are infinite. But so far, no analysis of the issues confronted by improvising ensembles and no effective approach to resolving those issues rivals the essays and lexicon of directives Lawrence Douglas "Butch" Morris prepared for *The Art of Conduction*.

Acknowledgments

Daniela Veronesi

It has been a great privilege for me to participate in the evolution of this book, in collaboration and friendship with Butch Morris. Being part of this project has opened new doors to my appreciation of music – from inside the creative process – in ways I could have never imagined; for this, and for sharing with me his passion and curiosity for music and life, I will always be grateful to Butch.

When I first met him in New York in late 2002, I knew nothing about Conduction. But over the next decade I had the opportunity to listen as well as *watch* Butch conducting on stage, work with him on a provisional Italian translation of his *Conduction® Workbook*, and later assist him during some workshops in Italy. This gave me a unique familiarity with this extraordinary way of making music together, and allowed me – from a peripheral, yet revealing, backstage perspective – to be part of it.

As time went by, I became more and more involved in Conduction, and not just as an enthusiastic listener. I found that my academic interest in languages and social interaction added a new dimension to my collaboration with Butch and my fascination with his way of working, especially in the intimate setting of the workshops. There, I had the chance to observe the challenges Conduction posed for ensemble *and* conductor, as well as witness the palpable thrill they all experienced when it was "happening." How much trust, skill, and imagination must it have taken to make it "happen"? What exactly was the nature of Butch's conducting gestures, so precisely codified on paper in his Conduction Lexicon, and yet so expressive and natural when used in the midst of practice and performance? Butch and I talked a lot about these issues; he was always ready to answer questions, and he never let you go without asking one in return.

I see *The Art of Conduction – A Conduction® Workbook* as a way of continuing those intense conversations, as well as an open invitation to anyone – be they a musician, teacher, or scholar – to join in. Together with the Lawrence Butch Morris Legacy Project, I am deeply thankful to all those who provided support, talked things over, read, wrote, or offered comments and suggestions. In doing so, they have made it possible to honor Morris's legacy with this book, and to offer it for all the many conversations, musical and non-musical, to come.

A small team of people was initially involved in making this book happen: Alexandre Morris, Alessandro Cassin, J.A. Deane ("Dino"), Allan Grau-

Preliminaries

bard, and myself. I owe the biggest debt of gratitude to Alexandre Morris, who enthusiastically believed in our endeavor from the very beginning, and was committed to fulfilling his father's wish to complete his book on Conduction and make it available to the music community. Thanks to Alexandre's openness, trust, and generosity, I was also able to consult Morris's unpublished, private writings: handwritten notes, sketches, and older versions of the *Conduction® Workbook* that I did not have from my own correspondence with Morris – an amazingly rich and revealing source of information that was crucial in gaining clarity and understanding as we revised the manuscript.

I am also indebted to Alessandro Cassin, who supervised the whole editorial project, and was a constant presence behind this book. Over the past few years, as we struggled to put it together, Alessandro was my biggest supporter, dealing with the many practical aspects – from fundraising to legal matters – that needed to be constantly addressed, and providing guidance and constructive criticism on each chapter of this book, and at every stage of the project. His personal committment, materially, intellectually, and emotionally, was invaluable to me, and he has been essential in bringing this work to completion.

As co-editor of the chapters "The Art of Conduction" and "Introduction to the Conduction Lexicon," Allan Graubard has been a treasured ally in this undertaking, and has my gratitude; so has Dino, who joined forces with me in revising the Conduction Lexicon, and putting together other chapters in the book. When he offered to "help" very soon after Morris's passing, he didn't know how much work – and innumerable discussions on Skype and over email – this would involve. For his dedication, and his openness and sensitivity in discussing – repeatedly – even the tiniest detail, I am very grateful to Dino, and I'll always treasure the gift of his kind soul and friendship.

During the revision of Morris's lexicon – illustrated in chapter 4 – a number of musicians generously gave us feed back, helping Dino and myself to refine it draft after draft, and to whom goes our thanks and appreciation: Henry Threadgill, Donato Cabrera, Kenny Wollesen, Stephanie Richards, Douglas Wieselman, Andrea Parkins, Jean-Paul Bourelly, Myra Melford, Brandon Ross, and Steve Coleman. Special thanks also to Cliff Korman and Mark Zanter who, at an early stage, provided the extensive criticism we needed to move forward.

Then, as *The Art of Conduction* was taking a more definitive shape, I was fortunate enough to have the assistance of Laoise Mac Reamoinn, who copyedited the entire revised manuscript, with sensitivity and brilliant attention to detail, patiently pondering options and solutions with me. Her questions, comments, and suggestions made the text more readable and hopefully more useful. To her, my heartfelt thanks.

Concetta Nasone and Massimo Golfieri – who took care, with openness, skill, and creativity, of the not easy task of designing the book in a way that would best convey Morris's ideas and educational goals – I would also like to acknowledge and thank here. They have both been great companions in this enterprise. Luciano Rossetti, who generously provided photographic material for the project, taking the time to repeatedly search his archive, I am as grateful.

Special thanks to David Hammons, who allowed us to base the cover on his artwork, and who brought the idea of this book to Brendan Dugan and Karma. Alfio, Amiya, Margit, Daniela, and Silvia, and many others too numerous to list here, I deeply thank for constantly encouraging me during the past three years.

This project would not have been possible without the generous support of a number of institutions and individuals. Together with the Lawrence Butch Morris Legacy Project I would like to express my deepest gratitude to Jack Tilton and the Tilton Gallery, and to Ahmet Uluğ, Cem Yegül, Ayşegül Turfan, and Pozitif, who believed strongly in Morris's work and in the very idea of this book, and provided the material conditions to bring it to conclusion. For their invaluable support, our thanks also to all listed as "Contributors to The Art of Conduction" (see p. 21).

When Butch and I were revising the "Conduction Lexicon" for what would be our last time together, in early 2013, he asked me if I wanted to "take care" of his book, and gave me the following advice: *Make it clear, elegant, and "travelable."* I hope that our team, and all the people who joined us along the way in this extraordinary, challenging, and revealing journey have come close to fulfilling that wish.

Contributors to *The Art of Conduction – A Conduction® Workbook*

- Jack Tilton and the Tilton Gallery
- Ahmet Uluğ, Cem Yegül, Ayşegül Turfan, and Pozitif
- David and Chie Hammons
- Vittorio Albani
- Scott A. Barton
- Corrado Beldì
- Antonia Belt
- Alessandro Cassin
- Corinne Clarac
- Helga Davis
- Elena Del Rivero
- Brendan Dugan
- Elizabeth Karp-Evans
- Bob Gorry
- Colleen Grove
- Don Heffington
- Sinisa Mackovic
- Christian Marclay
- William McIntyre
- Steve and Linda Miller
- Senga Nengudi Fittiz
- Kate Peoples
- Belle Place
- Brandon Ross
- Graziella Rossi
- Massimo Simonini
- Kim Smith
- Jeannette Vuocolo

About This Book

Daniela Veronesi

The Art of Conduction is a theoretical introduction as well as a practical guide to Conduction® – a process for ensemble music-making – as conceived and developed by composer, conductor, and arranger Lawrence D. "Butch" Morris, over the course of his long musical career.

Conduction – based on a codified set of hand signals representing specific instructions for musical interpretation – is designed to enable conductors to direct an ensemble either with or without notation.

Offering, as it does, the chance to conduct, orchestrate, and play music in real time, Conduction appeals not only to conductors, composers, instrumentalists, and music educators drawn to improvisation, but also to those engaged in classical interpretative traditions of written music. By providing musical coordinates for ensemble dialogue, it affords new space and favorable conditions for interaction to those engaged in improvising music, and also, as a natural extention and evolution of traditional conducting, offers the means to broaden interpretation and notation through the orchestration and (re)arrangement of written music – *while it is performed*. Conduction establishes a common language that can be employed within and across genres; in Morris's vision, it bridges the gap between notation and improvisation – as well as between musical styles and traditions – while drawing on and enhancing each individual musician's culture, interpretative skills, fantasy and creativity.

Beginning in the late 1970s, Morris applied Conduction across widely diverse musical communities including jazz, classical, electro-acoustic, and pop, as well as a broad spectrum of traditional instrumentalists from North America, Europe, Asia, Africa, and the Middle East. Internationally regarded as a leading innovator at the confluence point of jazz, new music, improvisation, and contemporary classical music, Morris has taught professional musicians and music students all over the world. This book is a detailed description of Conduction and how it works, as well as a rich account of the extraordinary man who brought it to a wider musical world.

Making Conduction available for musical praxis and education with a handbook that would illustrate its principles in detail – and carefully avoiding standardizing it as a "system" – was a goal Morris pursued with strong commitment. He first outlined it in the booklet that accompanied his 10-CD collection *Testament*, and he continued to develop and refine the concept, particularly in recent years, as he prepared what he called his *Conduction® Workbook* for publication.

The Art of Conduction is the result. Published posthumously, as it is, this book also embodies the efforts of a team of Morris's longtime collaborators

1 Preliminaries

to continue his legacy. By following his notes, directions, recommendations, pointers, hints, and other clues, in letter and spirit, they delivered a completed version of his original manuscript, augmenting it with further documentation to provide readers – both familiar and unfamiliar with Conduction – with a deeper look into Morris's personal explorations of ensemble music, and how Conduction can be taught, learned, and practiced in pedagogy and performance.

In "Preliminaries," assorted contributors – including practitioners as well as former collaborators – shed light on Morris's work, offering historical and musicological perspectives as well as more intimate insights into the practice of Conduction. Conversely, in "The Art of Conduction," it is Morris himself who relates how he first came to work on the idea of Conduction as a way of establishing common ground between orchestral notation and improvised music, developing a musical practice that, based on both collective decision-making and individual expression, would make an orchestra "as flexible as an improvising trio."

Then, in "Introduction to the Conduction Lexicon," Morris goes on to fully elucidate the principles of his "vocabulary for communication" between conductor and ensemble, and reflects further on the process of using his codified lexicon of signs and gestures – the Conduction Lexicon – in ensemble music making. He goes on to discuss what participating in such a process involves, in terms of ensemble interplay, individual choice, and distribution of responsibility from the perspective of the conductor, the ensemble, and individual instrumentalists, in practice and performance.

"The Conduction Lexicon" represents the core of this work: brief, precisely detailed descriptions of each physical Conduction instruction Morris developed. These instructions – a series of signs and gestures called *directives* – are classified and grouped in sections, illustrated with drawings, and include descriptions of how each sign/gesture is physically produced, as well as a delineation of both their function ("Signification") and usage ("Explanation").

Additional information on how instrumentalists might address selected directives is also provided here ("Supplementary Note") and, where it applies, a special note is offered ("Nota bene"), suggesting how a given directive may be utilized in more nuanced and complex ways for advanced practice, and/or indicating how conductors can use alternative hand signals, when needed.[1]

"Personal Notes," which includes an interview with Morris, personal entries from his original notebooks, and a glimpse into his private correspondence, was compiled with the dual aim of giving readers a chance to engage with a more personal, intimate dimension of Morris's work, also to preserve these unique reflections, discoveries, and pointers on Conduction that might otherwise be lost.

Similarly, "How to use the Conduction Lexicon," which I wrote with J.A. Deane, offers, alongside Morris's own writings, additional practical suggestions for conductors and music educators who want to incorporate Conduction within their own praxis.

And finally, two supplementary chapters contribute biographical information on Morris and comprehensively document his work with Conduction. The "Conduction Chronology" comprises full details of the performances and personnel on all Morris's numbered Conductions, while the "Conduction Discography" gives specifics on their recordings.

---

[1] Further details on the structure and organization of the Conduction Lexicon are given in "Editor's Notes." Please note: signs and gestures are presented one at a time in the Lexicon – examples of how they can be combined and layered in real time will be made available online in a collection of annotated video materials.

Editor's Notes
Daniela Veronesi

"Conduction" – as Morris states in this work – "is a medium of practice, requiring realization in physical rather than theoretical form." The same, in a sense, also applies to this book itself. Though it does offer a theoretical introduction to Conduction, *The Art of Conduction* primarily delineates its practical application in pedagogy and performance – as a tool taught, implemented and experimented, within the very physical context of musical interaction.

All those directly involved with this project were well aware of this, and when Dino and I began to edit "The Conduction Lexicon" itself – Chapter 4 of this book – we were conscious of the importance of bearing such educational and practical perspectives in mind. Moreover, given the distinct nature of our different experiences with Morris and with Conduction, our aim was not only to gain a broader as well as deeper understanding of Conduction, but also to reduce any risk of imposing our individual biases onto the original manuscript.

And so, our work has been to preserve, clarify and reconstruct, while consistently seeking to strike a balance between the clear, concise articulation of the lexicon and our commitment to maintain that unique openess to interpretation that Morris saw in each and every Conduction directive.

The following is an account of the editorial decisions that were made in the course of completing this work.

Minor and Major Revisions
For the most part, the original manuscript illustrating the Conduction Lexicon underwent minor editing. In a few cases, however, more substantial interventions – the rephrasing of single passages within a given directive, integrating information, and the rearrangement of directives in their entirety – were necessary.

In order to allow the reader to distinguish the original from such major revisions, the latter are highlighted with a double grey line (▤).

Classification of Directives
Since it was part of a work in progress, the "Classification of Directives" available in the original manuscript was still provisional – and incomplete. From my own experience collaborating with Morris on various drafts of his *Conduction® Workbook* over the years of its evolution, I know that for him the "Classification of Directives" was something to be refined as the practice of Conduction developed in the years to come.

Nevertheless, what was in the manuscript was, for the most part, structured and defined in detail and, though Dino and I were all too aware of the risks involved in any editorial decision we might take, we undertook to complete it as to include it in this book – with some integrations and revisions. In so doing, our aim has been not so much to "faithfully reconstruct" Morris's music theory approach to Conduction – some directives had not been classified yet, and some categories included directives that had not been fully elaborated on - rather, to provide practitioners of Conduction with a tool to navigate the lexicon in the clearest possible way.

The revision of the "Classification of Directives" – a task accomplished primarily by Dino – has, therefore, involved the creation of new categories, as well a re-classification of existing directives. In the original version, for instance, "Upbeat," "Downbeat," "Yield," and "Pedestrian" – now to be found under *Directive Activation* – appeared at the beginning of the classification as stand-alone instructions; a category entitled *Punctuation and Accent* included the directives "Staccato" and "Glissando," which seemed, to us, to fit more appropriately into *Articulation*, just as "Accent," which is now classified under *Time-Tempo/Pulse-Rhythm*. Consequently, *Punctuation and Accent* has been removed from the classification, together with the directive "Marcato," which was listed there but not elaborated on.

"Ground/Trap-Sample-Loop," originally listed under *Articulation*, has been moved to *Events*, which also includes "Accompany Me/Imaging/Shaping" – formerly classified under *Evolutionary Transformations*. "Melodic Movement (Melodic Information-Cantilena)" and "Graphic Information (Literal Movement)," originally paired in a specific, self-titled section (*Expressions of Melodic, Graphic and/or Phrasing Intent*), have been re-classified, respectively, under *Articulation* and *Events*. "Tension," which was not classified, has been included in *Dynamics*. Finally, for the sake of clarity, all directives applied in conjunction with notation are now collected in a new section entitled *Score-Related Directives*.

Directive Structure and Nota bene

The way each directive is presented to the reader – namely the description of the hand signal ("Sign," "Gesture" or "Sign/Gesture"), a "Signification," an "Explanation" and a "Supplementary Note" – reflects its depiction in the original manuscript.

However, in the course of rearranging information in these categories within each directive entry – with the goal of gaining consistency throughout the whole lexicon – we realized that in some cases the original manuscript had included instructions and suggestions that would require advanced comprehension and practice. Since that might introduce unnecessary complexity and even give rise to misunderstandings if applied at an early stage of teaching and learning the lexicon, we added a further category – to include such information – that we called "Nota bene." This is intended for the benefit of conductors and ensembles substantially familiar with Conduction, for deeper exploration of a particular directive, often in conjunction with other directives, in the context of advanced practice.

In editing the directives, our guiding principle was that information be presented in a progressive way, be it simple or complex, essential or supplementary. To this end we also used "Nota bene" to provide conductors with alternative ways to show a given directive by means of hand signals. Thus, we also appended here certain signs or gestures included – as supplementary options – in the original manuscript, and even, in a few cases, added newer ones drawn from close observations of Conduction footage ("Whisper" and "Staccato"), and/or from Dino's own practice ("Yield" – Nota bene 2; "Staccato," "Accelerando-Ritardando with Hand").

Finally, and for integrity's sake, we included in "Nota bene" information that was stated elsewhere in the lexicon, consolidated from Morris's original notebooks ("Pedestrian," "Panorama/Fragment-Excerpt"), or that we derived from our own knowledge of Conduction, ("Yield" – Nota bene 1; "Capture-Continue;" "Spar/Phrase in Time" – Nota bene 2; "Tonal Center/Key;" "Accompany Me/Shaping/Imaging;" "Ground/Trap-Sample-Loop"), or vis-à-vis specific instrumentation ("Harmodulation/Transposition").

All listings under "Nota bene" that were added or strongly revised are highlighted with a double grey line. (═)

Signs and Gestures

In its current form, the Conduction Lexicon includes most of the original hand signals used to convey the Conduction directives. In cases of possible ambiguities and partial overlapping, we decided to slightly modify Morris's original hand signal (as in "Coda," "Discretionary Ending," "Distill," and "Call and Response,") in that we changed the hand orientation (facing conductor/facing ensemble) or, for instance, the gesture final position.

Additionally, when the sign/gesture description was still at a preliminary stage, we chose a sign that could iconically represent the directive's name ("Bridge"), or expanded the available description ("Notes to the Beat"). "Tremolo" and "Trill" – only listed in the original manuscript – were elaborated ex novo by Dino and added under *Effects/Instrument-Specific Directives*.

All signs and gestures that have undergone such changes have been highlighted with a double grey line (═).

Directive Names

Regarding directive names, minor changes were needed. In the interest of clarity, we decided to adopt one name only for those directives originally labelled with two synonyms ("Arpeggio/Arpeggiate" or "Resolve/Resolution" for instance); in the case of "Accent" – originally named "Accent/Stress" – we opted for the first term; and for "Develop-Reconstruct" (horizontal and vertical), which also appeared in the manuscript as "Evolve-Reconstruct," we oriented ourselves to Morris's own use in a number of documented Conduction workshops, during which the directive was typically introduced as "Develop-Reconstruct."

Nuanced Usages

Nuanced Usages is a heading we decided on for those directives we found could be better used by conductors and ensembles of well-established collaboration; *Nuanced Usages* has been applied to "Tension" (originally not classified), "Accent" (in provisional form in the original), and "Downbeat and Upbeat: Indicating Rhythm" (initially included under "Downbeat" and "Upbeat" respectively).

Directive Drawings

In the original manuscript, and in further available documentation, not all directives were provided with a corresponding picture. It was therefore decided – together with the other members of the team directly involved with the editorial project – to have all signs and gestures represented by drawings. These drawings were produced by Massimo Golfieri, using existing pictures realized by Jules Allen, and his photography class at the Department of Art and Design, Queensborough Community College, New York, in February, 2009; along with Dino's own visual examples.

As stated at the beginning of the section "Conduction Directives" (p. 54), signs and gestures are illustrated as directed from the conductor to instrumentalists located in a central position, in the middle line of the ensemble.

On Conduction: My Experience with Butch Morris

J.A. Deane

I met Butch Morris in late 1984 in New York, while performing next to him on one of John Zorn's game pieces – I was a thirty-four-year-old electric trombonist, he was thirty-seven and a cornet player. Within weeks of that first encounter he invited me to attend a concert he was giving at the Kitchen, doing something he called "Conduction." That concert on February 1, 1985, was Conduction no. 1 (*Current Trends in Racism in Modern America*), and sitting in the audience I remember thinking, "He is doing the same thing that I do with samplers, only he is doing it with live musicians!" By Conduction no. 3 (*Goya Time* – 6/13/85) I was playing in Butch's trio and in his large ensemble as an electric trombonist and "live-sampler," and over the ensuing twenty-eight year collaboration into the creative process he became one of my dearest friends on the planet.

While working with Butch, I soon introduced him to the idea of having a live-sampler in the ensemble and he developed a sign specifically for it. As a live-sampler I had to take a "big picture" view of the music and almost intuit the direction Butch was going in, in order to be ready to trap (sample) the appropriate motifs as the music progressed. I think it was my role as live-sampler – along with my growing understanding of the Conduction Lexicon – that later moved Butch to trust me to edit and sequence his recordings, first in collaboration with him (*Testament* 10-CD box set) and then on my own (*Holy Sea*, *Verona*, *Interflight*, *Berlin Conduction nos. 67, 68, 69*; *London Improvisers Orchestra Conduction nos 81–87*; *Sucht/Lust*, *Excessette*, *Butch Morris Trio Vol. I–II–III*; *Folding Space*). Editing compositions created through the process of Conduction deepened my understanding of musical form and, in about 1997, after performing in Butch's large ensembles for twelve years, I established my own Conduction group, in the hope that I would gain an even deeper understanding of the Lexicon from the other end of the baton.

The next sixteen years turned out to be quite an education: in composition, sociology, communication, "being in the moment," and Qi Gong. But the lesson that resonates deepest within me was the realization that sound equals energy. What I've learned personally, from my years performing with Butch, leading my own ensemble, teaching workshops around the world and, more recently, in articulating, together with Daniela Veronesi, the Conduction Lexicon for this book, is this: *Conduction is the essence of musical form.*

Conduction gives:

- the conductor the essential building blocks of music in a simple and immediate format;

- the instrumentalist the freedom and responsibility to create a unique voice within the ensemble sound;

- both conductor and instrumentalist the opportunity to create musical form completely in the moment;

- everyone involved (conductor, instrumentalist, and listener) the opportunity to experience wonder.

As for the "building blocks" that constitute Conduction – that is to say, how the Conduction Lexicon is structured – I remember that during my first years of conducting the desire to *add new signs* came up – an urge that any conductor using Conduction might legitimately feel at one point or another –, and I spoke with Butch about it. He told me that whenever he had an idea for a new sign he would always ask himself this question: "Is this something better served by notation?" I have always followed his advice, because it holds the signs and gestures of Conduction to a symbolic standard and avoids the introduction of *overly defined* ideas. Indeed, in all my years working with Butch I saw how he made it a point of steering clear of over-definition when teaching the art of Conduction, and I adopted that point. Over the course of eighteen years, only six new signs have passed this test in my own practice – "Cross Fade," "Duo Panorama," "Wipe," "Percussion," "Add/Interrupt," and "Pulse" – and made it into my work with the Conduction Lexicon.

    We know that in Conduction the conductor is responsible for providing structure and the instrumentalist is responsible for providing content. It is easy to assume that the conductor is *in control* of the ensemble, but what I have come to realize is that the *only* decision I make during a Conduction is the choice of the first sign. The ensemble interprets that sign and creates a musical response, and it is the manifestation of that symbol into sound that then informs me of what the next sign must be… and so, on it goes. An energetic feedback loop develops between the symbolic (conductor) and the sonic (ensemble), and through this energetic exchange, a musical form emerges *on its own*. To experience this state of unfettered group composition, the ensemble (conductor and instrumentalists) must be completely present and in the moment. Until you experience this for yourself, it's very hard to get your head around the idea of giving up control, but the moment you give up the *illusion* of control – that's when the *magic* happens. Trust me...

    Working with Daniela, to articulate the Conduction Lexicon for this book has been a challenging and rewarding experience, and I want to express my deepest appreciation and respect for her dedication to making this book a reality. Conduction is Butch's gift to music, but it was Daniela's passion that put this book in your hands.

THE ART OF CONDUCTION 1

An Exceptional Reciprocity

Allan Graubard

My first collaboration with Butch Morris began on West 57th Street in Manhattan. It was nightime, perhaps 1981. I was walking home and he was coming the other way. We knew each other from Berkeley, which is where I first heard him play in 1974, astonished as much by his command of his instrument (cornet) as by his delicacy in using it. Butch knew I was a poet but I doubt he had read much, if anything, of what I had written. It didn't stop him from asking if I wanted to join him at an upcoming performance, "Music for Poets," at a small theater on 18th Street. I was surprised but agreed. He told me he'd be up in a few minutes with his horn – he was living around the corner then – and we'd see what would happen.

A half hour later we were listening and responding: his music, my poems. It didn't stop in "real time" until he died over thirty years later. But then again, it hasn't stopped. And this book is one continuation of a profound creative legacy that Morris has left for us.

During these decades, through performance, discussion, libretto, good times, and text we fed our friendship. As Conduction developed, so did our capacity to describe it. Exploring a language infused by the colors and resonance of the *event* has enriched all I have written since.

From that first collaboration came "Modette," our initial effort to found a medium for Grand Music Theater, a phrase that Morris was fond of and which configured the expanse of his vision. Other performances and exchanges followed, including the book that accompanied the epochal 10-CD set, *Testament*. Our last several stage works – from the series "Folding Space," with large ensemble, to the choral octet[1] with string tentet of "Erotic Eulogy" – revealed ever new ways to engage the Conduction ensemble and chorus, or dialogic and solo voice. Each returned values intimate to the heart of music as they are to poetry, drama, opera, choreography, and the communities born from them.

Attuned to the immediacy of performance, and the relationships that arise, more traditionally set within a given text or libretto or constructing and deconstructing the same in performance, an expansive, dynamic space for collaboration established its authority.

Our fundamentals were clear: from sound came music; from silence poetry, dialogue, and song; from gesture choreography; from space sculpture; and finally mise-en-scène – the frame in which our dramas intensify, which often did mean a stage focused on the conductor and full ensemble, without other visual enhancement.

[1] I refer to the "Chorus of Poets" established and developed by Morris.

Preliminaries

In one sense "Modette" found its embodiment here, although in two US incarnations a simple set transfigured the emotional arc of the story; the last set floating inches from the floor. In another sense, our works thereafter partook of the potential for heightened interchange in which word, poem, libretto, or text formed and reformed in a lyrically fraught ensemble projection of poignant music.

As a writer, this meant that I gave up any claim to owning what I wrote. In performance, creation is key. And while dialogue spurs actors, libretto singers, or other text choruses, exactly how they deliver their lines and live their character is as much a product of rehearsal as it is of the moment, then and there, in that place with those people, ensemble, and audience.

In our later work, the aforementioned "Folding Space" and "Erotic Eulogy," meaning itself, a culturally protected province of language, exchanges values with sonics and the music that rises from it. Here, interchange works on various levels: the physicality of sound and music embraces the intelligibility of words and text. Suddenly one partakes of the other, each distinct yet each revealed anew. The significance ascribed to words and text gains the resonance of music, and the sound that allows an ensemble to make music. From that sound and that music, the capacity to signify gains and matures.

This, too, is what Morris meant by Grand Music Theater: the drama inherent in sound and music, which the conductor draws from the ensemble and the ensemble gives to the conductor, infusing and infused by the words and text performed.

My contribution to this book – as co-editor of the chapters written by Morris, *The Art of Conduction* and *Introduction to the Conduction Lexicon* – is of a piece with all of that; the distillation of an oeuvre through an exceptional reciprocity.

Conduction®:
The practice of conveying and interpreting a lexicon of directives to construct or modify sonic arrangement or composition; a structure-content exchange between composer/conductor and instrumentalists that provides the immediate possibility of initiating or altering harmony, melody, rhythm, tempo, progression, articulation, phrasing, or form through the manipulation of pitch, dynamics (volume/intensity/density), timbre, duration, silence, and organization in real time.

The Art of Conduction

2

Lawrence D. "Butch" Morris

The "Extra Dimension"

Blues, Jazz and Gospel have driven North American music of the 20th century from one end to the other, and they still do, giving birth to many offspring, re-inventing themselves time and again. But no matter what changes, this music continues to be a medium for individual expression and collective interaction, with its own characteristic spirit, which is swing – or rather, the essence of swing. Born from the elements of intuition, spontaneity, propulsion/momentum (a sense of continuity), combustion, ignition, interaction, transmission, and communication, this essence has been called the "extra dimension." Conduction's main concerns lie deep in the heart of this extra dimension; in it, musicians must think constantly on their feet, remaining continually open to change, split-second decisions, and accomplishment.

The orchestral community has often sought this extra dimension to rejuvenate its traditions. Yet, for all the theory and works written over the past hundred years or so, only a handful have utilized it by bringing jazz and music for orchestra closer, or by creating a music that can itself attain the unique status held by each tradition distinctively.

To find common ground between orchestral notation and improvised music, I believe one must return to musical fundamentals and identify those elements that allow all traditions to coexist. That is, to provide an opportunity for improvisers to improvise and for interpreters to interpret *the same material.* This, to me, is what Conduction makes possible.

The most common misunderstanding about Conduction is that it is only, or primarily, intended for the improvised music community. Although Conduction was incubated within this community and incorporates many of its ideas, it has grown far beyond it, to involve musicians with the most diverse musical backgrounds and concepts – from Western instrumentation, contemporary electronic technology and voice, to traditional instrumentalists from Africa, Asia, and the Middle East.

As musicians, we all share a common language. We may express ourselves in different dialects, vocabularies, categories, or styles, but the language is music. Whatever tradition it springs from, music has certain intrinsic properties beyond harmony, melody, and rhythm. Although some of these properties may ultimately resist analysis, music will always allow musicians to communicate from vastly differing perspectives. Is this information sufficient to begin a new era of investigation and collaboration? I believe that the answer is yes!

When I first started to work on the idea of Conduction, I was trying to understand how to make notation more flexible, how to give it more expressive range: as a conductor, I wanted to be able to modify written scores in real time – to construct, deconstruct, and reconstruct a composition, to change the pattern or order of sounds, and consequently the larger form.

I also wanted to figure out how to make an orchestra as flexible as an improvising trio – to have that kind of combustion and spontaneity and momentum and ignition – and the lexicon of signs and gestures I was developing offered such possibilities. Here was a way I could alter or initiate essential musical parameters like rhythm, melody, harmony, form/structure, articulation, phrasing, and meter, within any given written work.

Then, as I established and refined the lexicon, I eliminated notation altogether. Conduction was giving rise to new forms of collectively motivated and organized musical expressions, allowing me to pursue the goal of constructing music in real time, within the intermediate space between notation and improvisation. Over the years I have often gone back to notation, and have utilized the Conduction Lexicon both without and with written music; this latter practice I have called "Induction."

What has emerged from my investigations is a procedure that not only addresses composition from a notational or improvisational point of view, but also one that is intimately connected to how each musician interprets the signs and gestures through which I conduct. It is only the instrumentalist who can bring "meaning" to those signs and gestures, as it is only through the dialogue within the ensemble that we can contribute to their possible evolution.

In its present phase, Conduction is a lexicon of directives (signs and gestures), an analogous procedure of musical representation and organization: it is form and forum, product and practice. It serves as a conduit for the transmission of symbolic information, and it motivates musicians to render, arrange, and construct, evolving their own vision and tradition, and participating in a decision-making process in which responsibility is dispersed within the ensemble.

The future of ensemble music must evolve to include individual sensibilities and the opportunity for everyone to find their expression. As a vocabulary for communication, Conduction offers a new array of tools to instrumentalists, composers and conductors, and opens new doors, enabling us to realize – through self-expression – our individual and collective freedoms.

For more than thirty years, Conduction has given me the privilege of enjoying the intermediate space between notation and improvisation from the inside, and I've acquired new skills and perspective in the process. Working with my vocabulary of visual signs, the Conduction Lexicon, has engendered a deeper exploration of a manner of communicating in music, and with music, that did not begin with me but has been here since ancient times.

Indeed, the practice of "Chironomy" – that is, hand movements – to stimulate ensemble music, existed as far back as 1500 BC, or earlier, as discussed by Elliott Galkin in his *A History of Orchestral Conducting: In Theory and Practice* (Pendragon Press, 1989). Galkin writes: "In its earliest applications chironomy was intended to indicate the course and characteristics of melody through the use of specific spatial movements." In effect, it served as a substitute for notation, constituting the earliest known system of visual signs to shape musical direction.

Since the mid-20th century others have broken ground in this area. I note the following, but more emerge every year: Lukas Foss (Improvisation Chamber Ensemble), Leonard Bernstein (*Three Improvisations for Orchestra*, Columbia Records LP 6133, 1965), Sun Ra, Frank Zappa, Earle Brown, Alan Silva, Doudou N'Diaye Rose, Charles Moffett, and Walter Thompson. However, there are differences between how I view our sonic future and musicianship and what these great musicians have done. Simply put, I do not draw stylistic lines between the ensembles, communities or musicians I choose to work with or the music I make. Conduction is constitutive in practice, rather than prescriptive.

It has always been my desire that Conduction be an act of communion, a place where *all* musicians from any background could navigate and give of themselves in an earnest engagement of minds. I'm by no means suggesting Conduction as an alternative to existing musical and music-educational methods or styles. Rather, I view Conduction as a neo-functionalist approach to ensemble music, and as an investigation of a new social logic that can unite and enhance existing traditions.

I see potential for Conduction. Whether embraced as a concept, a new skill, a way of understanding, a type of collective identity, virtuoso attainment, ensemble evolution, conductor as composer, as an extention of all things musical, or an expansion of the musical canon, there is much to be achieved. More than ever, Conduction is a viable supplement for music, musician, and education. I offer this as my contribution to the "extra dimension."

THE ART OF CONDUCTION 2

Comprehending Conduction

My interest lies in the area where the interpretation of the symbolism that generates notation meets the spontaneity of improvisation: an intermediate space where the potential for new life – an expansive range of expression that has long gone untouched – prevails, and where ideals and ideas can incubate for the continuum of the musical canon.

It is not – and never has been – my intention to use Conduction to redefine music or music theory, or to standardize Conduction as a system. I wish, rather, through Conduction, to stimulate a way of making and thinking about music that can expand the concept of musicianship and musicality in the individual and in the ensemble, that supplements and augments given forms with a greater appreciation of possibility, and refines the qualitative standard for what ensemble music is and can be.

With music I wanted to take a picture of the moment. How could I write music today, take it five thousand miles away, and not only make it reflect what I wrote, but also make it relevant to the environment it would be performed in? To my mind, neither notation, nor improvisation *alone* could manage that.

Notation and improvisation have developed distinct traditions as if they did not fundamentally enrich each other; we know, of course, that they do. Conduction facilitates this enrichment by locating and exploring new capacities for the conductor, composer, and instrumentalist. As music notation is symbolic of music, Conduction – with its lexicon of signs and gestures – is symbolic of notation, with this difference. Conduction does not express with the same kind of precision that we expect from ensembles that interpret a notated score. That "precision" has a unique cultural bias is something we accept; however, it is not something that need determine value in one tradition to the exclusion of other possibilities.

New requirements and scales of evaluation call for a new social logic; one that governs collective intimacy in the immediacy of creation. Why sustain the differences between notation and improvisation? To what end do we make music in ways that "fit" in the one or the other tradition? Conduction is my response to these questions, and it is a response animated as much by regard for proven forms as by a will to evolve the potential available to us: enhanced musicianship, discovery of structure and substance within the arc of the performance, the evolution of a musical practice based on new reciprocities between conductor and ensemble, instrumentalist and conductor, instrumentalist and composer, and between composer and the audience that enters this encounter.

2 The Art of Conduction

The bridge that Conduction builds between notation and improvisation fuels interest; with this, we can identify and exploit the strengths and weaknesses of both, and in the process depict core limitations in each. There are as many rewards as questions here, but none, it seems, as significant as those which open pathways, both individually and collectively — pathways shuttered previously by custom or fear. And I refer to the exclusionary focus of most musical traditions and to the fear of compromising collective, ensemble, or personal identity.

Conduction concerns transmission, communication, and expression; a common ground where all culture and style cohabit, not only by way of their distinctiveness, but also in how each contributes, in an ensemble, to a unique encounter. More intimately, it concerns a capacity of musicianship for new skills with new principles. In Conduction, the art of composition and the immediacy of performance become interdependent, while the language of music cultivates and integrates all vernaculars and traditions open to, and within, the ensemble.

Conduction asks us not to obscure the music we possess by constraining it exclusively to style or genre, nor to limit the imagination of the music we *can* possess by reusing given forms. It adds a dimension to music and music theory by promoting collective interpretation and personal interaction in a real-time environment. At the same time, by stripping away predispositions to value this or that style or tradition in music, we construct a mirror to the kinds of relationships that subsist in society, and the potential of music to challenge and transform them; a community in microcosm that functions through all its metaphorical concepts.

Conduction is a highly vivacious, adaptive medium, which can be perfectly responsive to each new work mode an ensemble may face; the music draws participants from diverse traditions and cultures, and their dialogues are poignant, often profoundly so. Conduction is also a model in and for evolution, one that allows its participants to modify the art, along with its significance. I know well from my experience over the years that as new directives entered the lexicon, so new individual and collective responses and perspectives evolved.

Conduction embraces a sonic arena in which to construct, deconstruct, and reconstruct with and from the basic properties of pitch, duration, intensity and timbre. As a process of transmission based on forms of interpretation and elaboration, variation, transformation, and revelation, it has become an organon for the investigation of essence and experience, both individually and collectively.

Primed by an "extra dimension," which motivates us to engage and respond within and beyond defined territories, Conduction invokes a continuum that thrives in a real-time transmission of relationships and meaning; the spontaneity and precision that we need to ignite and combust order and organization within sonic thought. Neither method nor process, Conduction is a *practicum* that *reveals* in practice.

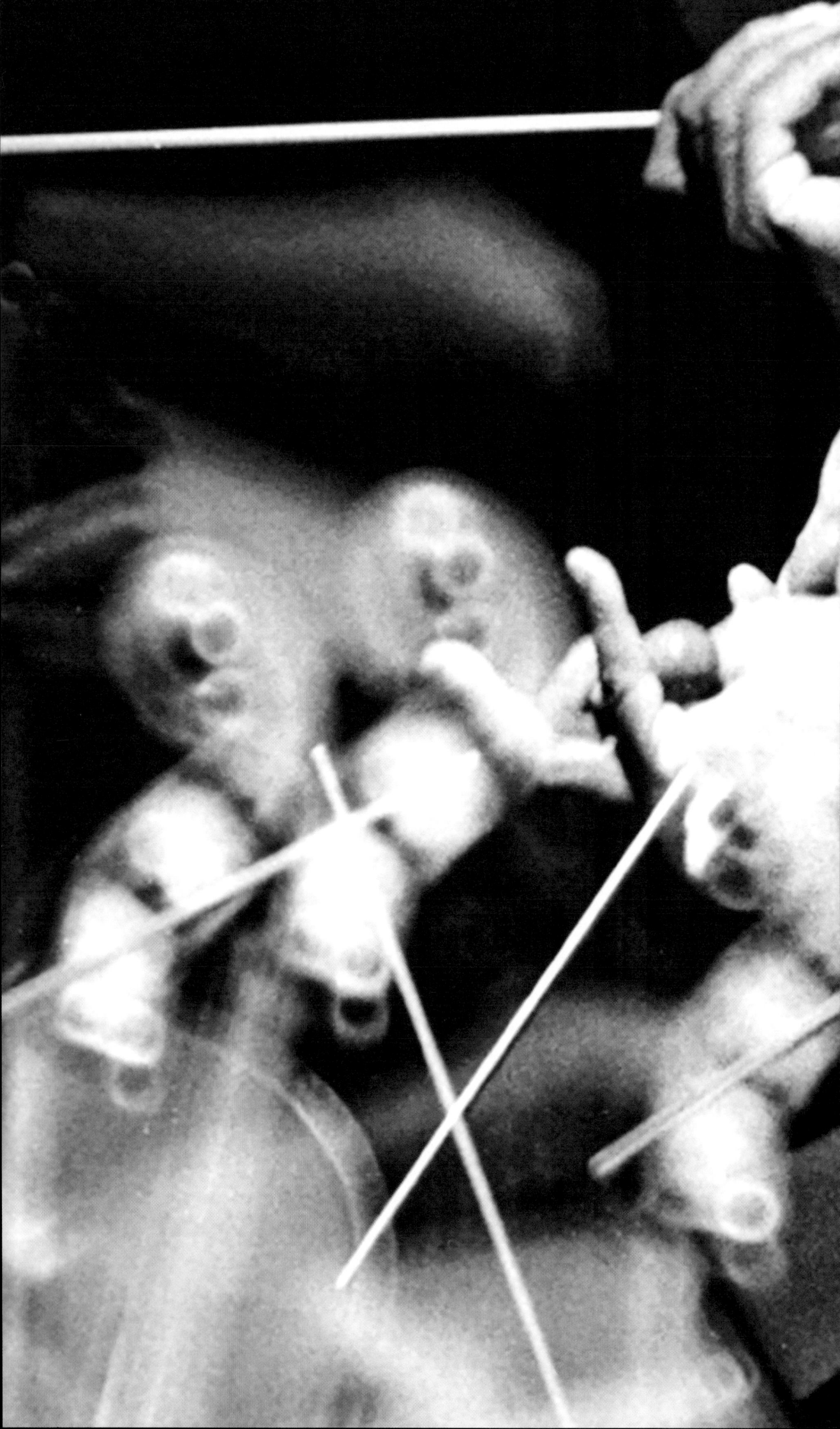

Introduction to the Conduction Lexicon

3

Lawrence D. "Butch" Morris

Directives

Conduction is based on a lexicon of instructions called "directives:" visual analogous representations of musical sound, which the conductor conveys through signs and gestures, and to which instrumentalists respond with musical content.

The Conduction Lexicon can be utilized within all musical forms, styles, and traditions. As a bridge between notation and improvisation, it enables any ensemble to arrange an infinite number of interpretations from the same notation, as well as create compositions without notation.

The Conduction Lexicon is structured in a) a set of cues that govern entrances and endings, (illustrated in the section "The Process of Conduction: Basic Parameters"), and b) directives that serve as creative tools of production, manipulation, clarification, continuation, and change (detailed in the section "Conduction Directives").

Directives are conveyed through a series of signs and gestures. In the Conduction Lexicon, signs are meant as static hand (baton) signals, and gestures as hand/arm (baton) movements. Directives conveyed through *signs* are first shown, and then activated by a downbeat (baton/hand); directives conveyed by *gestures*, conversely, are to be interpreted in real time. Signs have a preparatory function and indicate the direction to be taken – where we are going, what is about to happen; gestures visually express or demonstrate sonic ideas. Signs can also be followed by gestures (indicated in the lexicon as "sign/gesture"), in which case gestures act as a downbeat.

Once it is established to whom directives are addressed, the conductor can give them in any order and combination to any individual, group, section, or part of the whole ensemble, and thereby activate them as multiple directives. The arrangement of the directives, as provided by the conductor in real time, builds the structure and form of the composition in progress.

The conductor is responsible for structure and form, and the instrumentalists for content.

Each directive has a given signification, or "meaning," which provides parameters for interpretation; depending on the nature and direction of the music as it unfolds, instrumentalists are asked to define and give *content* to that meaning in *context*.

In such process, discretion is key: there is not merely one way to interpret directives, and instrumentalists may rely upon any musical means when deciding how directives should or could be represented sonically. The Conduction Lexicon is descriptive rather than prescriptive; its function is not to set limits, but to test boundaries. Directives are indeed interrogative in nature, in that they ask the instrumentalist: "What does this sound like in this situation, at this time?" And, "What is the content you choose to place in this context?"

In theory and in practice, each directive is, like notation, a visual stimulus, and is generative or infusive in nature. Within the definition of directives, the way each directive is interpreted is at the discretion of the instrumentalist. In responding to a directive within a particular context, instrumentalists

Introduction to the Conduction Lexicon

actuate an expression of musical sense that relies on their own personality, intuition, and depth of understanding, as well as on the place – foreground, middle ground, background – that such an expression occupies within the ensemble. Thus, a new rationale for responsibility within the musical progression is constituted. Directives generate prospect, and each interpretation of a given directive prompts momentary orientation and self-development for the instrumentalist and the ensemble.

Finally – and equally vital for the life, stability, and growth of the ensemble's direction – is how attentively instrumentalists follow the conductor's entrance and ending cues when starting and closing their musical contribution. Here, precision and a fine temporal co-ordination with the conductor are paramount.

The Conductor

From the perspective of the conductor, Conduction is a continuation of traditional conducting with an added lexicon of instructions (directives) that amplify and broaden notation and interpretation. Conduction is a tool that allows conductors to shape music in performance, rather than in rehearsal, and infuse notation and interpretation with the latitude of improvisation – revealing a new way of coordinating sound, responsibility, and accountability with and within the ensemble.

The act of Conduction is the art of "environing:" the process of organizing people, things, conditions, or influences that interact within, or in proximity to, the work. Through Conduction, the conductor acquires, develops, and practices the capacity to initiate, sculpt, and at the same time benefit from the collage of information coming from the ensemble, and transform it into a coherent stream of structure and sub-structure, collective meaning, implication, expression, poignancy, and momentary logic – as well as capture and place sonic information within its own sense of organization, and invent new sonic order in the very moment it reveals itself.

In Conduction, the conductor is constantly active, informing the ensemble and always alert to its character and coordinates. By means of the Conduction Lexicon, the conductor clarifies directions ("where to go") and means ("how to get there"), assessing and asserting conditions by representing structure in the foreground, middle ground and background, and thereby providing form, structure and context for the instrumentalists' response.

Giving direction within Conduction is, of course, a matter of taste, aesthetics, circumstance, adaptation, risk, and choice; as a conductor, however, you are always aware that ultimately your real-time decisions can *only* be structural, and that Conduction is not only about how you move from one sign or gesture to another, but also about how you influence that movement, and, most of all, how the ensemble – and each and every instrumentalist – responds by providing content to the directives you give them.

In Conduction you can thus excavate and discover sonic individualities and differences, maximizing the range of encounters and events that may take place while constructing and deconstructing together, and so arriving at a specific immediacy and intimacy of place. Demonstrating these possibilities in workshops and practice sessions will be essential not only to prepare the ensemble for what may occur in performance, but also to enhance its interpretative and expressive skills while always satisfying its need for challenge.

As a conductor, you establish, and are accountable for, your own capacity to initiate, capture, and understand the direction of a construction; with each construction, you start fresh, delegating and coordinating responsibility within the ensemble in relation to the work at hand, the order and sequence of sonic developments, and events that take place as sonically meaningful.

In this way, not only do you develop a keen intuitive sense for overall sonic, dynamic, and structural placement, but also you become aware of how your use of the Conduction Lexicon and the information coming from the ensemble intimately affect each other; how it's necessary to consider any and all interconnections, consequences, correspondences, and variables that will alter as form proceeds; and how, in the course of constructing and deconstructing such states of equilibrium and imbalance, Conduction will display the musical form-making process at work.

While practicing Conduction, you will observe the cultural, social, scholastic, stylistic, and historical potential of the art, as well as behavioral differences in the individual and the collective. You will see such differences present themselves in the most revealing ways, as they both open and obstruct pathways to construction and extra-musical possibility.

Remember: Conduction is an art that flowers in contraction (for some), ambiguity (for others), and encounter (for everyone involved). By constructing, deconstructing, and contrasting composition at will, we forge an intermediate space, both intensive and extensive, for the evolution of ensemble music, and for a new virtuoso thus versed.

3 Introduction to the Conduction Lexicon

The Instrumentalist

Conduction is open to any instrumentalist interested in developing new skills and techniques of perception, orchestration, and arrangement in real time, and being part of a new ensemble intellect that bridges composition and improvisation. Conduction encourages musicians to engage in a collective decision-making process by drawing on their unique personality, history, and ability.

Team play and individuality are two essential elements in Conduction because as an instrumentalist you are asked to have – and find – your own subjective response to the conductor's directives, based on how you both perceive and interpret them on your particular instrument – woodwind, strings, brass, percussion, electronics, and so on – and on what the music or sonic environment demands, at any given moment, for and within the ensemble progression.

To contribute "anything" to the sonic environment does not serve Conduction; on the contrary, as an instrumentalist you are aware that your interpretation of directives is historic as well as momentary in terms of quality and use of the instrument, and that each contribution you make carries the weight of reinforcement of the overall construction.

From an instrumentalist's perspective, Conduction is the capacity to see, hear, capture, evaluate, elevate, and evolve sonic ideas. In Conduction, it is the instrumentalist's responsibility to "realize" music in any situation and to evolve individual and ensemble content, while developing multiple, distinctive approaches to the directives of the Conduction Lexicon. Their definition is broad enough to accommodate more than one sonic action.

The practice of Conduction asks that instrumentalists be receptive in three territories simultaneously: interpretation, improvisation, and Conduction itself, with its lexicon of signs and gestures. Just as you may be improvisational in your response to unforeseen circumstances in your daily life, so in Conduction you adapt and respond to the changing situations that emerge as music unfolds, with focus, inventiveness, tact, and a sense for what belongs and is needed to advance and support the music; always ready to respond to an occasion in which an encounter may take place.

Conduction is not about style; we can accept style as something we bring, not something we play, something that helps us determine our ideas of beauty. When you are not forced to be style-specific, what do you do? You go to where you are most comfortable. Conduction is about inviting instrumentalists to bring in their own "comfort zone," and then to release that comfort zone into an ever changing sonic environment to test and push it to further limits.

As you become familiar with the Conduction Lexicon and can identify directives in order to "translate" them into sonic content, you will engage with situations that reveal intent and performance, and find difficulties and enhanced capacities; concentration and a thorough understanding of the lexicon will enable you to navigate new sonic and structural possibilities, while drawing upon your knowledge, intellect, logic, intuition, risk, and daring.

Conduction offers instrumentalists a dynamic of empirical form, a way to contribute to the musical continuum, and a new responsibility within the ensemble. Conduction lets us explore and evolve our own sense of musicality and musicianship in a manner that avoids what we know, or have known, traditionally as "perfection." It says: "Do not play what you *think* the conductor wants you to play; play yourself, always consider what the ensemble is doing, come in with conviction, commit, never doubt, and have fun!"

The Ensemble

Conduction is an ensemble skill. I like to think of an ensemble as a human body, with each ensemble member as an organ that contributes in its distinct way and yet always in communication with all other organs, to the well-being of that body. This is key to Conduction: here, individuals – conductor and instrumentalists – are asked to be true to themselves *in full service to the ensemble*, always attending completely to what is appropriate for the direction of the ensemble.

When sonically defining a conductor's directive, each instrumentalist acquires a programmatic clarity, and starts to experience a personal judgment that relates to the judgment of others in the ensemble. It is from such perspective, as well as that of the relationship musicians have with their own instruments, that form and sonic content will originate, and whence the ensemble can reach internal coherence and equilibrium; and so find synchronicity and then let it go, to further explore.

The importance to the ensemble of both individual instrumentation *and* the individual can never be stressed enough; instrumentalists cannot merely access their experience within musical ensembles, but their understanding of the history of their particular instrument, and the role it has played will also inform what they can now bring to it. It is the mutual comprehension of this confluence that informs and reflects the independence of the collective, and gives Conduction the freedom it thrives on.

Conduction cultivates the analytical reasoning, intuition, and creative passion of each instrumentalist; it provokes a state of readiness and responsiveness conducive to the generation of the ensemble.

In this sense, the ensemble is also a kind of organization in transition, a heterogeneous state comprised of autonomous individuals. It is a collective in which both conductor and instrumentalists take joint responsibility for building greater fields of contingency and constraint, while inviting new references into existing cultural realities and personal limitations. A place inhabited for an exchange that both confirms and confers.

In the process of designing a unique and complete sonic construction for the environment we play in, working relationships develop that foster structural integrity, gradual progress, and the resolution of whatever issues this creative method might bring up. Complexities are a given. But individual contributions, allied with solidarity and unity of purpose, as well as the equal division of labor that Conduction naturally engenders, promote rich opportunities for specialization, camaraderie, self-criticism, and opportunities for exchange that may not generally occur in other forms of collective music-making.

Patterns of tradition are acknowledged as such, but aren't necessarily seen to advance the ensemble towards a new understanding of consequence and conquest (on this day, in this place, at this time); rather, the ensemble – and the music it creates – benefits from individual contributions that are not constrained by predetermined concepts of musicality.

Conduction opens up a range of possibilities previously unknown, barely known, or known far too well. Ultimately, Conduction is a way to explore ensemble music *as we are making it*: a state of risk, the distillation of immediacy, and a step forward in the evolution of music and musicianship.

Practice and Performance

Conduction is a medium of *practice*, requiring realization in physical rather than theoretical form. Here, practice is dedicated to procedure as much as it is dedicated to risk through knowledge, research, and experience. Practice reveals.

It cannot be overstated: it takes time for an ensemble to gain confidence and familiarity with the Conduction Lexicon, and more, even, to develop that acute sensitivity to rapport that is at the heart of Conduction. The dedication of extended periods of time to workshop and practice sessions is, therefore, essential to this process.

The purpose of the workshop is for conductor and instrumentalists to gain a clear understanding of what each directive of the Conduction Lexicon is and how it works, and to explore and demonstrate the opportunities for transformation in performance.

In the workshop, instrumentalists learn how directives evolve meaning, and begin their journey toward understanding how much they and their instrument can manipulate and expand capabilities within their musical precept. How, by building focus and acting within the definition of each directive, they can provide *the most significant* contribution to the ensemble *in context*, experiencing a kind of self-confrontation that demands their uniqueness and an awareness of their own musicality. They also learn how to "read" the conductor, in the same way the conductor learns how they respond and bring their musicianship and musicality into the process of Conduction.

The workshop does not have the goal of establishing probabilities in the light of performance; what occurs in workshop and practice sessions, of course, may not occur in performance. There are no systematic regularities here, only determination; to prepare ourselves for anything when we practice, and to deal with anything when we perform.

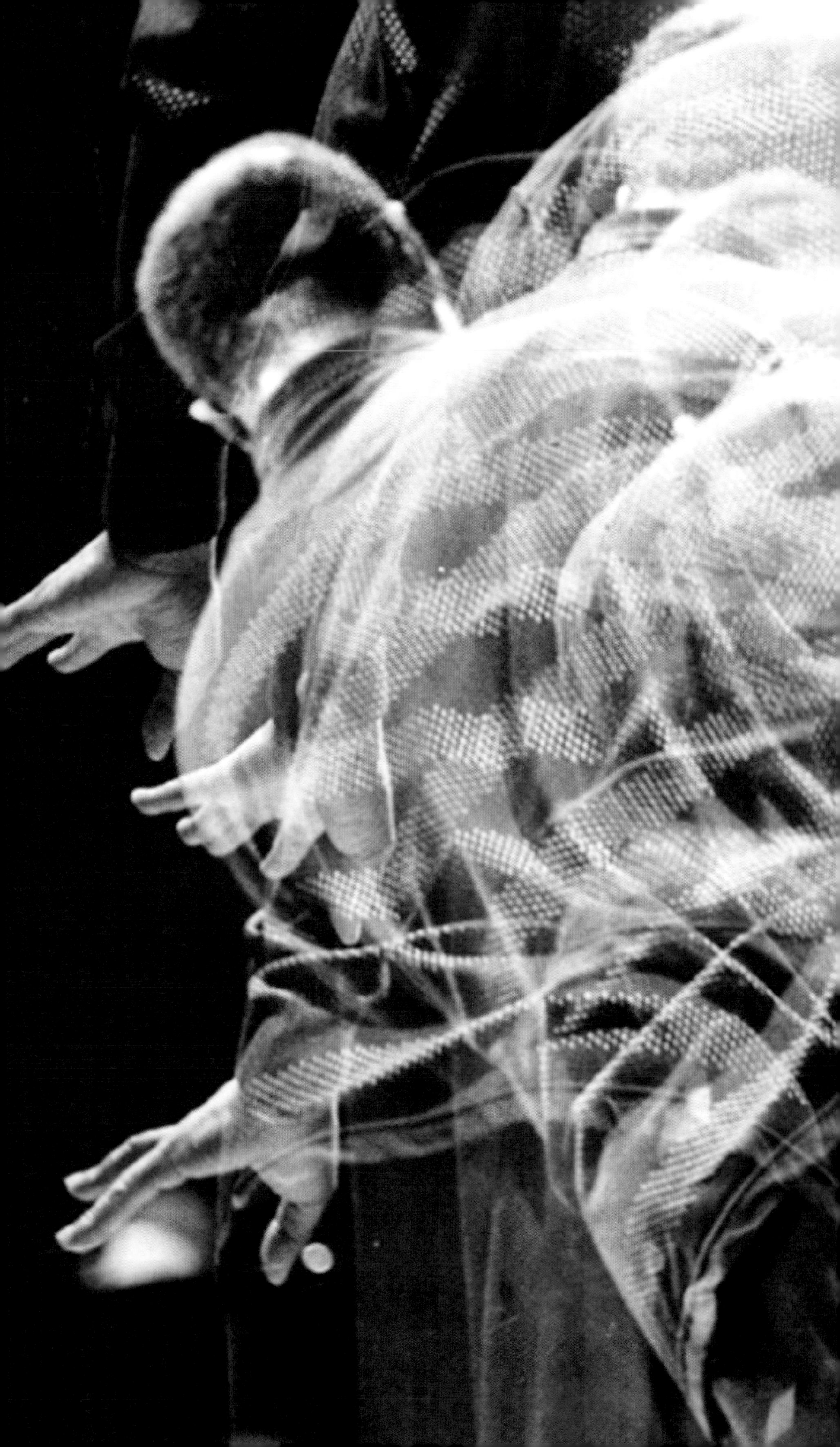

The Conduction 4 Lexicon

Lawrence D. "Butch" Morris

THE ART OF CONDUCTION 4

Classification of Directives

page	52	Entrance and Exits/Endings Specifications
	54	Directive Activation

- Upbeat
- Downbeat
- Yield
- Pedestrian

60 Directive Endings
- All Stop/Cut Off
- Discretionary Ending

64 Dynamics
- Real-Time Dynamics
- Next Directive Dynamics
- Whisper
- Nuanced Usages: Tension

70 Articulation
- Discretionary Sustain
- Pitched Sustain
- Melodic Movement (Melodic Information-Cantilena)
- Staccato
- Glissando

78 Repeats
- Repeat
    - Create/Construct
    - Imitate/Emulate
    - Echo/Reproduce
    - Shadow/Pursue/Follow
    - Copy/Replicate
- Capture-Continue
- Memory

84 Time-Tempo-Pulse/Rhythm
- Tempo Designation (Pulse-Tempo/Meter)
- Rhythm (Initiating)
- Proportional Tempo/Time
- Notes to the Beat
- Spar/Phrase in Time
- Nuanced Usages: Downbeat and Upbeat (Indicating Tempo/Rhythm)
- Nuanced Usages: Accent

4 The Conduction Lexicon

94 Tempo Modifications
- Doubletime
- Halftime
- Accelerando-Ritardando (with Baton)
- Accelerando-Ritardando (with Hand)
- Place in Time/Free of Time

102 Tonality/Pitch
- Change in Tonality/Pitch
- Change by Octave
- Harmodulation/Transposition
- Resolve
- Tonal Center/Key (Establishing)

110 Evolutionary Transformations
- Developments
    - Develop-Reconstruct (Horizontal)
    - Develop-Reconstruct (Vertical)
    - Distill
    - Spin
- Accompany
- Bridge

122 Events
- Panorama
- Panorama Fragment/Excerpt
- Panorama Hocket/Brief Contributions
- Graphic Information (Literal Movement)
- Accompany Me/Imaging/Shaping
- Ground/Trap-Sample-Loop
- Event
- Arpeggio
- Pedal/Splash-Crash
- Call and Response
- Breath

138 Effects/Instrument-Specific Directives
- Harmonics
- Stops
- Vibrato
- Tremolo
- Pizzicato
- Arco
- Strum
- Trill
- With Mute/Without Mute

150 Score-Related Directives
- Go Forward
- Go Back
- Section Designation
- Top
- Coda

The Process of Conduction: Basic Parameters

The essential parameters for the construction of a sonic composition – and vital to the practice of Conduction – are:

1) the designation of instrumentalists for directive execution (*who*);
2) the designation of the directive to be executed (*what*);
3) the activation of execution and the exit from execution (*when*).

Physical Sightlines (Field of Clarity)

The first act of a Conduction workshop is to define clear visual lines of communication between the conductor and the individual instrumentalists, wherever they are physically placed in the ensemble. This is crucial for transmitting and receiving information in all ensembles, and even more so in Conduction, where it is also the physical sightlines that must be understood and exposed in ensemble play.

In simple terms: each instrumentalist's body occupies a specific space in the ensemble, and each instrumentalist must recognize when the conductor is identifying her/him – either by pointing and/or making definite eye contact within that particular space – and that her/his presence is therefore being sought. Only by establishing such a field of clarity can identification ambiguity and confusion be avoided.

Giving Directives: Entrance Specifications

From the conductor's perspective, entrance specifications, preparation, and the execution of directives unfold as follows:

1. Individual(s)
   Who: point to and/or look at individual instrumentalist.
   What: show directive.
   When: give upbeat/downbeat in the direction of the individual.

2. Groups
   Who: any combination of instrumentalists that may be dispersed throughout the ensemble. Indicate which instrumentalists you want to be part of the group by pointing to and/or looking at each of them individually.

4 The Conduction Lexicon

What: show directive.
When: give upbeat/downbeat in the direction of the last instrumentalist indicated in the group.

3. Section(s)
   Who: instrumentalists sitting next to – or in immediate proximity of – each other. Indicate by pointing, while drawing a horizontal line through all of the instrumentalists in the section(s) that you want to take directive.
   What: show directive.
   When: give upbeat/downbeat in the direction of the section(s).

4. Division of Ensemble
   Who: through a slicing motion with the left and right hands, separate or divide the ensemble into parts or segments.
   What: show directive.
   When: give upbeat/downbeat in the direction of the designated part(s) or segment(s) of the ensemble.

5. All/Tutti
   Who: for everyone in the ensemble. Indicate with arms outstretched, left and right, waist high.
   What: show directive.
   When: give upbeat/downbeat.

Nota bene | Designation of directives (*what*) may precede designation of instrumentalists (*who*); designation of directives and of instrumentalists may also be indicated simultaneously by pointing the directive toward instrumentalists.

Exits/Endings Specifications

Exit specifications may be given to individuals, groups, sections, parts, or segments of the ensemble (previously designated or in a new combination for the purpose of exiting), or they may be given to the whole ensemble, to stop the contribution being performed in that moment (see details under "Directive Endings" on p. 61).

Nota bene | All Conduction directives are described from the conductor's perspective. Signs and gestures are illustrated as directed from the conductor to instrumentalists who are located in a central position and in the middle line of the ensemble. Based on the size and the layout of the ensemble, and on where addressed instrumentalists are located within it, the conductor will show a directive (sign or gesture) to his/her right or left on the horizontal axis, as well as higher (back line) or lower (front line) on the vertical axis.

ⓐ Conduction Directiv[e]
Directive Activation

- Upbeat
- Downbeat
- Yield
- Pedestrian

Upbeat

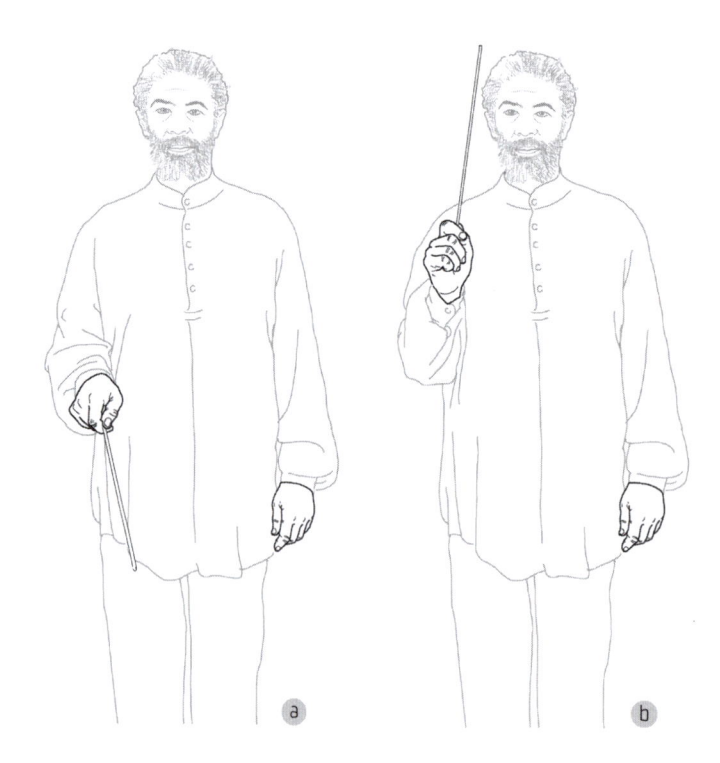

(a)   (b)

Gesture	An upward stroke of the right hand (baton).
Signification	To prepare to activate a directive or multiple directives.
Explanation	Given after a preparatory directive, the upbeat precedes and anticipates the downbeat as one complete movement.
Supplementary Note	When deemed useful, instrumentalists may, in the act of the upbeat use all forms of anacrusis, appoggiatura, acciaccatura, pick up, roll off, lead-in or grace notes at their discretion.
Nota bene	The upbeat may also be given with the left hand, or with both hands.

4 The Conduction Lexicon

Downbeat

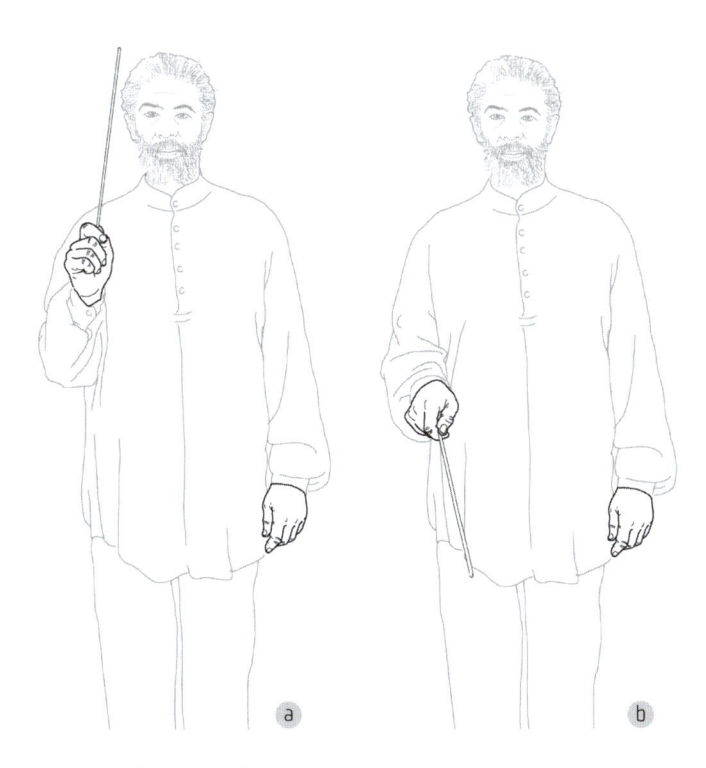

a   b

Gesture	A downward stroke of the right hand (baton).
Signification	To activate a preparatory directive.
Explanation	All preceding directives are superseded by subsequent directives; the downbeat closes the current directive and opens the new one.
Supplementary Note	The downbeat is given with a larger gesture than all preparatory information for the purpose of indicating uniformity, clarity and precision.
Nota bene	The downbeat may also be given with the left hand, or with both hands. For additional kinds of downbeats for activating preparatory directives, see *Directive Endings*, *Evolutionary Transformations* and the section, *Types of Downbeats*.

Yield

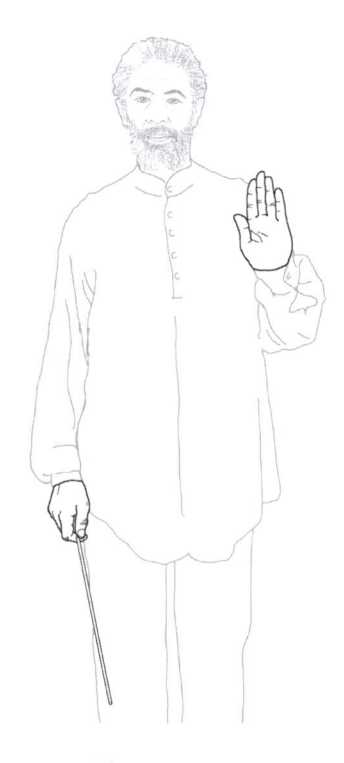

Sign	Left hand, palm facing instrumentalists, fingers extended upward.
Signification	Pay attention; stand by. To prepare instrumentalists to receive a forthcoming directive for imminent interpretation and execution. Indicates that a change or alteration will occur.
Explanation	The "Yield" sign is given prior to initiating rhythmic or graphic instruction (see, for instance, "Rhythm-Initiating"), or when multiple directives are distributed, in order to give instrumentalists ample time to recognize, understand, and interpret forthcoming preparatory directives.
Supplementary Note	If the instrumentalist is contributing at the moment the "Yield" sign is given, she/he should continue her/his contribution while paying strict attention to the directive that follows "Yield," then execute that directive upon a downbeat.
Nota bene 1	After giving the "Yield" sign, the conductor may want to give rhythmic or graphic instruction several times before giving the downbeat for execution.
Nota bene 2	The "Yield" sign may also be given with the left hand palm facing the conductor.

4 The Conduction Lexicon

Pedestrian

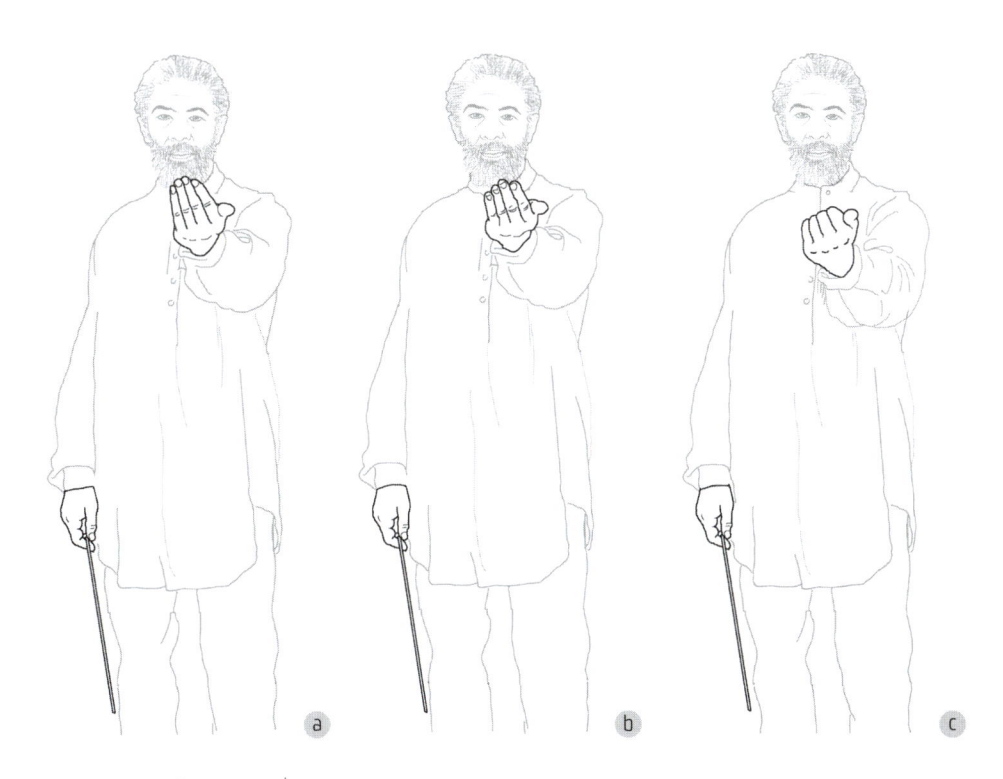

a b c

Gesture	A wave of the left hand, as if to beckon, *come in*, addressed to the instrumentalist being asked to act as a "Pedestrian."
Signification	The Pedestrian's primary concern is to contribute to the overall integrity of the construction in progress and to find or create situations for elaboration and development.
Explanation	The Pedestrian influences the sonic environment of the ensemble by establishing new relationships or nurturing already existing ones and building within them; she/he qualifies and/or quantifies ensemble information or introduces new information into the ensemble. To enhance, influence, and foster development; to orchestrate, score, and arrange; to contribute overall.
Supplementary Note	Response to this directive is at the discretion of the instrumentalist; no downbeat is given. The Pedestrian is temporarily free of all ensemble directives and resumes her/his place in the ensemble only when specifically addressed a new directive.
Nota bene	The Pedestrian is asked to affect the music of the ensemble, and this can be done in numerous ways that the Pedestrian must explore on his/her own. It is not necessary that she/he takes the ensemble over or is even heard outside of her/his immediate space. A feature by the Pedestrian may be arrived at, but never assumed.

(a) Conduction Directives | Directive Activation • Pedestrian

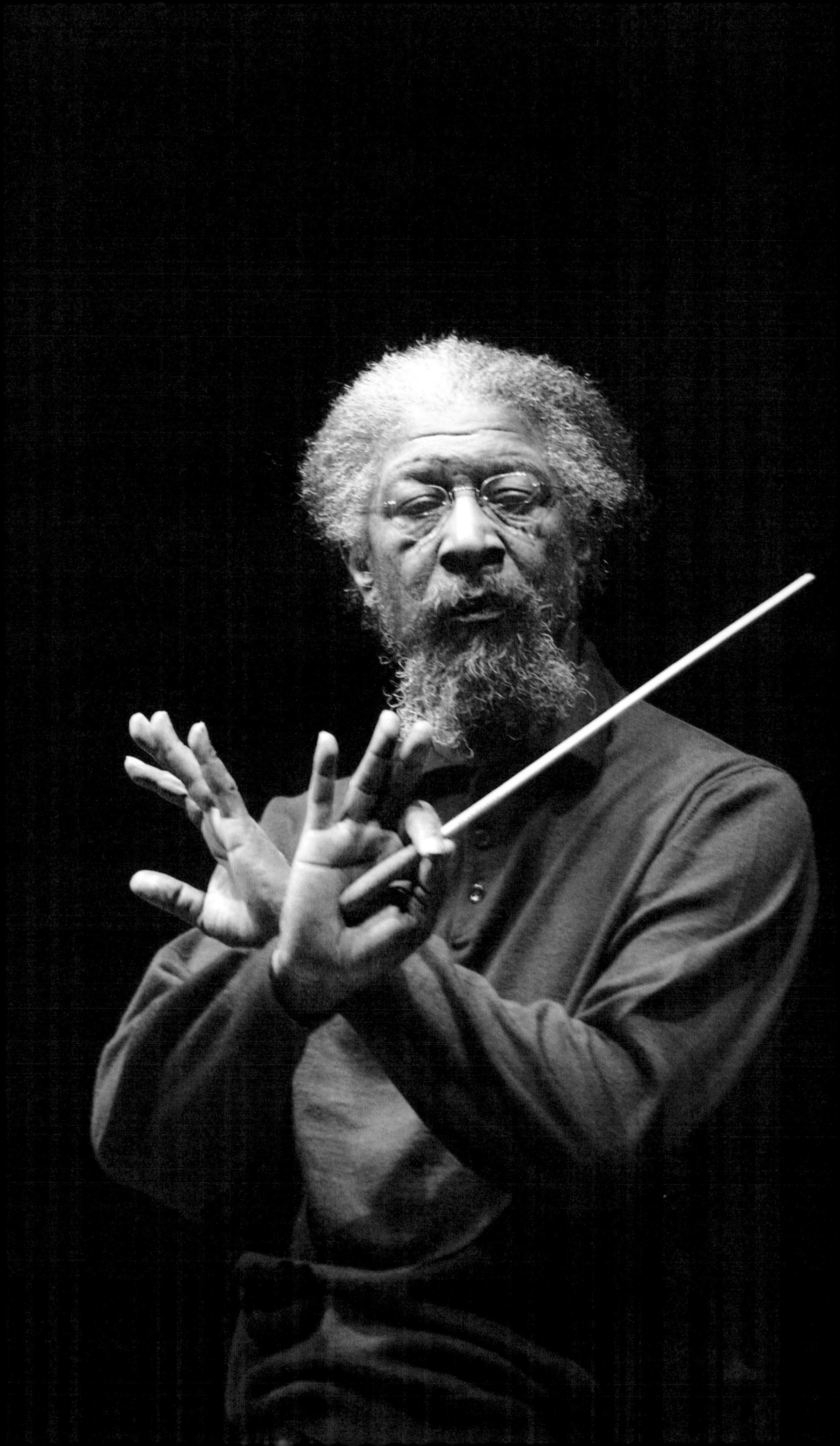

The Conduction Lexicon 4

b Conduction Directives
Directive Endings

- All Stop/Cut Off
- Discretionary Ending

All Stop/Cut Off

Sign/Gesture	Crossed arms at upper chest, palms facing outward toward ensemble, followed by uncrossing of arms, left to left side, and right to right side, ending at waist height.
Signification	Indicates that contributions will stop at the moment this directive is given.
Explanation	When the conductor's arms are crossed in the "Stop" position, all instrumentalists prepare to bring their contribution to an end; when the conductor uncrosses arms, they stop their contribution. The directive may be interpreted as immediate or gradual, depending on the speed or slowness – i.e., the intensity – of the sign/gesture given by the conductor.
Supplementary Note	The directive may be given with a smaller gesture to indicate groups, sections or individuals ("Cut Off"); groups, sections or individuals may also be indicated to stop their contribution by a horizontal movement of the right or left arm.
Nota bene	When a new preparatory directive is given just prior to the "All Stop/Cut Off," this may also be used as a downbeat to stop the current contribution and begin the new one simultaneously.
	Similarly, the "All Stop/Cut Off" directive may act as a downbeat indicating that designated groups, sections, parts of the ensemble, or individuals execute a new directive, and simultaneously indicate that other instrumentalists stop their contribution.

Discretionary Ending

a   b   c

Sign/Gesture	Left hand, palm facing the designated instrumentalist(s) at left shoulder to face level, closing hand to fist as it moves downward to hip height.
Signification	To bring contributions to an end at the instrumentalists' discretion.

Conduction Directives · Directive Endings · Discretionary Ending

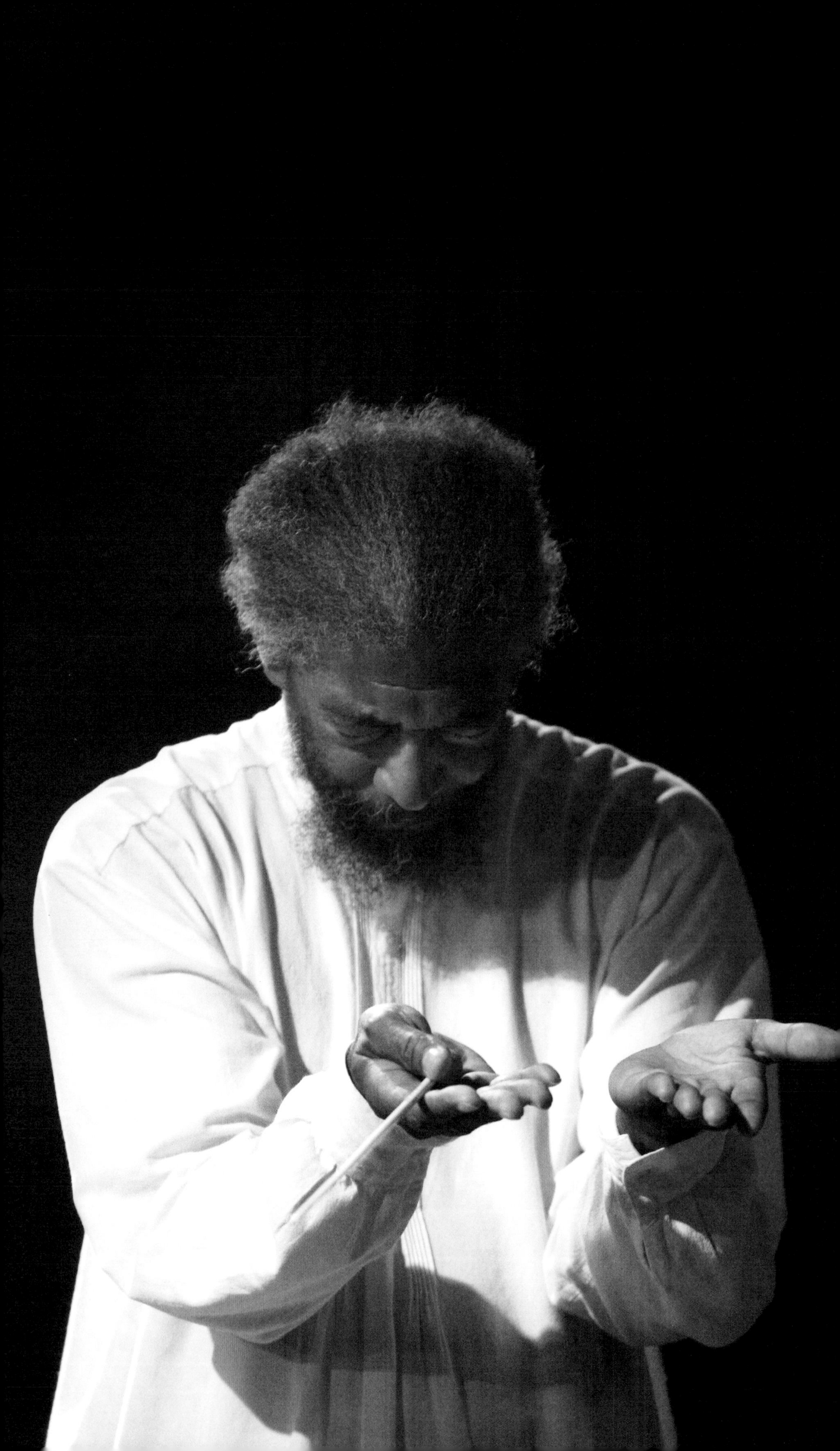

The Conduction Lexicon — 4

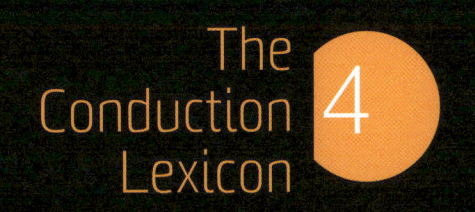

C Conduction Directives
Dynamics

- Real-Time Dynamics
- Next Directive Dynamics
- Whisper
- Nuanced Usages: Tension

THE ART OF CONDUCTION 4

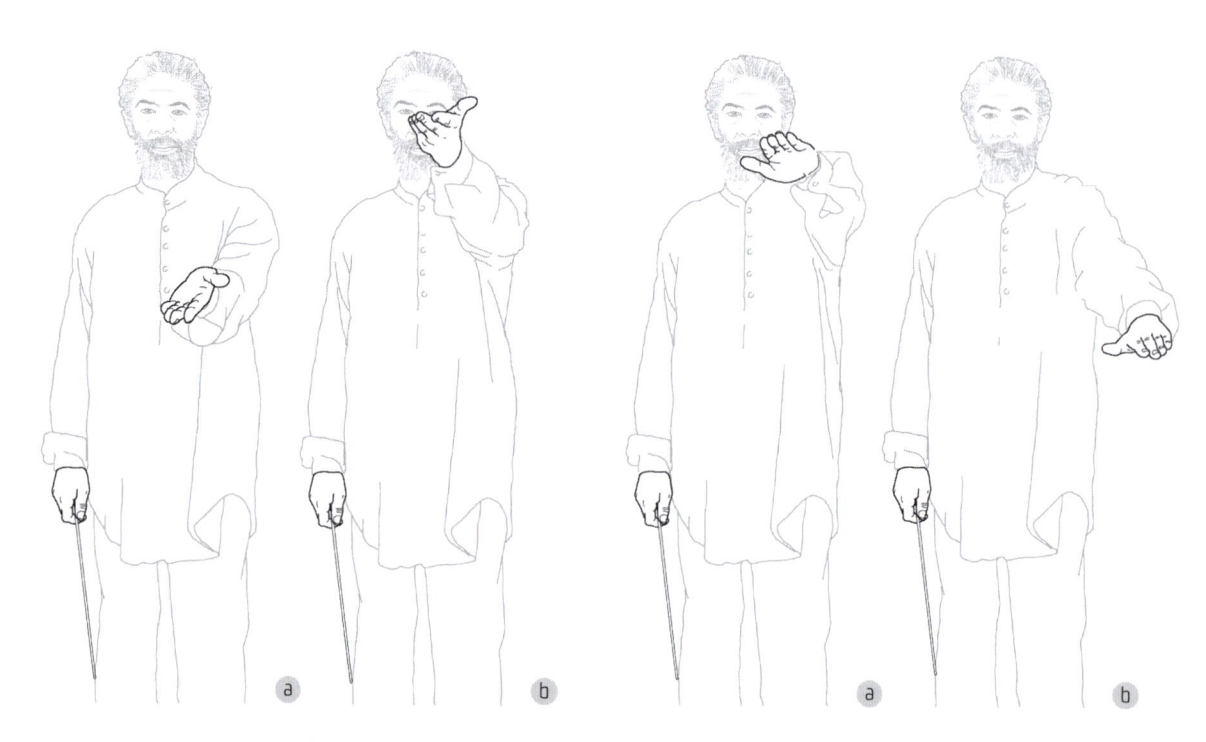

Real-Time Dynamics

a b a b

Gesture	Palm(s) raised face up for louder dynamics; palm(s) lowered face down for softer dynamics.
Signification	To implement real-time change in dynamics – i.e., energy, volume, balance/equilibrium, power, force, tension/intensity – from *fortissimo* to *pianissimo*. Executed without a downbeat, response is immediate.
Nota bene	The directive may be given with either hand or both hands.

Dynamics • Real-Time Dynamics

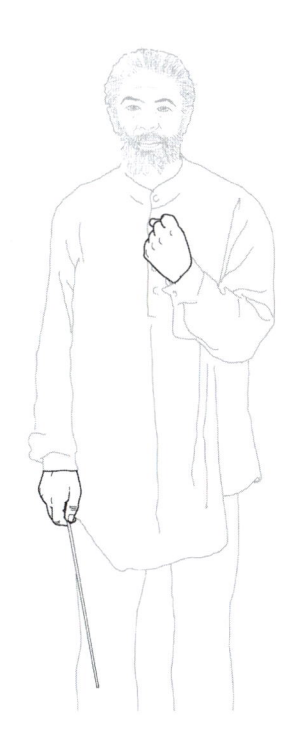

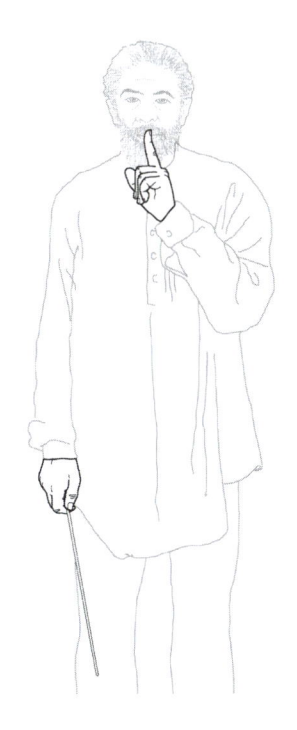

Next Directive Dynamics

Sign	Left hand, clenched fist in chest area for *fortissimo*; index finger to lips for pianissimo.
	Executed with a downbeat.
Signification	To implement change in dynamics (*ff-pp*) related to a forthcoming directive.

Dynamics • Next Directive Dynamics

THE ART OF CONDUCTION 4

Whisper

Sign	Left hand touching throat.
	Executed with or without a downbeat.
Signification	Indicates that the instrumentalist is to contribute at the lowest possible volume, and that her/his contribution should be expressed surreptitiously, as in ghost notes.
Nota bene	The directive may also be indicated by pointing the left index finger to the throat.

Dynamics • Whisper

4 The Conduction Lexicon

Nuanced Usages: Tension

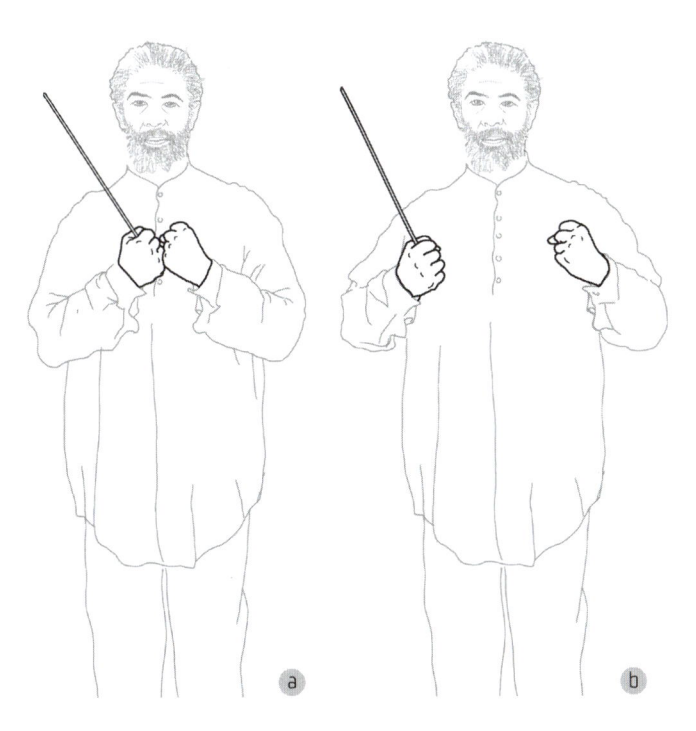

a b

More nuanced dynamics can be reached through the directive "Tension," which may be particularly suited to conductors and ensembles with a well-established collaboration.

Gesture	Both hands in fists on chest, with elbows separating to the left and right.
Signification	To produce or amplify tension/intensity or exaggeration.
Explanation	As the conductor pulls his/her fists left and right, the instrumentalist "exerts," intensity but not volume; with the return of the fists to the chest, intensity is released. Response is immediate, no downbeat is given.

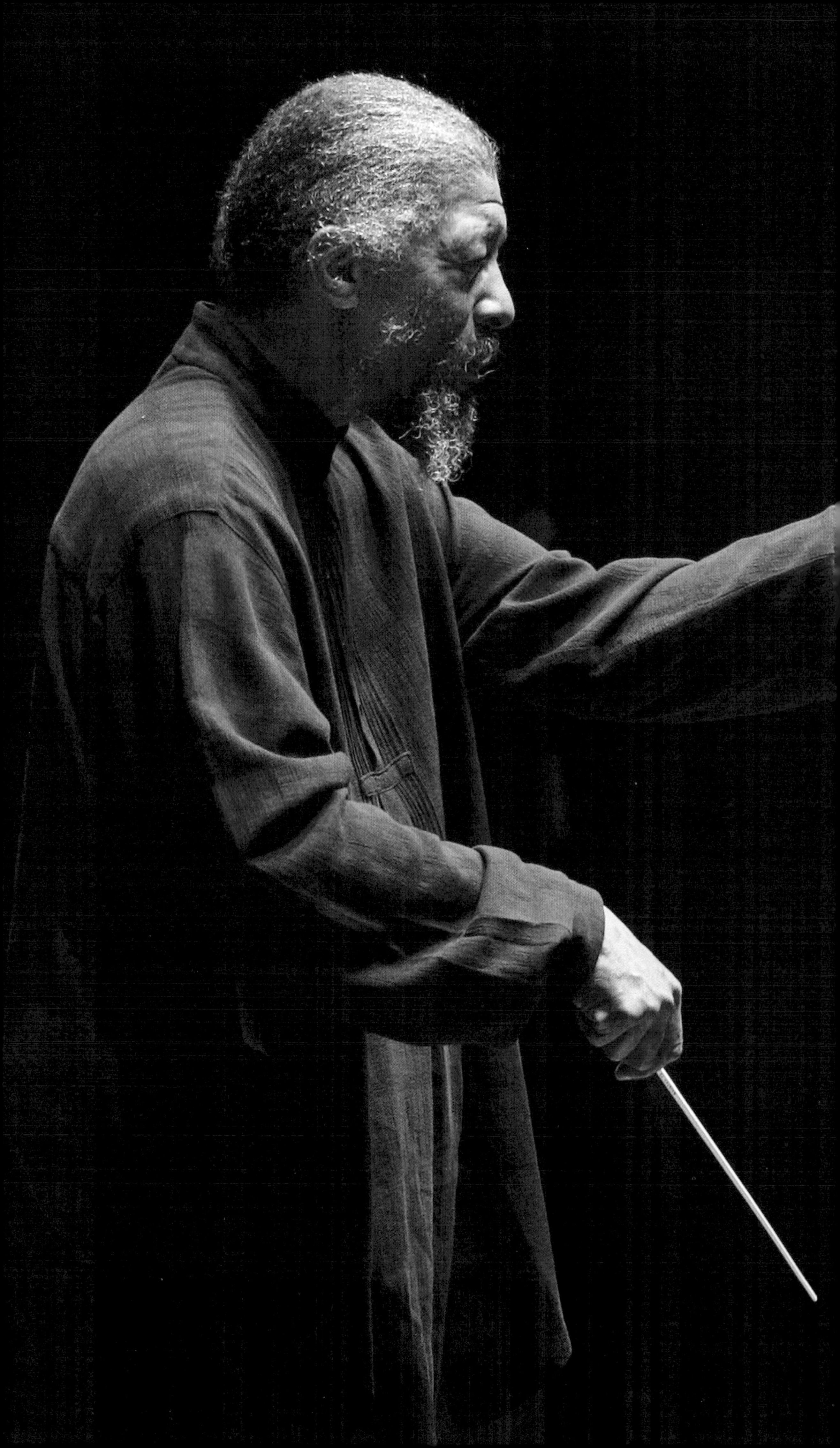

The Conduction Lexicon 4

ⓓ Conduction Directives
Articulation

- Discretionary Sustain
- Pitched Sustain
- Melodic Movement
  (Melodic Information-Cantilena)
- Staccato
- Glissando

THE ART OF CONDUCTION 4

Discretionary Sustain

Sign	Left hand, palm up, arm extended, approximately waist high.
	Followed by a downbeat.
Signification	Continuous sustained sound/pitch, at the discretion of the instrumentalist.
Explanation	The sign for "Sustain" is given, followed by a downbeat, to commence continuous sound/pitch. The sound/pitch may be changed each time a downbeat is given, and is always at the discretion of the individual.
Supplementary Note	It is suggested that as soon as instrumentalists hear how their sound fits into the ensemble sound, they immediately figure out what sound should follow to facilitate the best possible progression.
Nota bene	This directive may also be given to prolong individual sounds/pitches in notation.

(d) Conduction Directives | Articulation • Discretionary Sustain

4 The Conduction Lexicon

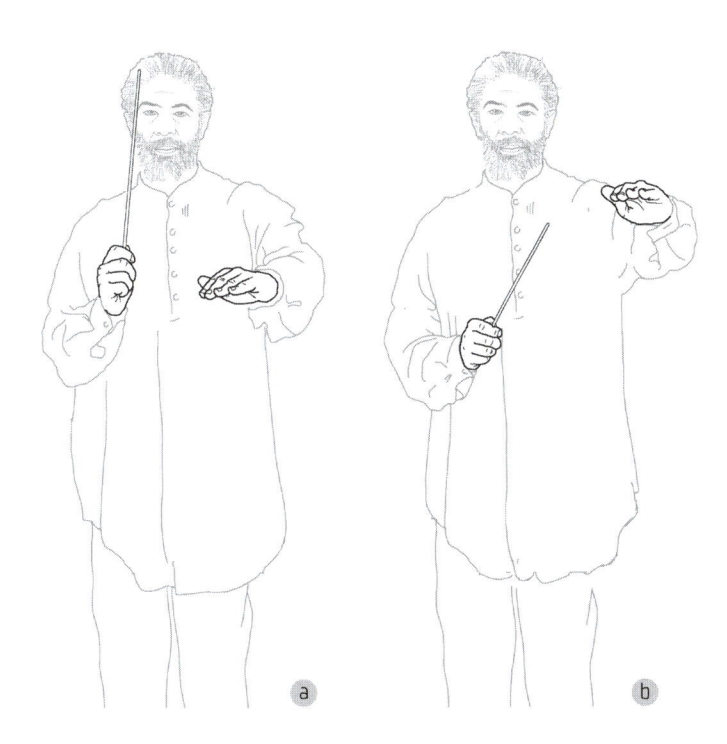

Pitched Sustain

a   b

| Sign | Left hand, palm down, arm extended. Moving in the general area from lower-waist to eye level for proximity of relative pitches – lower waist to eye level indicating a sonic range from low to high.

Followed by a downbeat. |
|---|---|
| Signification | Continuous sustained sound/pitch, relative to the position in space of the left hand. |
| Explanation | The sign for "Pitched Sustain" is given, followed by a downbeat, to commence continuous sustained sound/pitch.

The sound/pitch may be changed each time a downbeat is given, according to the conductor's lowering or raising of the left hand. |

(d) Conduction Directives | Articulation . Pitched Sustain

THE ART OF CONDUCTION 4

Melodic Movement
(Melodic Information-Cantilena)

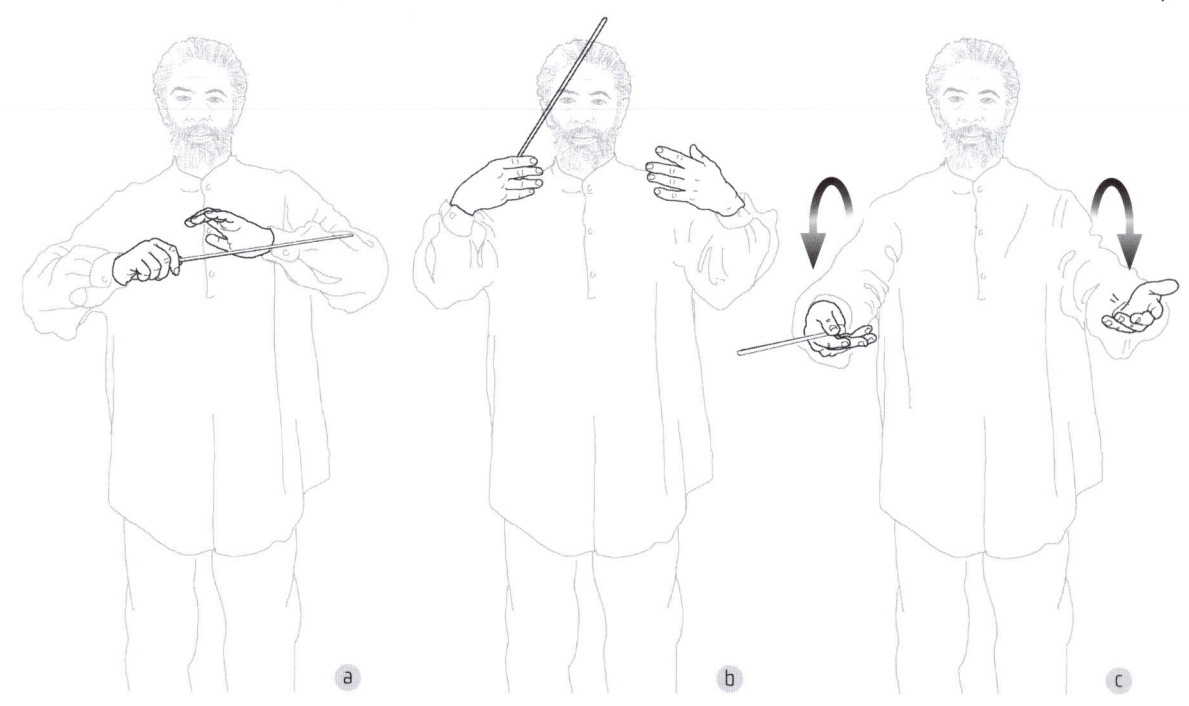

a   *b*   *c*

Sign/Gesture	Elbows spread, to the left and right, parallel to the floor with palms facing mid-chest area, moving upward and outward toward the ensemble.
Signification	A melodic intention/description, to be interpreted in real time.
Explanation	After the sign for "Melodic Movement" is given, the conductor transmits – by way of gesture – suggestions of a possible melodic arc. The conductor uses this directive to arrange melodic sequences by phrase. The instrumentalist is at liberty to interpret the conductor's expressions of melody; utilizing rests and silence whenever appropriate, she/he casts melodic ideas, interpretations, articulations, and accounts based on the conductor's real-time gestural descriptions. The first movement of the baton/hands following the designation of "Melodic Movement" acts as a downbeat for the activation of the directive.
Supplementary Note	All information should be executed in a space, time, and tempo that can be *articulated clearly*.

(d) Conduction Directives | Articulation • Melodic Movement

Staccato

Gesture	Right hand or baton held vertically, parallel to the body, above the right shoulder, producing short strokes.
Signification	Given as a small preliminary instruction, this indicates that the following sounds/pitches are to be articulated as short staccato. To be followed by larger gestures (short strokes) with the right hand or baton, chest to waist high, which also satisfy a downbeat requirement.
Explanation	The sound/pitch is to be changed each time a downbeat is given, following the arc of the hand or baton in space. The lower the hand (baton), the lower the pitch of the instrument; the higher the hand (baton), the higher the pitch of the instrument.
Nota bene	"Staccato" may also be indicated by the left hand in vertical position, from chest to waist height, fingers extended toward the ensemble, while a downbeat is given with the baton (right hand).

Conduction Directives | Articulation • Staccato

Glissando

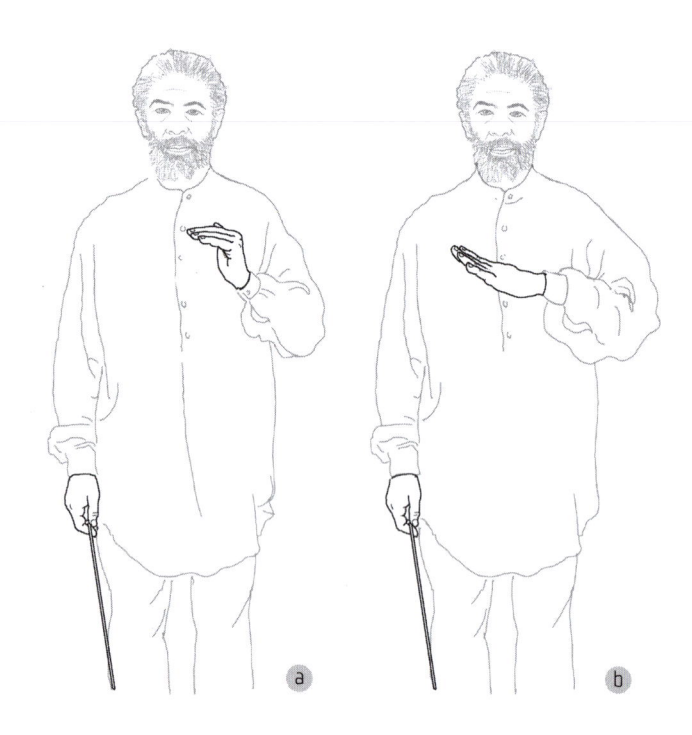

Gesture	Left hand, palm facing down, chest high, creating a wavelike motion (≈). Executed with or without a downbeat.
Signification	A gliding/sliding effect by tying all sounds/pitches together.

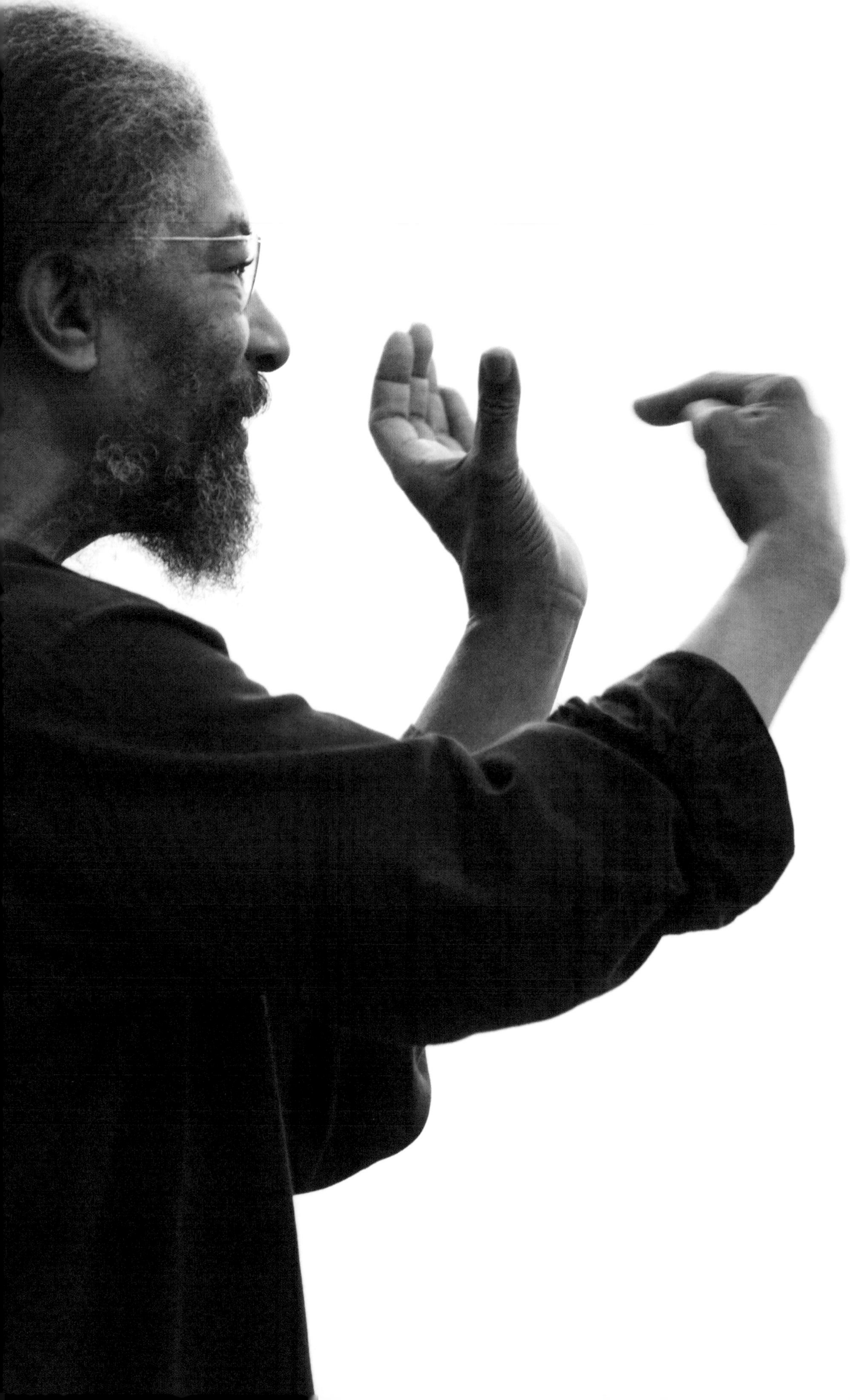

The Conduction Lexicon — 4

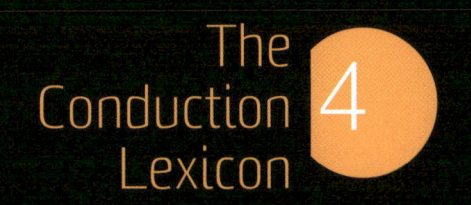

ⓔ Conduction Directives

Repeats

- **Repeat**
  1. Create/Construct
  2. Imitate/Emulate
  3. Echo/Reproduce
  4. Shadow/Pursue/Follow
  5. Copy/Replicate

- **Capture-Continue**

- **Memory**

THE ART OF CONDUCTION 4

Repeat

Sign	Left hand forming the letter "U."
	Followed by a downbeat.
Signification	To create, emulate, echo, imitate, or follow information/content, if not verbatim then by contour, outline, gesture or rhythmic graft, texture, timbre, and dynamic.
Explanation	There are five circumstances in which this sign is used:

1. Create/Construct:
   If the instrumentalist is *not* playing when the "Repeat" sign is given, she/he must construct content – be it sonic, melodic, rhythmic, or any combination thereof, and for any given duration – that is then repeated and established into the immediate collective sonic constructive order (i.e., "create something that repeats").

   When constructing a Repeat, the instrumentalist is advised to take all the time needed to do so, and to remember that the use of rests may be incorporated into the construction. Each instrumentalist determines the beginning (the "one") of their repeated information.

Nota bene	This directive may also be given with (time-based) pulse-tempo (i.e., "repeat in this tempo", or "repeat in time") in which case it is suggested that any time-based repeated content be represented as rhythm (rather than beat).

4 The Conduction Lexicon

2. Imitate/Emulate:
If there is information to be imitated/emulated from any source, the "Repeat" sign may be given to the instrumentalist with the left hand, while the information to be imitated/emulated will be identified by the conductor either by pointing with the right hand in the direction of the source (i.e., "repeat that") or through a gestural emulation of that sound.

3. Echo/Reproduce:
If an instrumentalist is playing, and the desire is to repeat/capture previously played information from that same instrumentalist, she/he is given the "Repeat" sign and then pointed to. The act of pointing satisfies the downbeat requirement for that same information to be echoed or reproduced (i.e., "repeat what you just played").

4. Shadow/Pursue/Follow:
If there is information of a continuous nature (neither repeated nor recurring), that information can be "shadowed," "followed," or "pursued" (as close as possible to the source contribution), in that the pursuer is given the "Repeat" sign and the source contribution is identified by the conductor by pointing with the right or left hand in the direction of the sound to be shadowed.

Nota bene — The instrumentalist being shadowed (possibly a Pedestrian) is at liberty to lead her/his pursuer(s) in any direction.

5. Copy/Replicate:
If there is an ensemble pattern (phrase, passage, or structure) that has been established, the "Repeat" sign may be given to indicate that this is the pattern to be replicated. The "Repeat" sign is shown for the duration of the pattern, or for as long as is needed to establish the pattern. The conductor may "trace" the pattern, by way of gesture, to demonstrate the rhythm of the movement, and give a downbeat to establish order.

Supplementary Note
(applies to all "Repeats" except "Shadow/Pursue/Follow")

Each instrumentalist can repeat (only) what they have processed from what they hear, have heard and understood from the proceedings and its direction. Nevertheless, when executing a Repeat (i.e., "Create/Construct" or "Imitate/Emulate") instrumentalists should attempt to capture the very essence of the sound that is repeated, from timbre and texture to arc and duration, sonic range and dynamics, to silences and rhythm, as it applies to their own instrument.

Once any (repeated) information is established, the instrumentalist is at liberty to elaborate/embellish it independently, while maintaining the integrity of her/his initial contribution and never losing sight of her/his original idea.

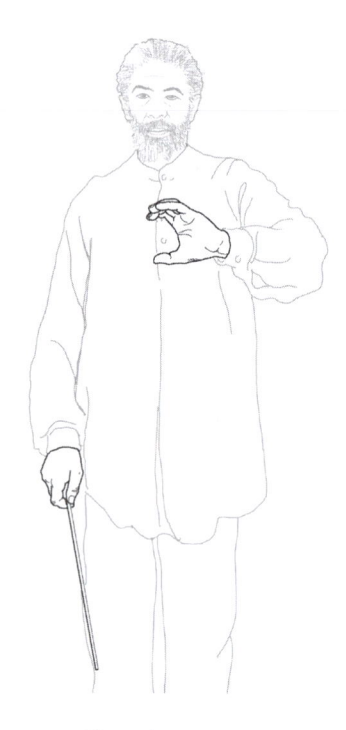

Capture-Continue

Sign	Left hand forming the letter "C," chest high; right hand designating the content to be captured.
Signification	Indicates that the instrumentalist is to capture the current content and to continue along these lines of investigation and discovery.
Explanation	When the "Capture-Continue" sign is given, the instrumentalist assesses what she/he is contributing and pursues and procures this (new) musical direction. No downbeat is given.
Supplementary Note	"Capture-Continue" differs from the "Repeat" sign in that it applies to a contribution that is already in a transformational state and remains so until a new directive is given.
Nota bene	"Capture-Continue" can also be addressed to designated groups, sections, or parts of the ensemble.

Memory

Gesture/Sign	Left hand numerical designation to forehead, followed by the display of the same numerical designation with finger(s) pointing upward and palm facing instrumentalists, head high. "Memory One:" one (index) finger; "Memory Two:" two (index and middle) fingers, etc. Followed by a downbeat.
Signification	For the recall and the return to designated information.
Explanation	Whatever the instrumentalist is contributing when the "Memory" designation is given, is what she/he recalls (and returns to) when that designation is repeated.
Supplementary Note	Any information designated and assigned as "Memory" is available for recall and re-evaluation at any time. The precision of "Memory" lies in the detail of remembering and returning to the exact point and moment of designation.

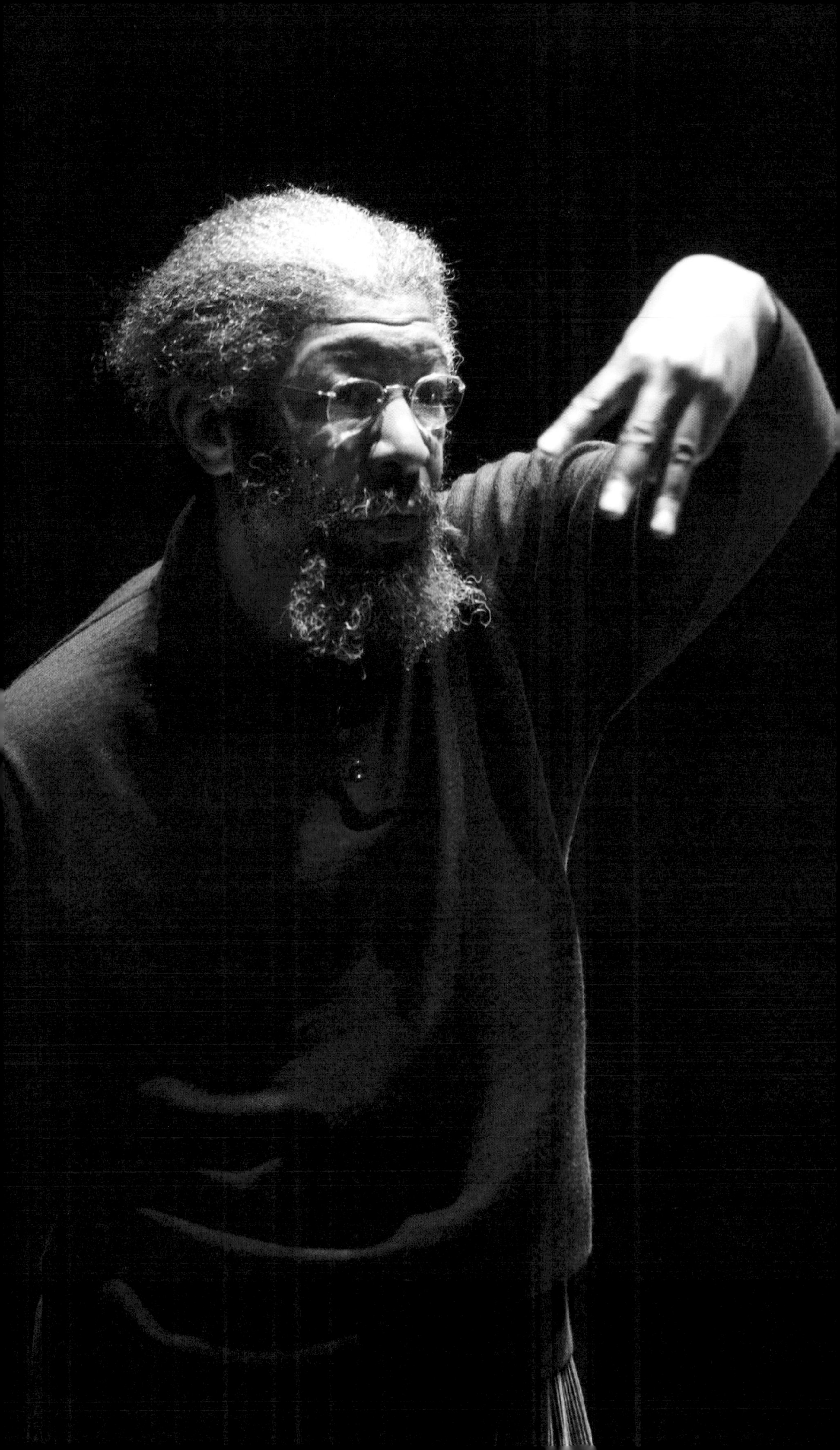

The Conduction Lexicon 4

ⓕ Conduction Directives
Time-Tempo-Pulse/Rhythm

- Tempo Designation (Pulse-Tempo/Meter)
- Rhythm (Initiating)
- Proportional Tempo/Time
- Notes to the Beat
- Spar/Phrase in Time
- Nuanced Usages: Downbeat and Upbeat (Indicating Tempo/Rhythm)
- Nuanced Usages: Accent

Tempo Designation (Pulse-Tempo/Meter)

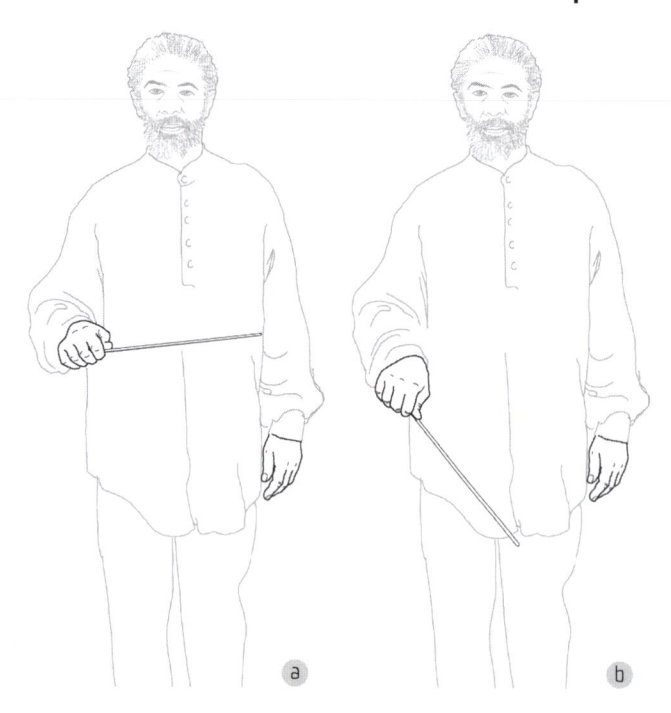

a   b

Gesture	Right hand or baton, facing right to left (perpendicular to the body) close to the chest area, beats desired pulse.
	Followed by a downbeat with the left hand.
Signification	To establish a pulse/tempo, a meter indication, or a meter modification.
Explanation	The pace of the tempo is indicated with the right hand as 1, 1, 1, 1 in even beats (none stronger than the other unless desired). The left hand may accent "1" when making a distinction between 2, 3, 4, etc.
	To indicate meter (measure): while the right hand marks time, the left hand indicates the beginning of the meter (or measure) with a stronger downbeat (accent/stress).
Supplementary Note	In all cases, this directive should be understood as constructing rhythm within the designated tempo.

4 The Conduction Lexicon

Rhythm (Initiating)

a   *b*

Gesture	Right arm/hand close to the body, waist high, taps and shapes the intended rhythmic gesture. Preceded by the "Yield" sign and followed by a downbeat.
Signification	To imply, initiate, define, or clarify rhythmic information or pattern.
Explanation	To define a new rhythm to be performed by designated instrumentalists, the conductor demonstrates it through rhythmic gesticulation with the right hand; to clarify an existing rhythm, the conductor emulates it with the right hand while pointing with the left hand in the direction of the rhythm to be imitated. In both cases, the right hand (baton) repeatedly taps and shapes (in mid air) the intended rhythmic gesture as preparatory information, while the left hand marks "1" or the beginning of the rhythm to be played.
Supplementary Note	When interpreting "Rhythm," each instrumentalist is at liberty to choose her/his own pitches.
Nota bene	"Rhythm" may also be given with the left hand, or with both hands.

(f) Conduction Directives | Time-Tempo-Pulse/Rhythm • Rhythm (Initiating)

Proportional Tempo/Time

Sign	Left hand, finger(s) pointing downward toward the floor, palm facing the conductor, waist to chest high, indicating: 1. index finger: SLOW (tempo); 2. index and middle fingers: MEDIUM (tempo); 3. index, middle, and third fingers: FAST (tempo); 4. index, middle, third, and fourth fingers: MACH (very fast tempo). Followed by a downbeat.
Signification	To designate a relative change of tempo.
Explanation	In changing the tempo of their contribution according to the conductor's indications, instrumentalists respond to the directive in a way that can be articulated clearly.
Supplementary Note	To bring information back to the original tempo and content, the "Reconstruct" gesture (horizontal) is given (see "Develop-Reconstruct" on p. 113).

4 The Conduction Lexicon

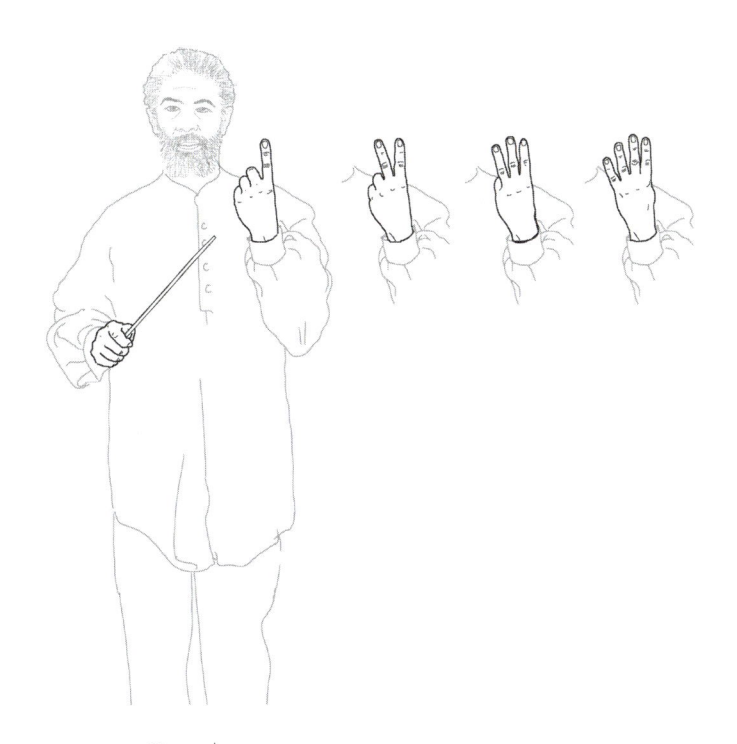

Notes to the Beat

Sign	Left hand, palm facing the conductor, one to four fingers extended upward, while the right hand (baton) beats the desired tempo. Followed by a downbeat.
Signification	To indicate how the designated tempo is to be divided (one finger for quarter notes, two fingers for 8th notes, three for triplets, four for 16th notes).

Conduction Directives | Time-Tempo-Pulse/Rhythm • Notes to the Beat

Spar/Phrase in Time

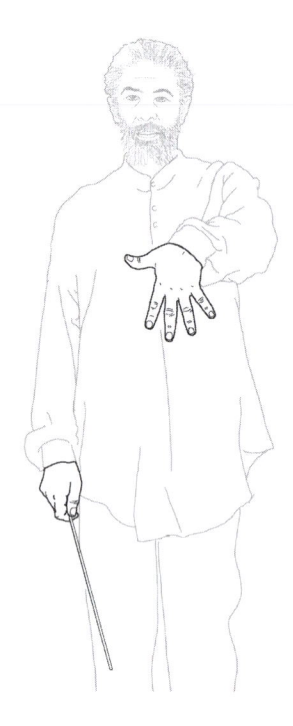

Sign/Gesture	Left hand, all fingers pointing downward toward the floor, palm facing the conductor, waist to chest high, followed by a tempo designation. Followed by a downbeat.
Signification	A monologue of rhythmic and melodic phrasing whose primary function is to imply tempo. Phrases, fragments, and syncopations that represent the flow of pulse/tempo, punctuated by *pauses*. To spar or bandy, as can be articulated clearly.
Explanation	When the "Spar" sign is given, and the conductor establishes a tempo (either through "Tempo Designation" or "Proportional Tempo/Time"), the instrumentalist casts rhythmic syncopations and melodic ideas/interpretations, employing dynamics, accents and pauses in the given tempo. The collective result is a discourse of rhythmic counterpoint with *the primary purpose and function of propelling the ensemble.*
Supplementary Note	All information is executed in a space, time, and tempo that can be *articulated clearly*, by utilizing pauses and rests whenever appropriate, all within the standard notation system (whole note through 64th note).

4 The Conduction Lexicon

Nota bene 1 — The directive can also be connected to gestural real-time descriptions the conductor produces with the baton, as in "Graphic Information" (see p. 128). In that case, after the sign for "Spar" is shown and a tempo designation given, the instrumentalist contributes as if scatting on her/his own instrument by interpreting the movement of the baton as it transmits and determines phrase/form, graphic contour, and accent.

The position of the baton indicates the sonic register on the instrument: the lower the baton, the lower the pitch on the instrument; the higher the baton, the higher the pitch on the instrument. When the baton stops, the instrumentalist stops.

Nota bene 2 — The directive may also be executed in connection with "Melodic Movement" or "Panorama."

Nota bene 3 — If the conductor does not designate a tempo, the instrumentalist may establish a tempo and play phrases accordingly.

Nuanced Usages: Downbeat and Upbeat (Indicating Tempo/Rhythm)

Downbeats	Downbeats (with baton/hand) may indicate pulse, mark time/pulse, or meter; they may also be used to indicate rhythm or correlating accents, to stress any fragment of a rhythm or a beat that is not an upbeat.
Upbeats	Upbeats (with baton/hand) may indicate rhythm, pulse, or correlating accents, to stress any fragment of a rhythm or a beat that is not a downbeat.

4 The Conduction Lexicon

= Nuanced Usages: Accent

To create or move the accent placement within the current content, the conductor can draw upon various forms of bodily expressions (a gestural visualization, whispered singing, etc.) through which he/she indicates location and type of accent. The following sign may also be used, with or without a downbeat.

Sign | Left hand on right shoulder.

Nota bene | Moving the accent placement may also be left at the discretion of the instrumentalist.

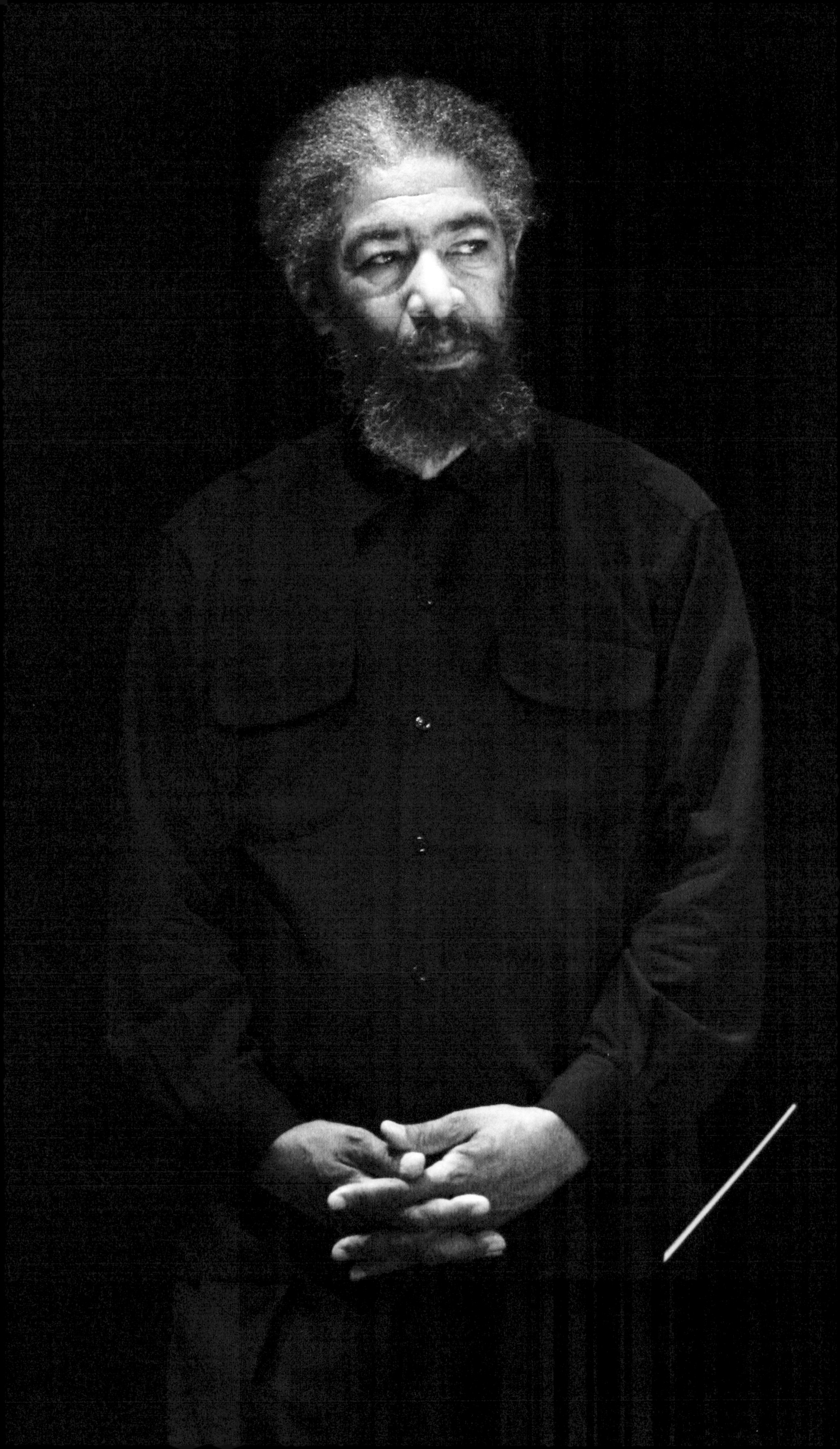

The Conduction Lexicon — 4

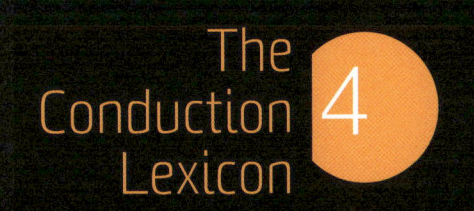

⑨ Conduction Directives
Tempo Modifications

- Doubletime
- Halftime
- Accelerando-Ritardando (with Baton)
- Accelerando-Ritardando (with Hand)
- Place in Time/Free of Time

THE ART OF CONDUCTION 4

Doubletime

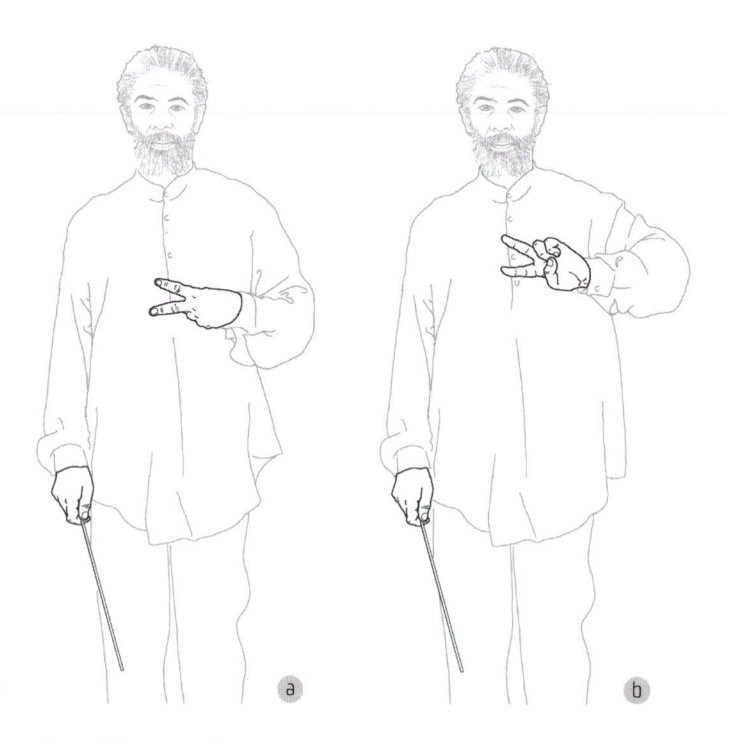

a   b

Sign/Gesture | Back of the left hand facing the instrumentalist, index and middle fingers spread and pointing to the right at mid-chest or upper waist area, then hand turned to expose the palm toward the instrumentalist, rotating upward.

Followed by a downbeat.

Signification | Indicates that the instrumentalist is to play her/his contribution in doubletime.

Nota bene | To bring information back to the original tempo, either the "Halftime" sign (see opposite) or the "Reconstruct" gesture (horizontal) may be given (see "Develop-Reconstruct" on p. 113).

(9) Conduction Directives | Tempo Modifications • Doubletime

4 The Conduction Lexicon

Halftime

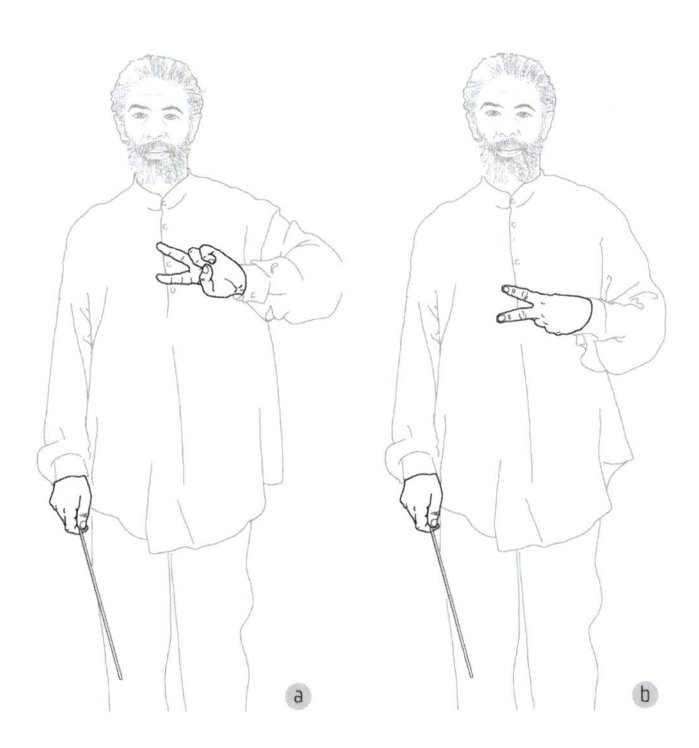

a   b

Sign/Gesture	Palm of the left hand facing the instrumentalist, index and middle fingers spread and pointing to the right at mid-chest or upper waist area, then hand turned to expose the back toward the instrumentalist, rotating downward. Followed by a downbeat.
Signification	Indicates that the instrumentalist is to play her/his contribution in halftime.
Nota bene	To bring information back to the original tempo, either the "Doubletime" sign (see opposite) or the "Reconstruct" gesture (horizontal) may be given (see "Develop-Reconstruct" on p.113).

(9) Conduction Directives | Tempo Modifications • Halftime

Accelerando-Ritardando (with Baton)

Gesture	Right hand or baton facing right to left (perpendicular to the body), close to chest area, beating desired pulse.
Signification	To make immediate tempo modifications (faster or slower) by beating desired tempo.
Explanation	Response is immediate, no downbeat is given.
Supplementary Note	The directive may be preceded by the "Accompany Me" sign as preliminary information, indicating there will be a change of tempo.

Accelerando-Ritardando (with Hand)

a   b

Sign/Gesture	Left hand, palm facing instrumentalist(s), waist to mid-chest high, pushing forward for faster, and backward for slower.
Signification	To make immediate tempo modifications (faster or slower).
Explanation	Response is immediate, no downbeat is given.
Nota bene	"Accelerando/Ritardando (with Hand)" may also be indicated by the left fist (palm down) pointing at instrumentalist(s), waist to mid-chest high, pushing forward for faster, and backward for slower.

THE ART OF CONDUCTION 4

Place in Time/Free of Time

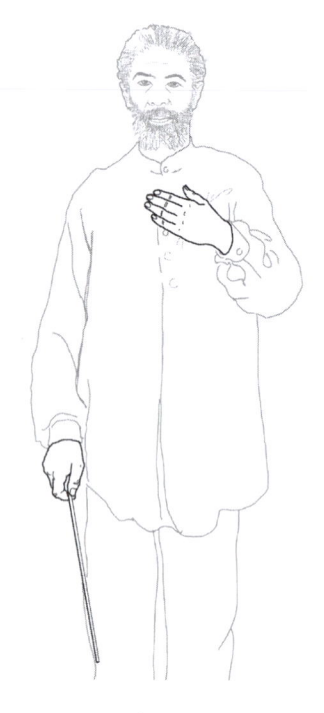

Sign	Left hand on heart.
	Followed by a downbeat.
Signification	Indicates that the instrumentalist is either to place her/his contribution in a designated or discretionary time/pulse, or to take that contribution free of time/free of pulse.
Explanation	If the instrumentalist is contributing in time/pulse when this directive is given, she/he is to contribute the same information free of time/free of pulse upon a downbeat.
	If the instrumentalist is contributing free of time/free of pulse when this directive is given, she/he is to contribute the same information in time/pulse upon a downbeat.
Supplementary Note	Time/pulse may be designated by the conductor, or left to the discretion of the instrumentalist.
Nota bene	To bring information back to the original state (in time or free of time), the "Reconstruct" gesture (horizontal) may be given (see "Develop-Reconstruct" on p. 113).

Conduction Directives — Tempo Modifications • Place in Time/Free of Time

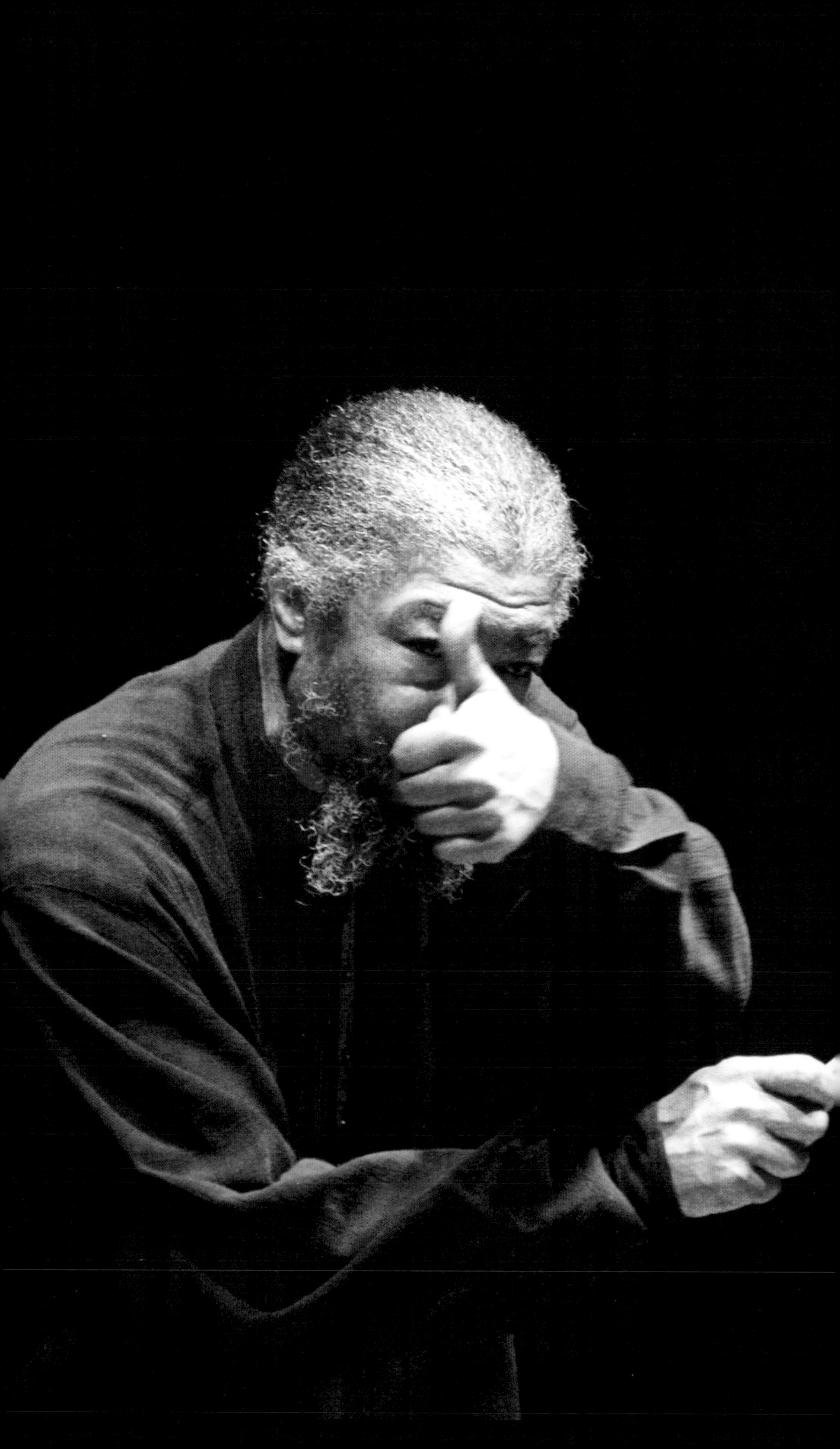

The Conduction Lexicon 4

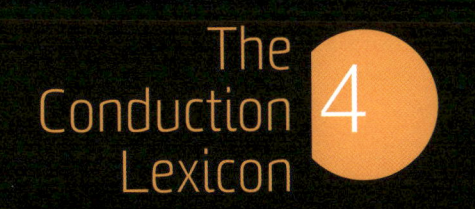

(h) Conduction Directives
Tonality/Pitch

- Change in Tonality/Pitch
- Change by Octave
- Harmodulation/Transposition
- Resolve
- Tonal Center/Key (Establishing)

Change in Tonality/Pitch

Sign	Left hand in fist, thumb pointing upward for higher sonic range; thumb pointing downward for lower sonic range.
	Followed by a downbeat.
Signification	To transpose, transfer or shift whatever the instrumentalist is contributing to a higher or lower sonic range.
Explanation	Depending on which sign is given, the instrumentalist "moves" what she/he is playing up to a higher, or down to a lower pitch, tonality, or tonal center. The extension of the change in tonality is at the instrumentalist's discretion.

Change by Octave

Sign	Left hand, thumb pointing upward with little finger downward for higher octave; thumb pointing downward with little finger upward for lower octave. Followed by a downbeat.
Signification	The "Change by Octave" sign indicates that whatever the instrumentalist is contributing will be played either one octave up or down.

Tonality/Pitch • Change by Octave

Harmodulation/Transposition

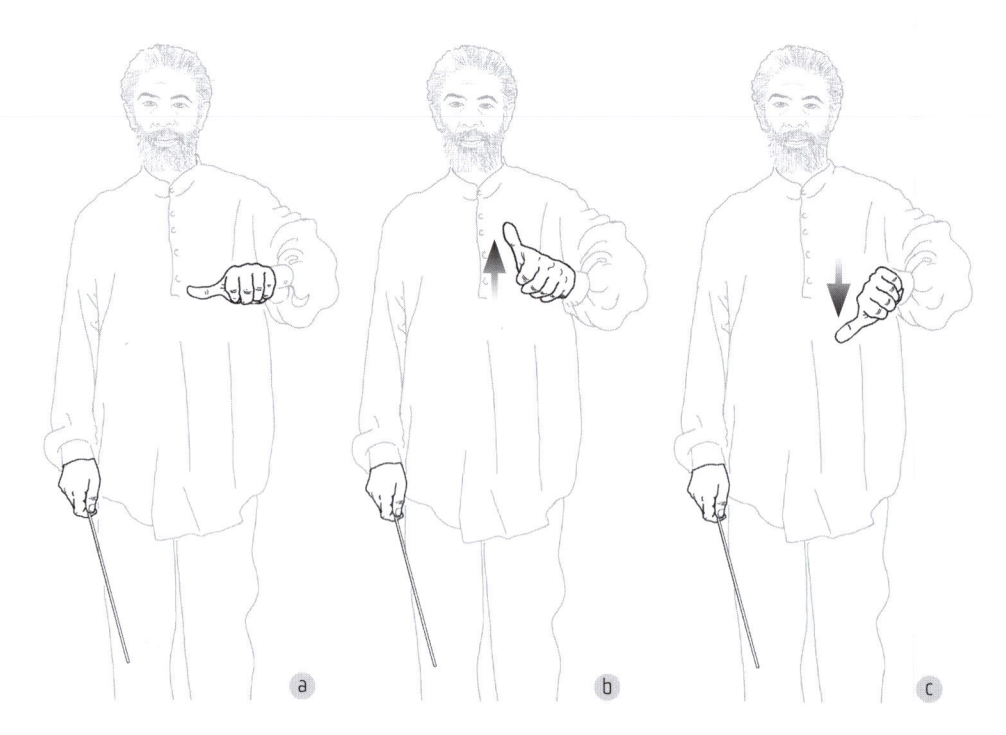

a b c

Sign/Gesture — Left hand in fist facing the ensemble, thumb pointing right, then rotating thumb upward or downward.

Signification — To "migrate," harmodulate, transpose sonic information from one tonality to another in real time.

Explanation — As the conductor progressively turns the thumb of the left hand up or down, the instrumentalist "migrates," harmodulates, transposes her/his information through a tonality, pitch, tonal center, or key to another. The first movement of the thumb activates the directive.

Nota bene — The directive can be achieved by thinking of the whammy bar on a guitar or the pitch bend on a synthesizer.

Resolve

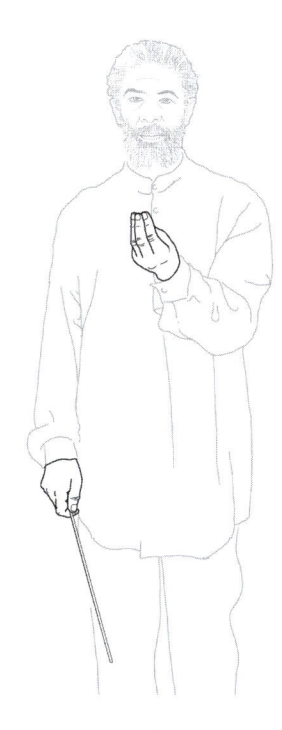

Sign	Cupped left hand, all fingers and thumb touching at their tips, facing upward in the center of the chest.
	Followed by a downbeat.
Signification	To resolve a contribution to its tonic, tonal, or key center.
Explanation	If the instrumentalist's contribution is of a sustained nature, he moves to a resolved sustain; if the instrumentalist's contribution is of a "moving line" nature, he moves (transfers the content) to a final cadence, that is, to a moving line resolution. When instrumentalists see the "Resolve" sign, they begin to position themselves toward resolving their content.
Supplementary Note	The tonal independence of each instrumentalist will determine the ensemble's tonal concord. However, if (one) tonal center has been established, everyone moves to resolve on that center.

THE ART OF CONDUCTION 4

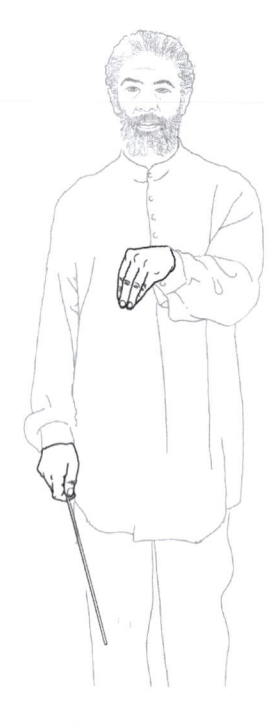

Tonal Center/Key (Establishing)

Sign	Cupped left hand, all fingers and thumb touching at their tips, facing downward in the center of the chest, followed by the designation of the instrumentalist whose key the conductor wishes to move to.
Signification	Indicates what the tonal center (or key) is and where it is being established; instrumentalists are required to contribute from this harmonic viewpoint.
Explanation	Response is immediate; no downbeat is given.
Nota bene	The directive may also be used when working in conjunction with notated material.

(h) Conduction Directives | Tonality/Pitch • Tonal Center/Key (Establishing)

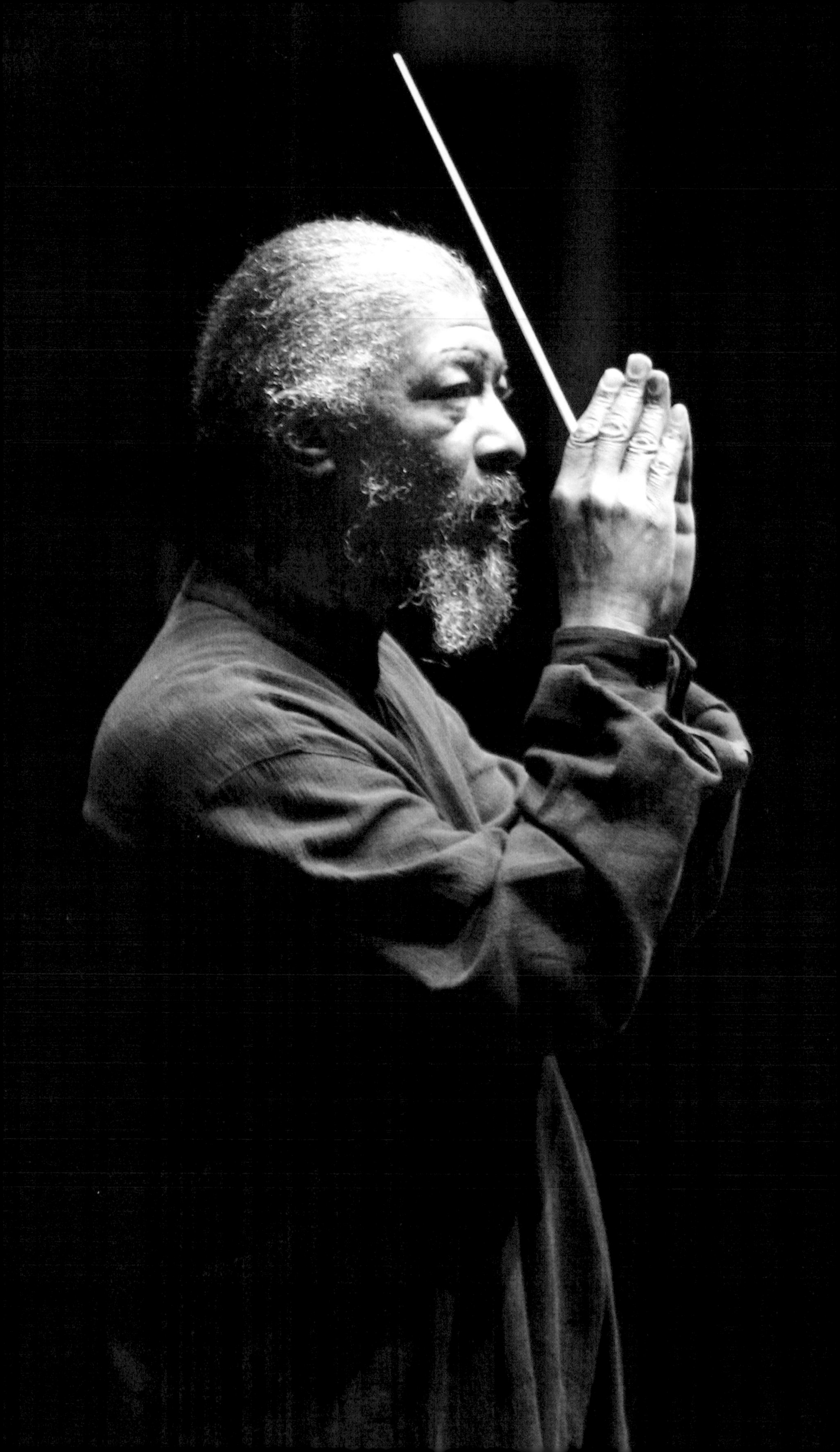

The Conduction Lexicon 4

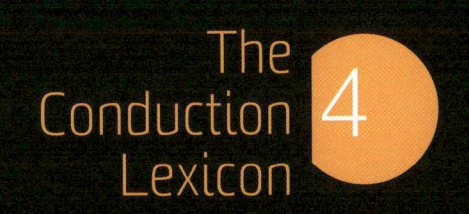

ⓘ Conduction Directives
Evolutionary Transformations

- Developments
  - Develop-Reconstruct (Horizontal)
  - Develop-Reconstruct (Vertical)
  - Distill
  - Spin
- Accompany
- Bridge

Developments

All directives in the "Developments" category are processes of explaining, unfolding, and evolving the effectiveness of the contribution at hand; working out by degrees and revealing growth in stages.

The developmental transformation of sonic information/content is based on the nature and signification of the directive to which it is applied, on the way this is musically interpreted by instrumentalists, and on instrumentalists' conception of development.

The time taken to transform the information is at the discretion of each instrumentalist; the use of rests and silence of any duration is highly encouraged in all stages of development. The process of transformation should in any case unfold and evolve slowly in time.

All directives in the "Developments" category are transitory; they involve elaboration, disclosure, embellishment, adornment, manipulation, augmentation, or diminishment of subject, theme, form, or structure. Through them, instrumentalists bring individual meaning to the context of the directive at hand, elevating and evolving it within the ensemble sound.

Develop-Reconstruct (Horizontal)

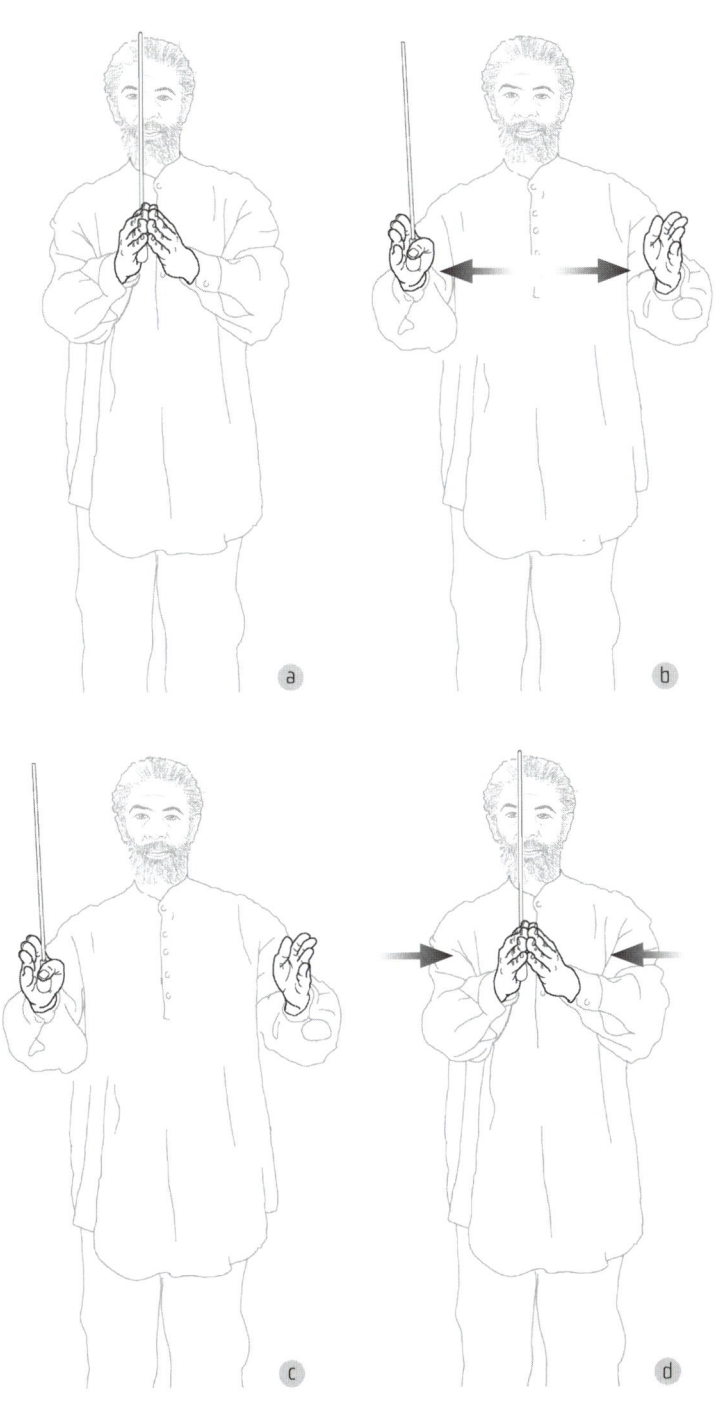

| Gesture | Hands palm-to-palm facing left and right, chest level, separating left and right for "Develop," and returning to the together position for "Reconstruct." |

THE ART OF CONDUCTION 4

Signification	The exploration, elaboration, exploitation, and subsequent reconstruction of existing information. To construct, deconstruct, develop, and reconstruct-retrieve specific (designated) content.
Explanation	Palms together designates the information/content to be developed, as perceived and conceived by the instrumentalist; the separation of the hands ("Develop") acts as a downbeat to begin the developmental process, while the rejoining of the hands ("Reconstruct") acts as a downbeat for returning to the initial information. Whatever the instrumentalist is contributing when the "Develop" gesture is given (for example, a sustained or a staccato sound, a repeat, a pedal, or silence) is *exactly* what he returns to when the "Reconstruct" gesture is given.
	The "Develop" gesture indicates that the instrumentalist is at liberty to explore the information/content that she/he is contributing at the time the directive is given, but should never lose sight of the original idea.
Supplementary Note	The degree of development may be seen as determined in stages by the expansion/contraction of the space between the hands.
Nota bene 1	The gesture for "Reconstruct" may also serve as a downbeat to bring information back to the original tempo (see "Proportional Tempo/Time," "Doubletime," "Halftime," "Place in Time/Free of Time").
Nota bene 2	If during the developmental process the conductor shows a new directive – for instance, "Repeat-Create/Construct" or "Memory" – the subsequent gesture for "Reconstruct" acts as a downbeat to activate the new directive. Furthermore, if the new directive is given to groups, sections, or parts of the ensemble only, the gesture for "Reconstruct" acts as a downbeat to activate the new directive for those designated instrumentalists, while instructing every other instrumentalist to reconstruct their initial information.

4 The Conduction Lexicon

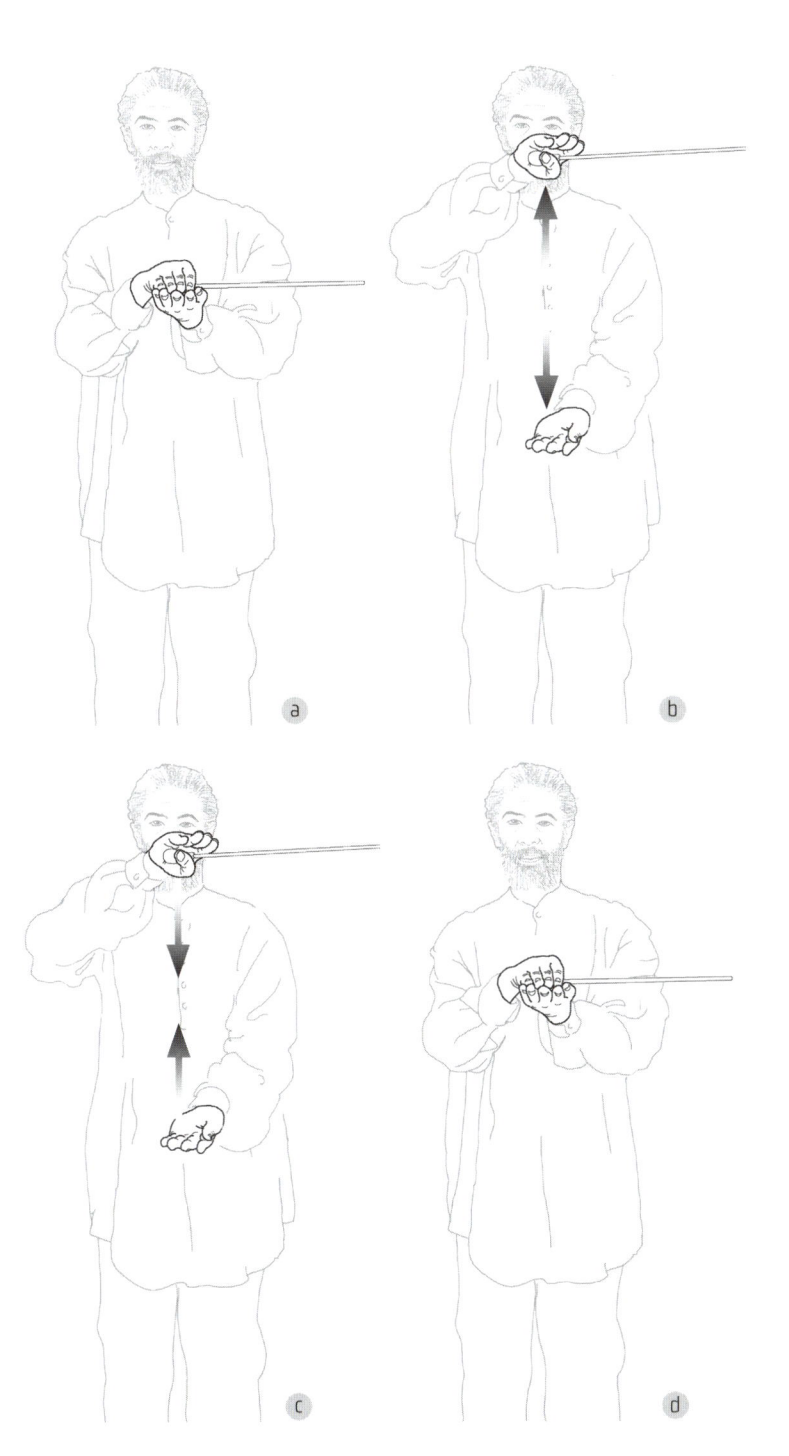

Develop-Reconstruct (Vertical)

a

b

c

d

Gesture | Hands palm-to-palm, facing upward and downward at chest level, spreading upward for "Develop" and downward for "Reconstruct."

Conduction Directives | 115 | Evolutionary Transformations • Develop-Reconstruct (Vertical)

THE ART OF CONDUCTION 4

Signification	To maintain the rhythmic idea (subject, theme, motif, or direction) of one's own contribution, while altering the harmonic/melodic/pitch content.
Explanation	Palms together designates the information/content to be developed, as perceived and conceived by the instrumentalist; the separation of the hands ("Develop") acts as a downbeat to begin the developmental process, while the rejoining of the hands ("Reconstruct") acts as a downbeat for returning to the initial information. Whatever the instrumentalist is contributing when the "Develop" gesture for harmonic/melodic development is given is *exactly* what she/he returns to when the "Reconstruct" gesture is given.
Supplementary Note	The degree of development may be seen as determined in stages by the expansion/contraction of the space between the hands.

4 The Conduction Lexicon

Distill

a   *b*

Gesture	Hands spread left and right pointing forward and closing to touch, index finger of right hand touching palm of left hand.
Signification	To condense a contribution/information/content.
Explanation	When the "Distill" directive is given, the instrumentalist reduces her/his contribution to whatever she/he deems most important or necessary, through (processes of) elimination. Such process of transformation will lead to a new concentration of information.
Nota bene	The "Distill" directive is not associated with a previous "Develop;" rather, it may be applied to instrumentalists' contributions such as, for instance, "Repeat" or "Pedestrian."

Conduction Directives | Evolutionary Transformations • Distill

Spin

Gesture	Left hand, index finger pointing upward, left shoulder high, making little circles.
Signification	To make rhythmic variations and re-arrangements on given pitches only.
Explanation	When the "Spin" directive is given, the instrumentalist re-arranges her/his contribution rhythmically, without altering the pitches. Response is immediate; no downbeat is given.

4 The Conduction Lexicon

Accompany

Sign/Gesture	Left hand, index finger pointing to left ear, right hand (baton) pointing toward the information/content to be accompanied.
Signification	To direct focus to a particular instrumentalist or area of sound, for support.
Explanation	The instrumentalist accompanies existing designated information by supporting and or reinforcing it from a sonic (melodic, rhythmic, or harmonic) and/or structural perspective. The instrumentalist's entry into "Accompany" is at her/his discretion; no downbeat is given.
	To listen to, assist, complement, the and interact in a supportive manner with the indicated activity.

Conduction Directives   Evolutionary Transformations • Accompany

Bridge

Sign	Left hand forming an arc (bridge) shape, face high, parallel to the conductor's body.
	Followed by a downbeat.
Signification	To span one section into another through change.
Explanation	The directive indicates a transmutational shift that is to take place in another key or tonal center; a section or movement that the instrumentalist transitions through modulation or harmodulation to a new tonality or tonal center.
Supplementary Note	Although attributed and connected with what precedes it, and a continuation thereof, the "Bridge" represents noticeable change. It is more assertive in its exposition, development, and chorus, and it is constructed as significantly intermediate, that is, as an arc that leads either back or forward, serving to advance the spirit and direction of the overall construction.

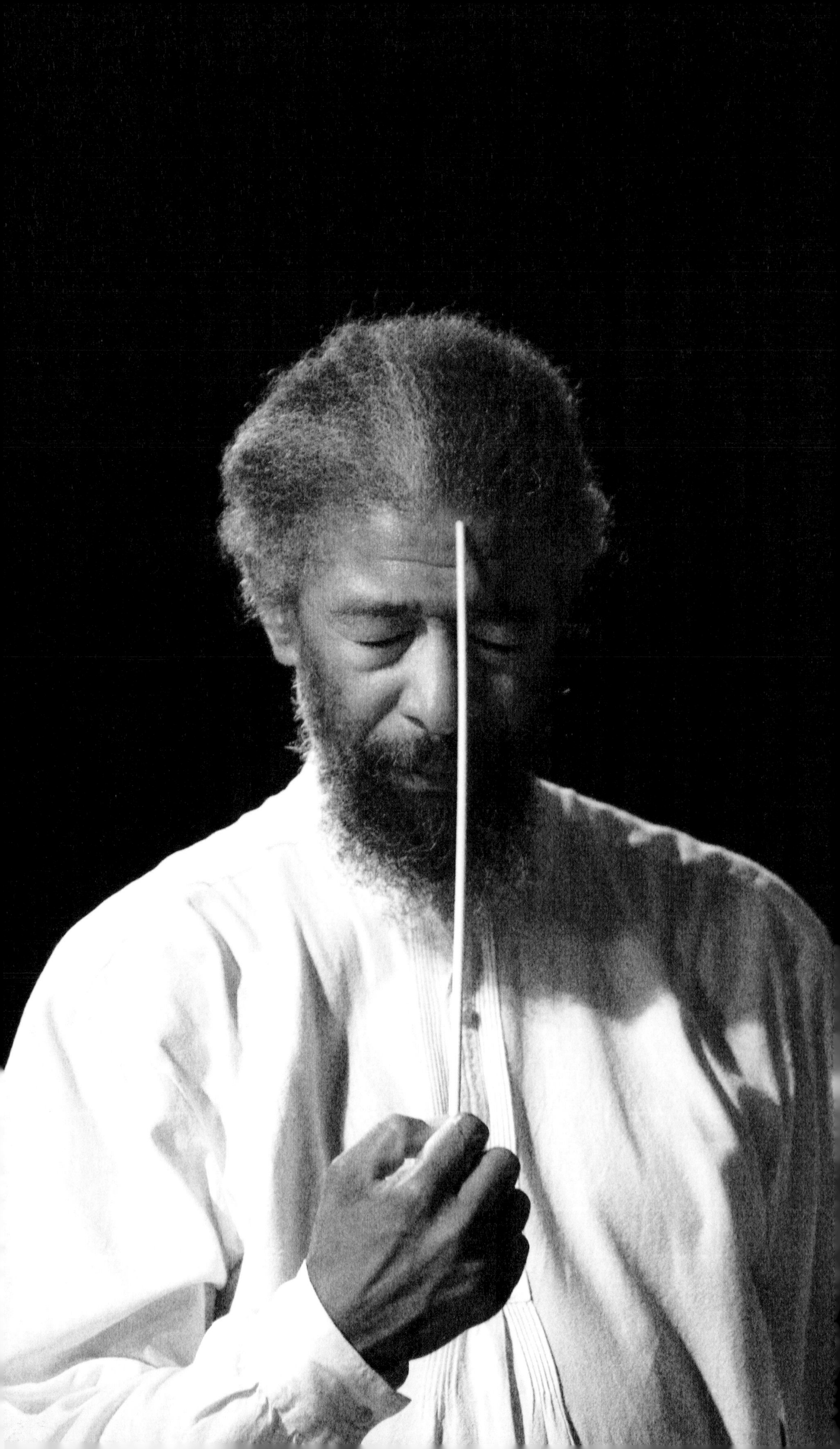

The Conduction Lexicon 4

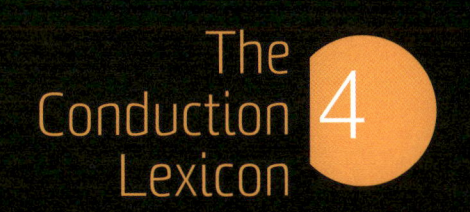

j) Conduction Directives

Events

- Panorama
- Panorama Fragment/Excerpt
- Panorama Hocket/Brief Contributions
- Graphic Information (Literal Movement)
- Accompany Me/Imaging/Shaping
- Ground/Trap-Sample-Loop
- Event
- Arpeggio
- Pedal/Splash-Crash
- Call and Response
- Breath

Panorama

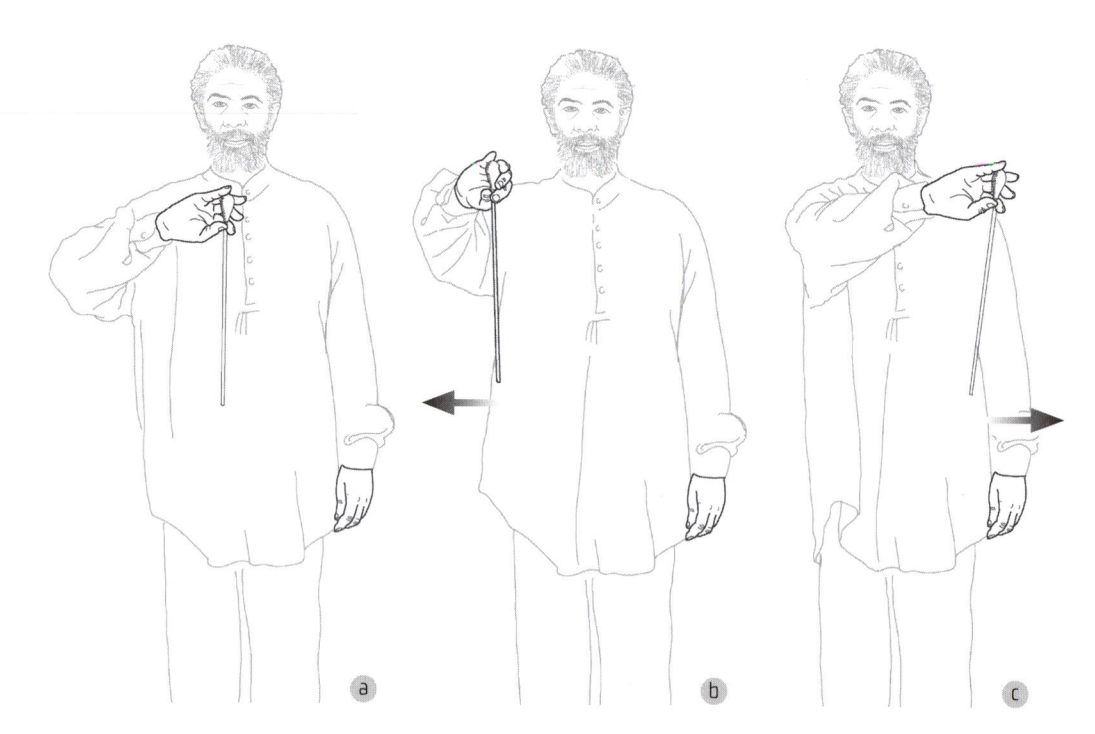

Sign/Gesture	Baton parallel to body, handle in chin area, pointing downward. After the panorama designation, the baton (or hand) is directed toward, and passed in front of, the instrumentalists.
Signification	Presence or absence of musical contribution. To start and then stop, or to stop and then start a contribution, when the baton or hand is directly in the "physical field" between the conductor and the instrumentalist.
Explanation	After the "Panorama" sign is given: 1. If the instrumentalist is *not* contributing (is at rest), she/he is required to start her/his contribution when the baton (or hand) enters her/his field, and to stop when the baton exits it. Instrumentalists are at liberty to change the content of their contribution each time the baton enters their field. 2. If the instrumentalist *is* contributing (is playing), she/he is required to stop her/his contribution when the baton (or hand) enters her/his field, and to resume playing when the baton exits it.
Supplementary Note	The first movement of the baton following the "Panorama" designation acts as a downbeat for the activation of the directive.

4 The Conduction Lexicon

Nota bene 1	Panorama 1: If the "Repeat" sign is displayed during the execution of the "Panorama," the instrumentalist immediately captures one sonic contribution and repeats the same one each time the baton enters her/his field. The conductor may, subsequently, designate the repeated panorama as a "Memory," and establish where the panorama begins by pointing to a given instrumentalist and giving a downbeat.

The beginning of the "Panorama" – the "one" – can be relocated by the conductor from instrumentalist to instrumentalist, so as to change the internal rhythm of the "Panorama." The "Panorama," though, will continue to move in the same, original direction. |
| Nota bene 2 | "Panorama" may also be moved into a developmental stage, for instance, through "Develop," and brought back to its original state through "Reconstruct." |

THE ART OF CONDUCTION 4

Panorama Fragment/Excerpt

Sign	Baton parallel to body, handle in chin area, pointing downward.
	Followed by a downbeat.
Signification	To break (up) or separate existing information, utilizing space between sonic contributions.
Explanation	If the instrumentalist *is* contributing when the "Panorama" sign is given and is followed by a downbeat, she/he is required to interrupt (stop-rest) her/his contribution, then resume the process of starting and stopping. After the downbeat, all entrances and exits (contributions and interruptions) are at the discretion of the instrumentalist.
Nota bene	The directive "Panorama Fragment/Excerpt" is about stopping a contribution rather than bringing it to an end.

Panorama Hocket/Brief Contributions

Sign	Baton parallel to body, handle in chin area, pointing downward.
	Followed by a downbeat.
Signification	To make brief contributions.
Explanation	If the instrumentalist is *not* contributing when the "Panorama" sign is given and is followed by a downbeat, she/he makes a brief contribution, followed by rest, then resumes the process of starting and stopping. After the downbeat, all entrances and exits (contributions and interruptions) are at the discretion of the instrumentalist.

Graphic Information (Literal Movement)

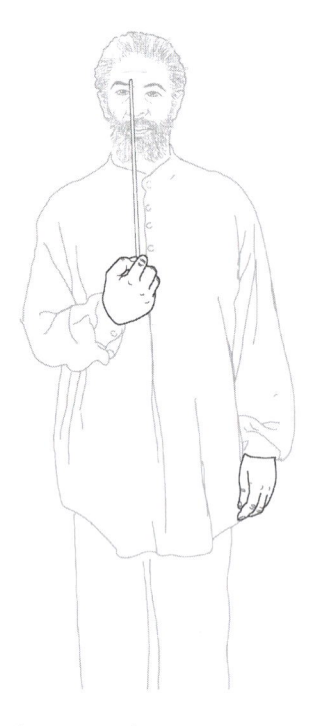

Sign /Gesture	Baton parallel to the body, in front of the face; baton handle in chest area, tip of the baton at forehead. After the sign for "Graphic Information" is given, the conductor traces visual patterns with the baton in midair.
Signification	A real-time literal sonic interpretation of graphic information.
Explanation	Each instrumentalist is required to "read" and interpret on their own instrument the movement of the baton as it transmits graphic information and determines phrase/form and graphic contour.
	The position of the baton indicates the sonic register on the instrument: the lower the baton, the lower the pitch on the instrument; the higher the baton, the higher the pitch on the instrument.
	After the sign for "Graphic Information" is given, the first movement of the baton acts as a downbeat. When the baton stops, instrumentalists stop.
Supplementary Note	The directive should be executed in a space, time, and tempo that allows for a clear articulation. Instrumentalists are encouraged to use rests and space whenever appropriate.

Accompany Me/Imaging/Shaping

Sign/Gesture	Left hand pointing to chest, followed by gestural illustrations of sonic/rhythmic ideas.
Signification	A developmental device to initiate or transform/modify sonic information/images through gestural suggestion/appropriation. Indicates that the instrumentalist is to interpret what she/he perceives in tandem with the conductor.
Explanation	This sign may be used in three instances:

1. Accompany Me:
   Indicates that the instrumentalist is receiving new direction at the moment the sign is given. The instrumentalist is to accompany, join, or follow the conductor's direction or place (see, for instance, "Accelerando-Ritardando with Baton").

2. Imaging:
   Indicates that the initiation of collaborative ideas will take place, based on the conductor's gestural suggestion. After the sign is given, the conductor displays a visual representation/illustration of a sonic idea, which is then elaborated on by the instrumentalists.

3. Shaping:
   Indicates that the collaborative development of (an) existing sonic idea(s) will take place. After the sign is given, the conductor gesturally captures

and appropriates an existing sonic idea, then applies a visual image/description for that same idea to be modified and/or redirected together with instrumentalists.

Supplementary Note (applied to "Imaging" and "Shaping")

The conductor, either by graphic or rhythmic contour, may initiate, modify, elaborate, and/or embellish sonic information by making it longer or shorter in duration, higher or lower in pitch, softer or louder in dynamic, foreground, mid-ground or background in depth.

Nota bene

"Accompany Me" may also be used to instruct designated instrumentalists to join the conductor in executing a directive currently being given to other members of the ensemble.

Furthermore, it may be used when multiple directives are distributed among the ensemble. In this case, while some instrumentalists are executing a given directive (for instance, a "Memory" or a section of a notated work), the conductor may address additional members of the ensemble with the "Accompany Me" sign, and give them a new, different directive (for instance, a series of "Sustains").

Ground/Trap-Sample-Loop

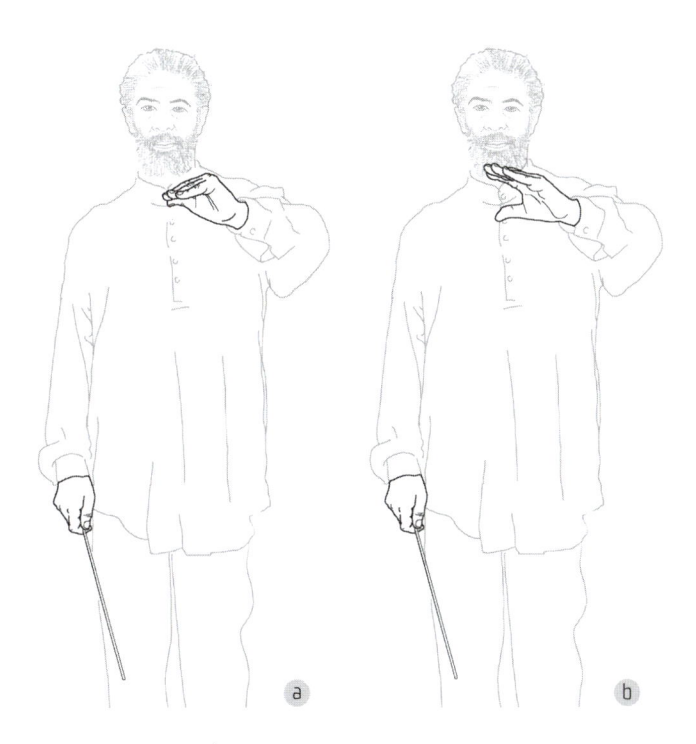

a b

Gesture	Left hand, four fingers meet thumb, at chest to chin level. Followed by the opening of the four fingers (for electronic instruments) or by a downbeat (for acoustic instruments).
Signification	For electronic instruments: to "trap-sample." For acoustic instruments: to prepare to "ground." The ground is a layer of sound that may or may not be a harmonic/enharmonic progression and that is a continuous and recurring variation of "sound fabric."
Explanation	For live samples and digital delays: to record, capture (trap/loop) general or specific information that is then continued. For acoustic and amplified acoustic instruments: to instate a vamp/bed (of sound) – ostinato, ground, or any combination thereof – that is continuous and recurring.
Nota bene	The activation of the directive may also be at the discretion of the instrumentalist.

Event

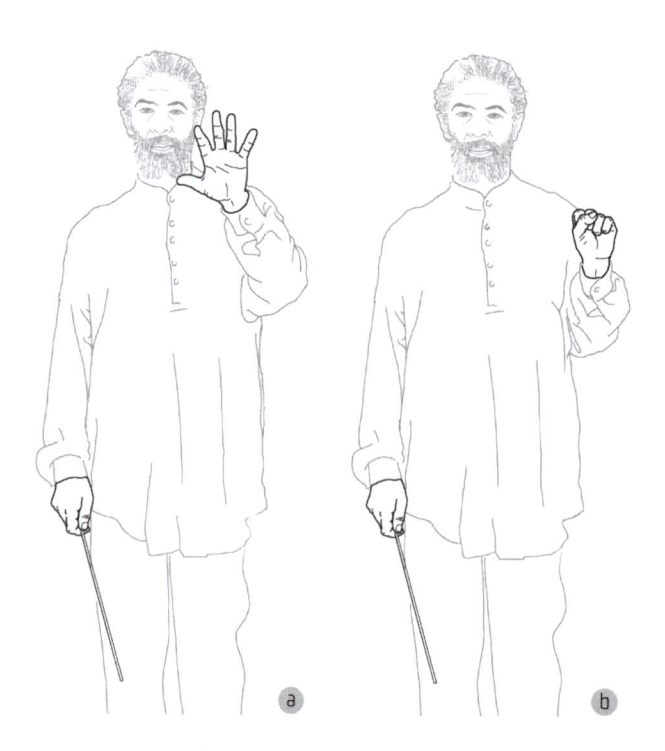

a b

Gesture	A grabbing motion/gesture with the left hand ending in a fist at mid-chest level (parallel to body), palm facing the ensemble.
	Followed by a downbeat.
Signification	To make contributions (in phrases) lasting the length of a breath and brought to an end.
Explanation	To create collective occurrence of individual circumstantial events.

4 The Conduction Lexicon

Arpeggio

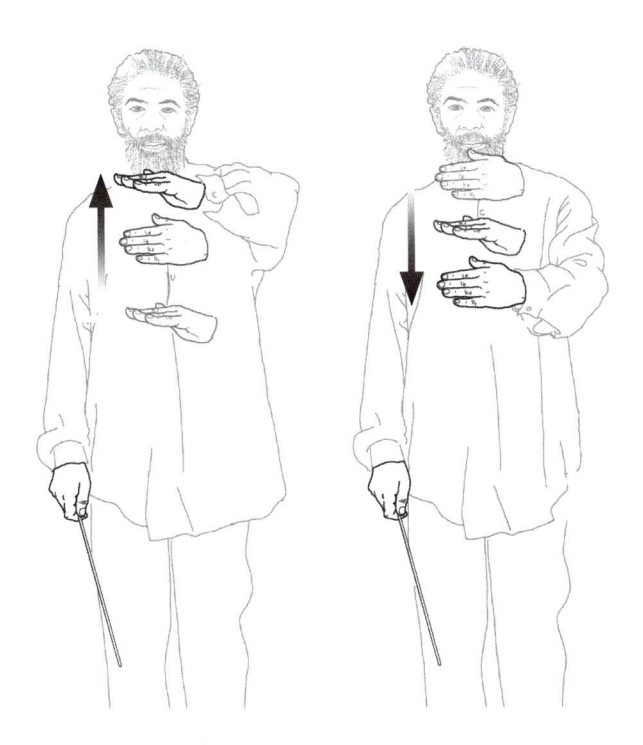

Gesture	Left hand, palm facing downward at chest level, quivering and moving upward (for an ascending arpeggio) or downward (for a descending arpeggio).
	Followed by a downbeat.
Signification	The creation and production of an arpeggio. Melodic succession of tones/pitches/notes/sounds, going either up or down, as indicated.
Explanation	When the "Arpeggio" directive is given, followed by a downbeat, the instrumentalist elaborates and embellishes whatever she/he is doing through arpeggiation.
Supplementary Note	The rhythm and duration of the arpeggio may be determined by the conductor, or be at the discretion of the instrumentalist.

Conduction Directives | Events • Arpeggio

Pedal/Splash-Crash

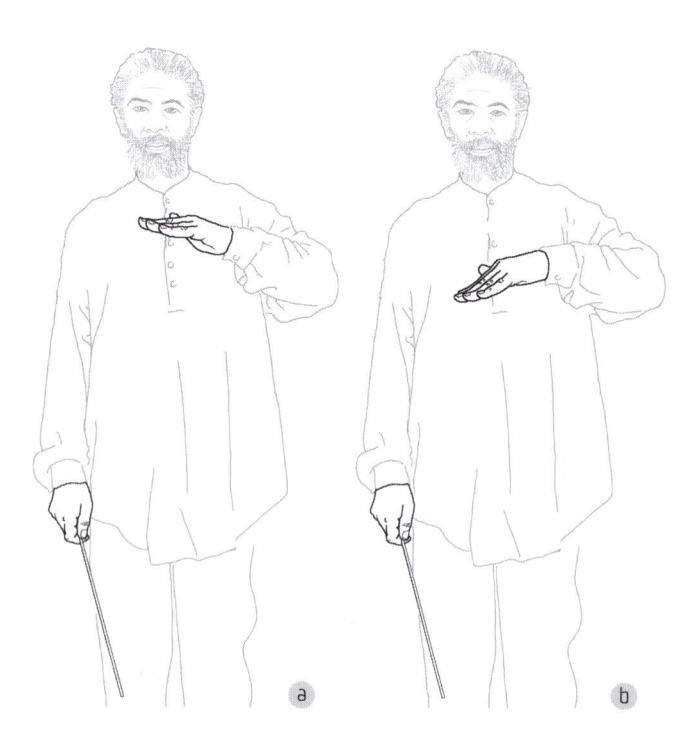

Gesture	Left hand, palm facing downward in front of chest, moving up and down from wrist.
	Followed by a downbeat.
Signification	Attack and decay (*diminuendo*).
Explanation	Pedal is an effect that can be achieved by thinking of a piano or vibraphone with the sustain pedal down; a strong attack and a natural decay, until all sound has diminished.
Supplementary Note	How each instrumentalist imitates and achieves this effect is dependent on how each perceives this notion on their particular instrument.

4 The Conduction Lexicon

Call and Response

Sign	Left hand, palm to left ear, while designating the "caller" with the right hand. Followed by a downbeat.
Signification	To establish exchanges between caller and responder.
Explanation	This sign indicates that an instrumentalist will be assigned to initiate and lead the call, while additional designated instrumentalists will respond to the call for the same duration. The "Call and Response" may be activated by either a single downbeat to the caller, or by separate downbeats to the caller and the respondents.

Conduction Directives | Events • Call and Response

THE ART OF CONDUCTION 4

Breath

        a   b   c

Gesture	Arms begin crossed at wrist, at waist level, then move upward or downward.
Signifiacation	An impulse of rising or falling phrase progression or harmodulation of motivic elaboration and/or embellishment that stimulates crescendo, tension/intensity, cadence, and anticipation.
Explanation	This directive is intended as a long pick up, upbeat, lead-in, or roll off for rhythmic, melodic, and/or harmonic impulse progression, in anticipation of a forthcoming event. Response is immediate; no downbeat is given.

Conduction Directives   Events • Breath

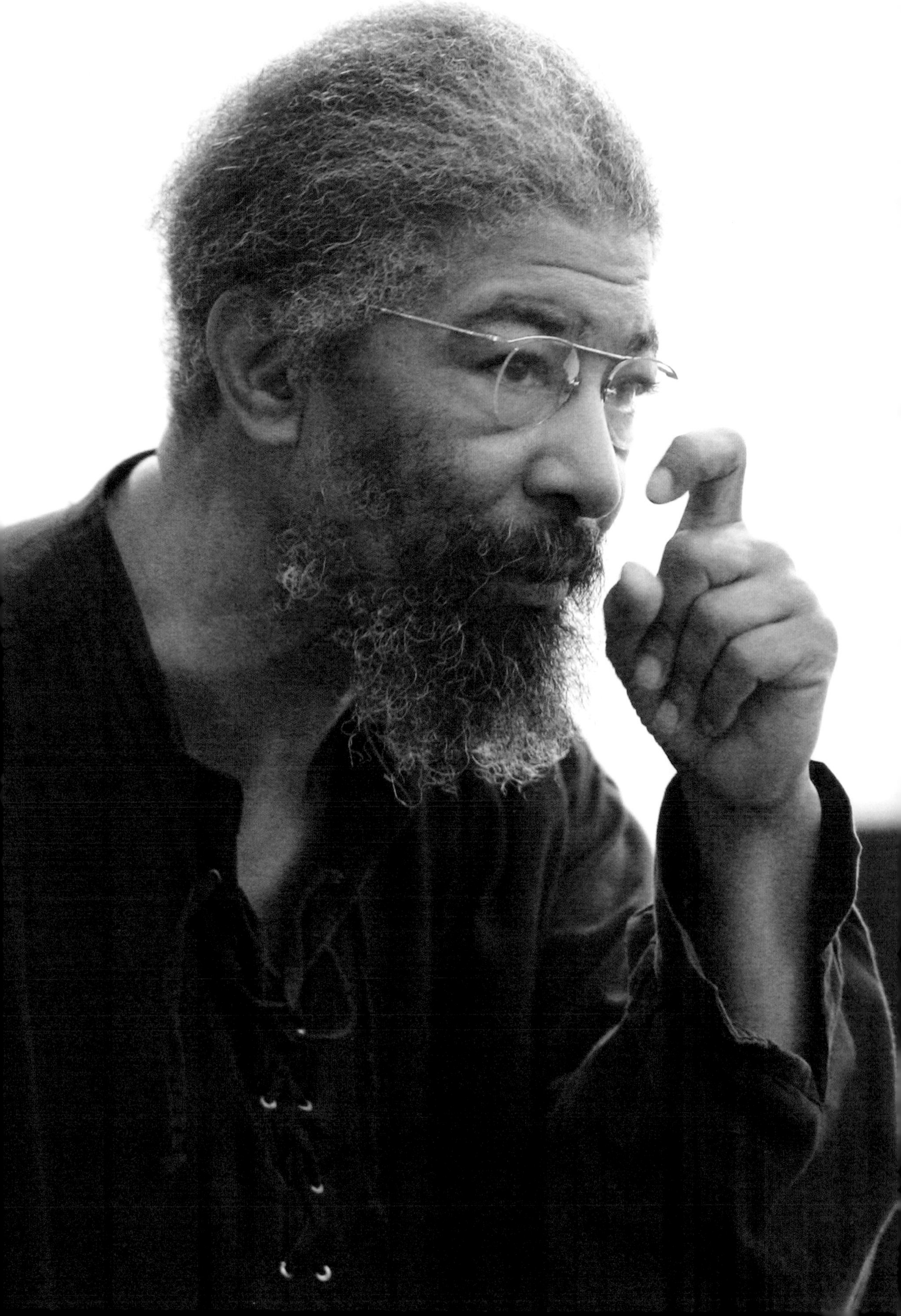

The Conduction Lexicon — 4

k Conduction Directives

Effects/Instrument-Specific Directives

- Harmonics
- Stops
- Vibrato
- Tremolo
- Pizzicato
- Arco
- Strum
- Trill
- With Mute/Without Mute

THE ART OF CONDUCTION

The following instrument-specific directives can be applied to any other Conduction directives, so as to attain a particular manner of execution (as, for instance, in a series of "Sustains" played by stringed instruments as "Harmonics" only).

Harmonics

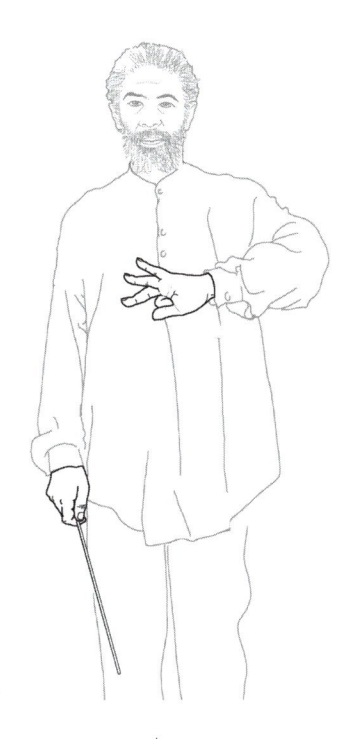

Sign	Left hand, thumb and index finger forming a small "o" at chest level.
Signification	To only use harmonics.

Stops

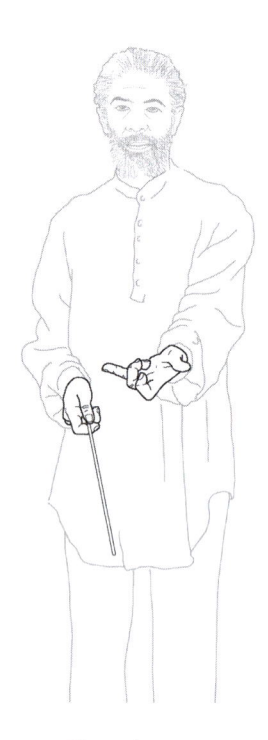

Sign	Left hand, fingers in palm at waist level. Two fingers for double stops, three fingers for triple stops, four fingers for quadruple stops.
Signification	To apply double, triple, quadruple stops, as indicated.

4 The Conduction Lexicon

Vibrato

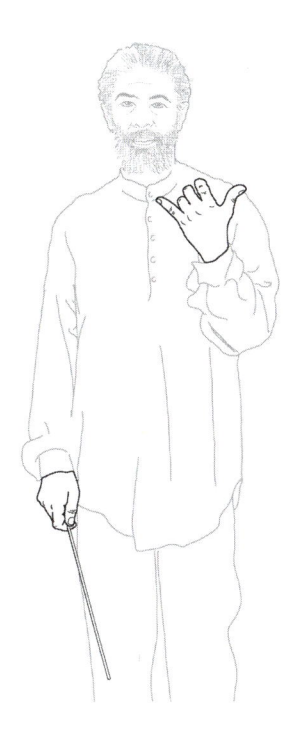

Gesture	Left hand, fingers oscillating (fluctuating) front to back (toward palm) at shoulder level.
Signification	To apply vibrato.

Effects/Instrument-Specific Directives · Vibrato

≡ Tremolo

Gesture	Left hand, palm facing hip, pointing downward, quivering.
Signification	To produce tremolo.

4 The Conduction Lexicon

Pizzicato

(a) (b)

Gesture	Left hand, index finger plucking, chest to face level.
Signification	To pluck the strings.

(k) Conduction Directives | Effects/Instrument-Specific Directives • Pizzicato

Arco

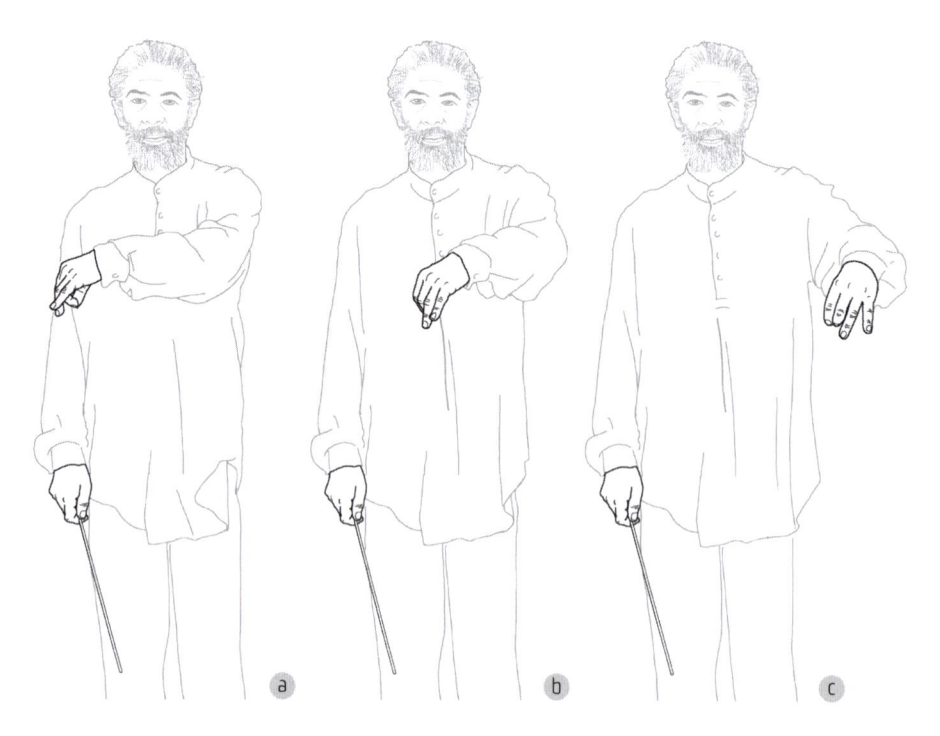

Gesture	Left hand, thumb, index, and middle fingers touching, moving right to left at chest level.
Signification	To use a bow.

4 The Conduction Lexicon

Strum

a b c

Gesture	Left hand strum/shake at neck level.
Signification	To strum (play rhythm).

Trill

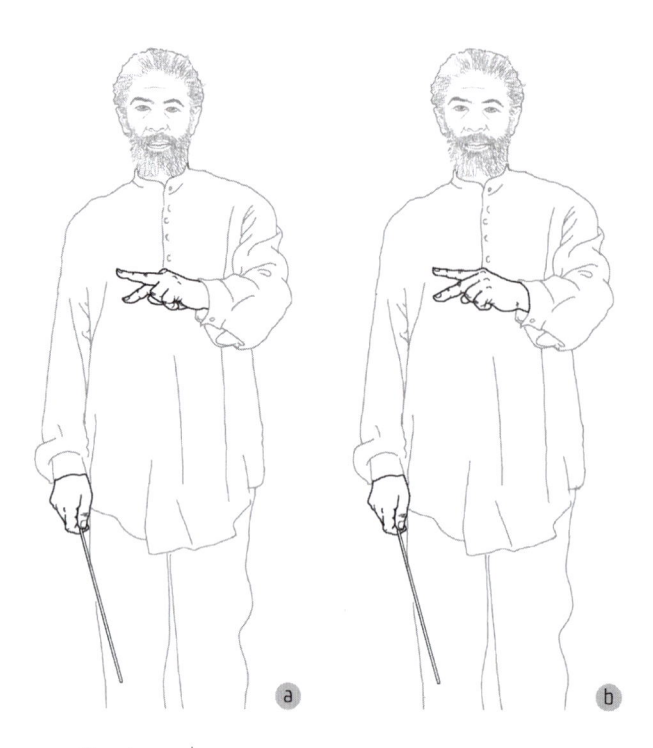

Gesture	Left hand, palm facing downward, index and middle fingers moving upward and downward, alternating, at chest level.
Signification	To trill between two pitches at a given tempo, at the discretion of the instrumentalist.

With Mute/Without Mute

Gesture	Left hand, as if with mute, putting in/taking out, at chest level.
Signification	To use a mute.

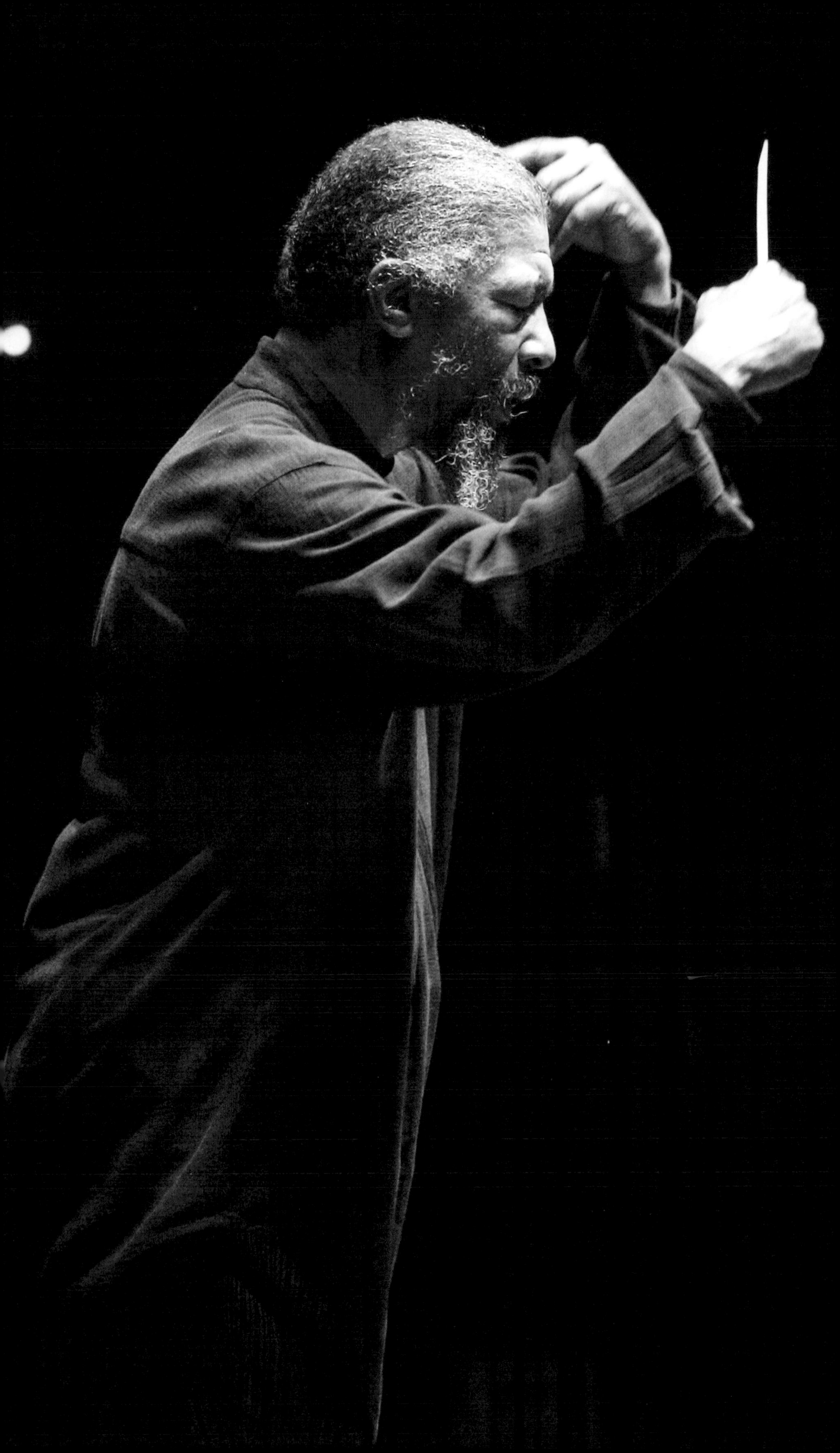

The Conduction Lexicon 4

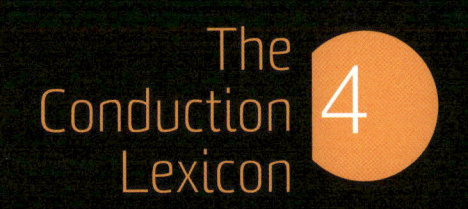

L Conduction Directives

Score-Related Directives

- Go Forward
- Go Back
- Section Designation
- Top
- Coda

THE ART OF CONDUCTION 4

Go Forward

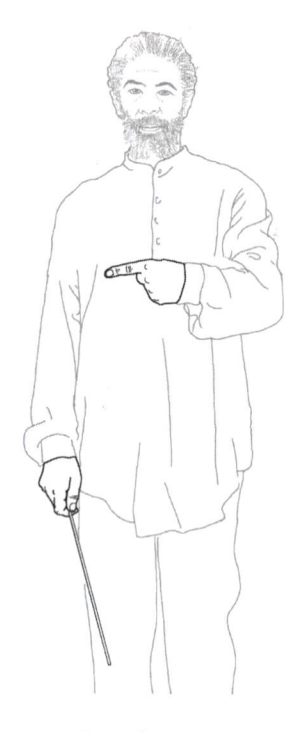

Sign	Left hand, index finger pointing to the right.
	Followed by a downbeat.
Signification	Indicates move on to the next section or phrase of a notated work.

Conduction Directives | Score-Related Directives • Go Forward

4 The Conduction Lexicon

Go Back

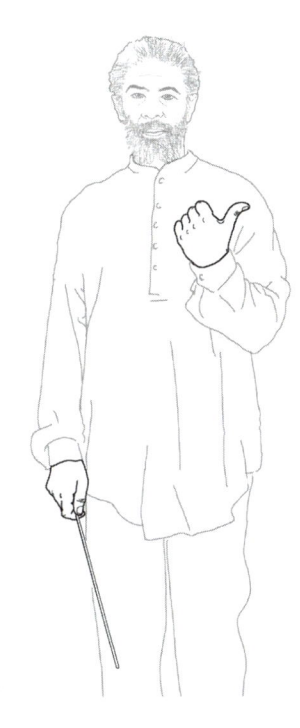

Sign	Left hand, thumb pointing to the left.
	Followed by a downbeat.
Signification	Indicates go back to the last section or phrase of a notated work.

Conduction Directives | Score-Related Directives • Go Back

Section Designation

Sign	Left hand numerical designation (1, 2, 3, 4, etc.), chest high. Followed by a downbeat.
Signification	Indicates go to designated section of a notated work.

Top

Gesture	Left hand, index finger touching the top of the head.
	Followed by a downbeat.
Signification	Indicates go to the beginning (section 1) of a notated work.

THE ART OF CONDUCTION 4

Coda

Gesture	Left hand, clenched fist, between head and shoulder high, facing the conductor. Followed by a downbeat.
Signification	Indicates go to the final section (coda) of a notated work.

Conduction Directives | Score-Related Directives • Coda

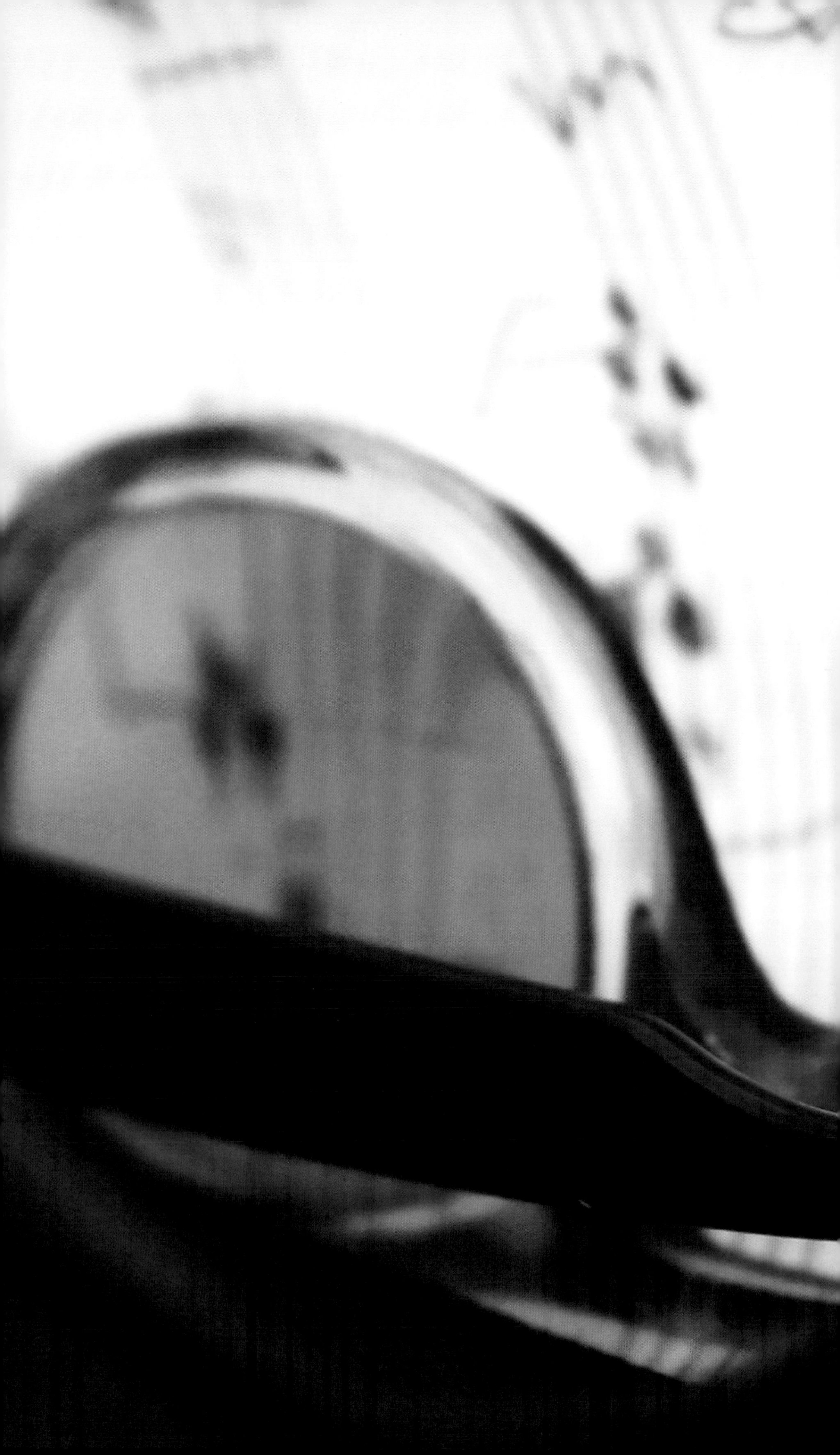

Personal Notes 5

Lawrence D. "Butch" Morris

An Interview with "Butch" Morris[1]

Precision and Economy

Precision is something that is very important to me and I think it's important to everyone. Precision and economy. I thought in the beginning I needed a sign to say this and a sign to say that, but really i needed to find the strengths and the weaknesses of both notation and improvisation, and *that* would dictate what the vocabulary would be. What exactly did I need the vocabulary to say that notation does not say? What could I produce in real time that neither improvisation nor notation could convey in real time? That is how the evolution of the Conduction vocabulary came about.

There are a number of other people that are using this or similar methods and they have completely different ideas about what they want from music. The interesting thing I've seen over the last thirty years is that more and more people are starting to conduct, in all sorts of different ways, particularly using some form of improvisational skill to support their conducting ideas, but all totally different from what I do. Everybody brings their personality to this, and there is room for that in music.

I don't need a sign that says "play a polka in C;" some people have a sign that says play a polka in C, or play a blues in F. Those are things that you can write down. I don't need to duplicate information that exists, it's not important to duplicate information. What's important is not only to wed these grand areas of improvisation and notation, but also to make of their union something more expansive. Then you really have something expressive to say.

Soloist

I have taken *soloist* out of my vocabulary; the *Pedestrian* sign means that you are at liberty to play whatever you want to play, but it just doesn't mean to solo. That's all many musicians know how to do; a lot of musicians don't know how to accompany the ensemble or give information to the ensemble, and until you understand this, it's hard to understand the breadth of this music. I'm interested in the individual, but I'm interested in the ensemble first.

Tonality

I never talk about tonality, I'm not necessarily interested in tonality in the beginning. My primary interest is in everybody trying to find the balance of that

[1] The following quotes are taken from a lecture Morris gave in Berkeley on February 5, 2007, as documented in the video "Improv:2: Understanding Conduction: An Informance with Lawrence "Butch" Morris," produced by Rova: Arts and filmed by John Rogers of Ideas in Motion. Interviewer Derk Richardson. Available online at RadiOM: https: //archive.org/details/IMP_2007_02_05#.Transcription, headings, and minor editing by J.A. Deane.

unique group. I don't want to project anything that can be written down; I want to get to what can't be written down.

Dynamics and Development

I, for one, believe that there's a lot of music in dynamics, dynamics alone, and when I perform I generally play with dynamics – you can do a lot of things with dynamics.

Never start developing something if you don't quite understand what it is. You play it until you know what it is – then you can develop it. I'm confronted with anarchists every day and I always tell them: it's best to know the law before you break it (in this case, the principle).

Rehearsal

We don't rehearse what we are going to perform, I just show the instrumentalists what the possibilities are. A symphony orchestra rehearses what they are going to perform and chances are, they're going to perform it like they rehearsed it. We're not going to do that.

Trust

This is new to a lot of people. I have thirty years of experience helping to evolve this kind of idea (and I see no end to working in this way). When I start showing someone who has no idea what to expect, of course they're kind of leery about this information I'm giving them, until they get into it, more and more, and slowly you build trust. In many ways, they have to be debriefed. There is a lot of trust involved with this.

You need musicians who will respond in a positive way. The worst thing that can happen in an ensemble is hesitation; it sounds full of doubt and the audience recognizes it as doubt. One thing I don't like to do is give examples. I explain the definition of the signs and the gestures, but if I give examples, musicians tend to do it like the example – you justify it, you take the responsibility for your response.

Every instrumental constellation is different, and if you take out one person from the ensemble and add a new person it's going to change the balance (the input) of that constellation. It's demanding: there's a lot to remember and there is a lot of responsibility to take, in constructing these ideas.

Conduction Lexicon

This is the music. The conduction vocabulary is symbolic of notation, just as writing is symbolic of speech. The more the musicians become comfortable with the vocabulary, the more they will give. The more they give, the better the ensemble will sound. The better the ensemble sounds, the higher the level of music we will make. The higher the level of music we make, the more joy we will experience. And joy is something I seek in this music. Joy.

Notes and Sketches[1]

Notes

SOUND/MUSIC: Not a prescription to be filled; sound has its own laws and its own logic; it also has accountability. (Wb, 2013)

Everyone has a sound within. This is the sound we bring out, what reflects our being. That sound (your sound) is the greatest benefit in life – listening to that sound and understanding that sound leads us to the right places at the right time.

Somehow, there must be a general attitude that beyond "traditional" sounds and timbres [...] "all" sounds can be simulated on "all" instruments – and the effort to play (to simulate) them, must exist. (Wb, 2009)

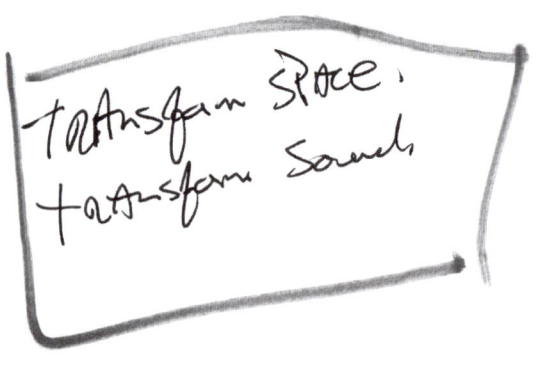

> *Transform Space.*
> *Transform Sound.*

Both composition and improvisation are (acts of) construction – they both confirm a musical need that supplies purpose to the act and art of making. It is the internal logic that coordinates structure. (Wb, 2013)

Improvisation is a skill and an asset to Conduction. Improvisation can only happen in real time: you don't "play" an improvisation, you can only prepare for it. In Conduction you prepare for the nature of improvisation; this is Conduction's relationship to improvisation.

> *Music Structures Sound in Space*

Improvisation is about solving problems creatively when the only solution is not at hand. Adapting to situations.

You don't teach someone to improvise. You show them the way to get in touch with their creative self.

---

[1] The following quotes are taken from Morris's available loose handwritten and printed notes. "Wb" stands for Conduction® Workbook in progress, and refers to an earlier version of the current book. A date presumed from content and the context of the quote is followed by a question mark. If not otherwise indicated, date is unknown. Omitted text is signalled through square brackets, as in [...]; text within square brackets has been added for the sake of clarity, while the use of quotation marks and underline reflects the original manuscript. Selection, arrangement, headings, and minor editing by Daniela Veronesi.

5 Personal Notes

To conceive of music as a whole and NOT a category.

[handwritten notes:]
The Point of Jazz is to Play together
To think together.
Combust
Ignite

The Role of Jazz is Deeper than Conversation
It could be dialogue – But Not only with the selves.
The Audience Also – And As Always, Something else Also.
& is Always About Playing "Music" –

Conduction

The language is music, the vocabulary[2] is Conduction.

A music that is "goal-directed" and "cooperative action." (Wb, 2009)

Conduction reconciles contradictions; it causes circumstances, it arranges moments, and it constructs situations. It is an interrogation of possibilities. (Wb, 2009)

As (musical) notation is symbolic of music, Conduction is symbolic of notation. But a transparent notation that can be read into (you can read between the lines). (2005?)

To evolve a more meaningful relationship between musician and music.

To allow each and every instrumentalist to find their emotional center – devoid of stylistic limitations. (2004?)

[handwritten diagram:]
Quantum Music – Sono Architecture
Coordinates
Notation [○] = Longitude – Built on a Horizontal Plane
Impulse [◇] = Latitude – Built on a Vertical Plane
Interpretation [⊕] = Meridian – Where these Planes Intersect.
The Highest Point of Perspective Power.

[2] The term "vocabulary," which Morris initially used in his writings, refers to the Conduction Lexicon of signs and gestures; both "vocabulary" and "lexicon" appear in later versions of the Conduction® Workbook dating 2009 and after. Eventually "lexicon" was chosen, as documentend in the latest available mauscript of early 2013.

What I often hear from people in the audience is how different the music can be from performance to performance. That nothing sounds the same, even though I only used a limited vocabulary. I must admit I do try to "push" or "pull" the music in different directions. I had to. Just to see what would happen. Not only with the music itself, but also the volatile nature of the ensemble. I wanted to keep (my) music "outside" so to speak – to keep it so everyone could have their own view with their own perspective.

The properties of (musical) sound (pitch, intensity, timbre, and duration) are "the" major contributors to a <u>real-time action</u>. And it must be a real-time encounter to enter the extra dimension. (2005?)

With Notation

To make notation "lucid," flexible, malleable.
To give the ideas of notation more expressive range.
The possibility for everyone to find their expression. (Wb, 2009)

> *→ Conductor in Pure form.*
> *(Meaning Nothing Between The transmitter And Receiver — No Notation).*
> *→ Conduction in Representative form. [INDUCTION]*
> *→ Conduction in static form (conduction Notation)*
> *(meaning the use of Notation)*
> *Induction is for the constant Reevaluation And interpretation of Notation.*
> *Music as an Intentional object of Perception.*

Subjective response to objective indication.

In its beginnings I thought of this method as a vehicle for improvisers only, but I soon understood how it could be of service to "music." Where all communities – no matter what culture, category, or style – could participate, bringing their own histories to the same vocabulary.

The purpose of Conduction is to express something that is not in notation nor in improvisation, but is unique to itself.
Not to create or replicate music as we know it, but to probe the unknown.

Conductor

For the conductor, Conduction is an attempt to discover the relationships (given) between forms of aesthetic thought in music and to seek an explanation for the fact that all substances of sounds and silence are indeed music. All substances of sound aspire to the condition of "music;" <u>all</u> earthly things aspire to the condition of music.

The conductor and each instrumentalist must see sound and hear movement.

The importance of capturing information as it happens – hearing and application. (Wb, 2008)

Each conductor must create his own patterns of expression.

> *The conductor must "Describe" with his eyes, face, head, arms, body —*

Nothing can be controlled [by the conductor] but structure. All else is supervision.

Instrumentalist and Ensemble

Music must exist in the mind and soul of the instrumentalist. Not "the" music but music in general.

Unlike [with] notation, [when] utilizing the Conduction vocabulary instrumentalists must represent themselves. (Wb, 2009)

For musicians, [Conduction] should be an opportunity to take advantage of a situation that will allow them to contribute from their perspective – to think of (their own) ways to sustain, repeat, construct, deconstruct, and so on, within the parameters of the directive. (Wb, 2009)

Each sign and gesture possesses an infinite variety of options that address either "how" or "what." How an instrumentalist interprets/addresses this information will tell much not only about the music, but also about the person making the music. Because the instrumentalist will always be confronted with a constantly changing landscape that cannot be anticipated – either structurally or sonically.

All instrumentalists are welcome to bring "their" style of playing; but they should also try to push beyond their limits into their fantasy, and to hear "all."

I care about what you hear and how you translate it.

I know that it's difficult to give what I ask of you on demand, but there is no other way to achieve the magic that we (can) possess. Please, don't contribute anything, any note, any phrase, any sound that you are not or will not be proud of. Because everything contributed by you represents you. It is indeed true that you can satisfy the directives in a number of ways, but please do not reduce your abilities to satisfy the demands; elevate your abilities, contribute nothing that you will not be proud of. We have remarkable (undiscovered) abilities at our disposal if we only take into account the things and sounds that we love. And the reason(s) we contribute to the musical canon in the first place. Our musical future and indeed the future of music (education, employment, and enjoyment) will be determined by what we contribute to it.

I need to "hear (and know)" how you think about music. What is crucial to the health of music is what you think about music, otherwise it will remain too conservative for growth. (2010?)

Contribution = the act of giving in real time.

It is not the improvisation that is magical, it is your understanding of music […]. To have a great understanding about how music is made. If you have this understanding you can make music with anyone. Your understanding of music and how you use it to interact with others – the strength of your dialogue/conversation. You are always in a state of dialogue: if you should (happen) to reach a state of monologue you should have some profound things to say. And in many ways it is up to the ensemble to get you there and keep you there.

> *You have to Ask Yourself Questions, And The Questions you Ask must Be Based on Need And Need Should Be Addressed.*

The instrumentalist must show restrain and tact. (Wb, 2009)

The ultimate goal for the ensemble is to attain a plural singularity, in which the quantitative and qualitative differences in interpretation intersect to achieve a "classic" bond of unity-accord-oneness – yet always striving for a perfection that can never be achieved. (Wb, 2009)

> *① To Get The Ensemble to Understand Ideas – – And to "Have" Ideas –*
> *② This is The Responsibility of Musicianship & Musicality.*

To get the ensemble to understand together, and to have an opinion together, even though each opinion can be different. (Wb, 2012)

…That the collective ensemble identity be/is premised on ideals and principles of sonic (and musical) order (as understood and practiced by the individual), rather than the roles of a single stylistic organization.

5 Personal Notes

[In workshops] I am not saying "do it like this," I am saying "understand it like this, then in performance use all that you know and all what you have just learned." (Wb, 2009)

Of course, every ensemble will be different in terms of musical capacity and understanding capability. The conductor must determine the order of learning the lexicon – to facilitate the experience of learning by doing. (Wb, 2008)

My proposition is that we see the sounds before we play them and before the audience hears them.

The Ensemble

Each musician [...] will come with their own baggage and history. So will the ensemble. The problems of interaction will be at varying strengths (in speaking musically). Who is polite and who is not? Who cares? Who listens and who acts like they are listening, and who doesn't listen at all? Who pays attention? Who uses the moment to compose and who doesn't?

To make the collective a priority i the music community.

Conduction Lexicon/Conduction Directives

The vocabulary must answer questions about unity and independence that notation and improvisation do not address.

Ephemeral metaphor: the directives are locations that only the instrumentalist can bring "meaning" to… in as much that their meaning is fleeting but the principle remains. Discourse and disclosure. (Wb, 2013)

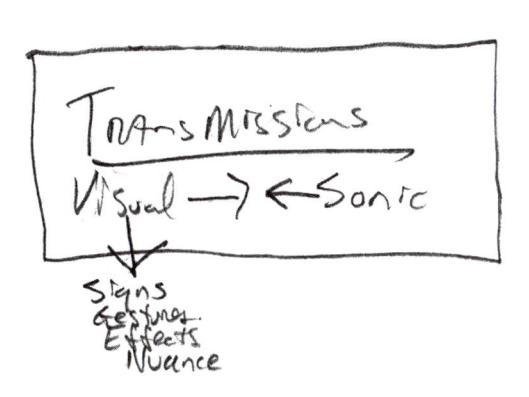

Transmissions
Visual → ← Sonic
Signs
Gestures
Effects
Nuance

Directives are coordinates – an intricate system of relationships. (Wb, 2009)

The action and movement of directives can only be understood in practice. (Wb, 2009)

> *The Conductor Brings structure through context*
> *The Instrumentalist Brings form through Meaningful context.*
> *Directive = Context.*

The Vocabulary

For me to develop [the Conduction] vocabulary, simplicity and precision had to play "the" major role [...]. Whatever the amount of signs and gestures, they had to be simple to understand and fluid in movement.

The vocabulary is the impetus to compose. Not just to improvise. Whether it be called instant composition, real-time composition or comprovisation.

This vocabulary should be used by all in accordance with the tradition to which one belongs, and to what it implies [...].

Lexicon as Stimulus

What makes the stimulus "tangible" – sound as movement, sound as "thing;" not a conditioned response. (Wb, 2009)

Signs and Gestures
Difference between sign and gesture: sign with left hand, gesture with right hand or both hands. (Wb, 2008)

Upbeat
Anything can happen on the upbeat. (Wb, 2013)

Downbeat
Traditional downbeat is related to pulse; in Conduction, it is related to execution. (Wb, 2009)

Left and Right Hand
To keep all directives to the left hand frees up the right hand to continue direction or beating pulse; therefore multiple indications may be given. (Wb, 2009)

Sustain
The sign Sustain means to play one continuous sound. The first problem is that of the instruments. A piano, a trumpet, and let's say a violin all have a si-

tuation that is vastly different from the next. How one interprets Sustain is up to the individual in the particular circumstance that Sustain may arise. Almost all the signs and gestures have their problems to solve and that is (basically) up to the musician.

Rhythm and Graphic Information
When I give the instrumentalist an idea, as I may do when I give rhythm or graphic contours, I am asking questions. I am asking the individual: "What is the rhythm of 'this'?" "What does 'this' sound like?" So as I am giving you this information, have an idea of what it sounds like to you and what the rhythm is, and when I give a downbeat for you to "interpret" or "translate" this information, execute your concept; no two interpretations will be the same. Hold on to your idea; don't let anyone or anything sway you away from it, or influence your judgment. (Wb, 2013)

Rhythm
Rhythm can also be interpreted melodically (not always on the same or one pitch). (Wb, 2013)

Repeat and Develop-Reconstruct (Horizontal)
When repeating (anything), we are repeating until we understand how our information/ideas are working in the fabric of sound… working with, against, around, and together. While repeating, identify "your one (1)," wherever that may be (perhaps at the beginning of your information/idea/phrase, although you might find it convenient to place it elsewhere, as long as you can identify "your one"). When this is understood [and the Develop gesture is given], you can begin to develop "precisely" the information on your own, in your own time (please use rests as you see fit). When the Reconstruct gesture is given you return to your motif/idea/information on "your one." (Wb, 2013)

Evolutionary Transformations [Developments]
In all cases of evolution it is both the signification of the directive and its content that is to be evolved. (Wb, 2009)

Evolve [Develop]
If the sign for Evolve [Develop] is given as an initial directive, the instrumentalist is obliged to evolve an idea (or information). When the directive Reconstruct is given, the instrumentalist is obliged to distill that information to its most important characteristics. (Wb, 2009)

Pedestrian
Pedestrian: where loitering is permissible. The idea of the Pedestrian is that s/he is able to bring something into the ensemble rather than "on top of" it – as the soloist has historically. To give the pedestrian broader judicious responsibility.

The musician that is Pedestrian is free from ensemble instruction, but is subject to the environment, until returned to instruction.

The Pedestrian is in a position of "high" prerogative. The Pedestrian can be a very influential contributor and a controlling factor to the overall, if he or she understands the nature and depth of this directive and the conductor.

The Skill of the Pedestrian

There are many musical, extra-musical, and psychological aspects to the Pedestrian's skill – if he understands his position. [...] How to instigate and insinuate (more) material. Unearth the innermost compositional workings. Feed the ensemble and the conductor. (Wb, 2011)

[...] Pedestrians are free to do whatever they want, however their "main" concern and responsibility should be to concentrate on strengthening the sonic environment around them by using the (sonic-musical) information that comes from the ensemble. In other words, to describe, modify or moderate (useful) sonic information that comes from the ensemble. A Pedestrian oversees ensemble information.

[handwritten note: What I Am After — Precission & Understanding, Spontaneity & Passion]

5 Personal Notes

Sketches: Ensemble Layout

Preparation

Everyone must see and understand the layout of the ensemble. Let them see it from your [the conductor's] point of view. (Wb, 2009)

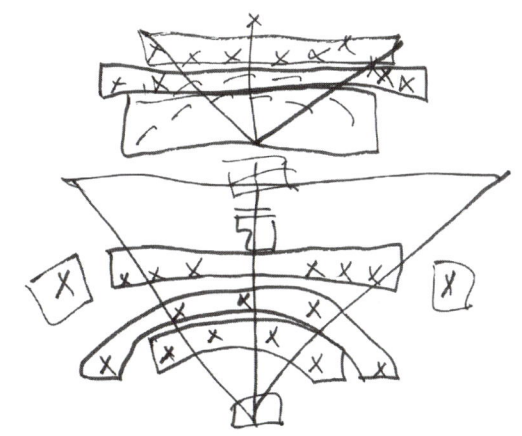

The "conductor's window"

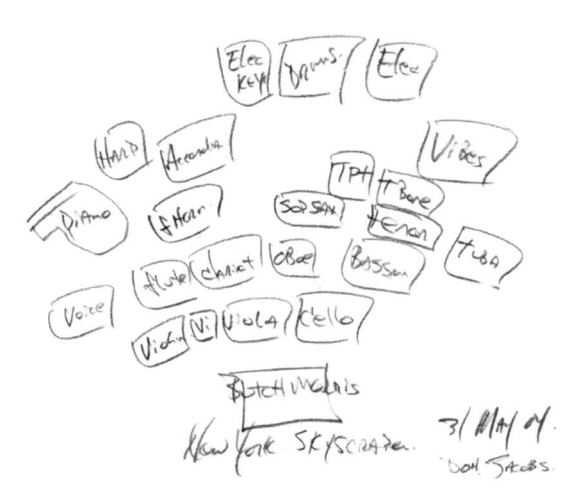

New York Skyscraper®, May 21, 2004, Vision Festival, New York

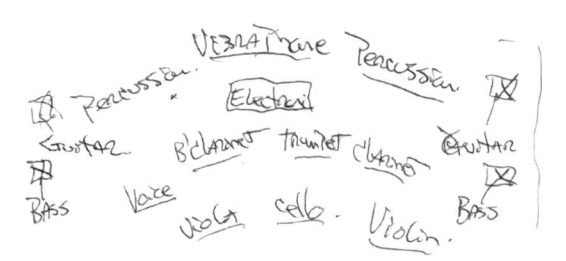

Lucky Cheng Orchestra, November 14, 2011, Lucky Cheng, New York

In Conversation[1]

November 4, 2012

dear Butch,

[...] I'm attaching an abstract for a talk proposal at a conference in september, where I'd like to analyse musicians' designations in Conduction, see what problems it involves for musicians and how it gets understood.

Would be nice to hear your feedback before I submit it.

Grazie!

Daniela

November 15, 2012

The initial meeting for a conduction workshop ensemble is a forum for the explanation and navigational principles of its practice. Beyond explanation and demonstration, it is up to the instrumentalist to decide <u>what</u> their contribution will be based on the information (directive) given them and the conversation they enter.

As multiples enter the conversation (as directed) they (learn to) decide how and <u>when</u> to.... then the quality of their contribution begins to take shape.

...as in learning to speak with family. <u>when to speak, when not.... what to speak, what not.</u>

Lawrence D. "Butch" Morris

November 16, 2012

Hey Daniela

[...] What I'm saying is that I've only, "only" had an ensemble for 10 days for them to learn this as theory.... for the most part, most instrumentalists are contributing in theory. Imagine what the beginner knows in theory and what Dino knows through experience in building an intimate history with me and the players. [...]

As you know, 10 days is not enough... a year or 2 may not be enough for a beginner. In time certain things like the intuitive aspects of instinct creep in that could not have happened before...

---

[1] Extracts from an email correspondence between Lawrence D. "Butch" Morris and Daniela Veronesi.

as I mentioned with family, the child responds to watching and hearing the family to learn how to act, talk, and (general) interaction. In time that child will take on its own persona with its own voice and strike out to take its own chances and risks. Whether that "forum" be a family or an ensemble the addition of one more can turn the tide in one direction or the other with their choice.

Lawrence D. "Butch" Morris

November 16, 2012

hey, I think we're on the same track... [...] but are you saying that with some ensembles you've experienced musicians who would enter whenever they want (and feel appropriate) and do whatever instruction they want? My only point here is that, as far as I understand, it is the Conductor who gives musicians the direction (Conduction directive), and also when exactly (downbeat) to take that direction...

Daniela

November 16, 2012

I'm saying with musicians with lots of experience ... like Dino, like Brandon and like Wayne Horvitz and Lê Quan Ninh and a few others, it only takes a nod of the head or nothing at all to "let them" figure out what to do and say. But I'm talking about good musicians with exceptional musicianship.
To me this is when the music begins and the theory is out the window.... that's where I want to go and that's what this is about.... getting somewhere. Workshop is one thing but high performance is where it's at. With musicians like that, the music could start with no indication from me.
BEST

Lawrence D. "Butch" Morris

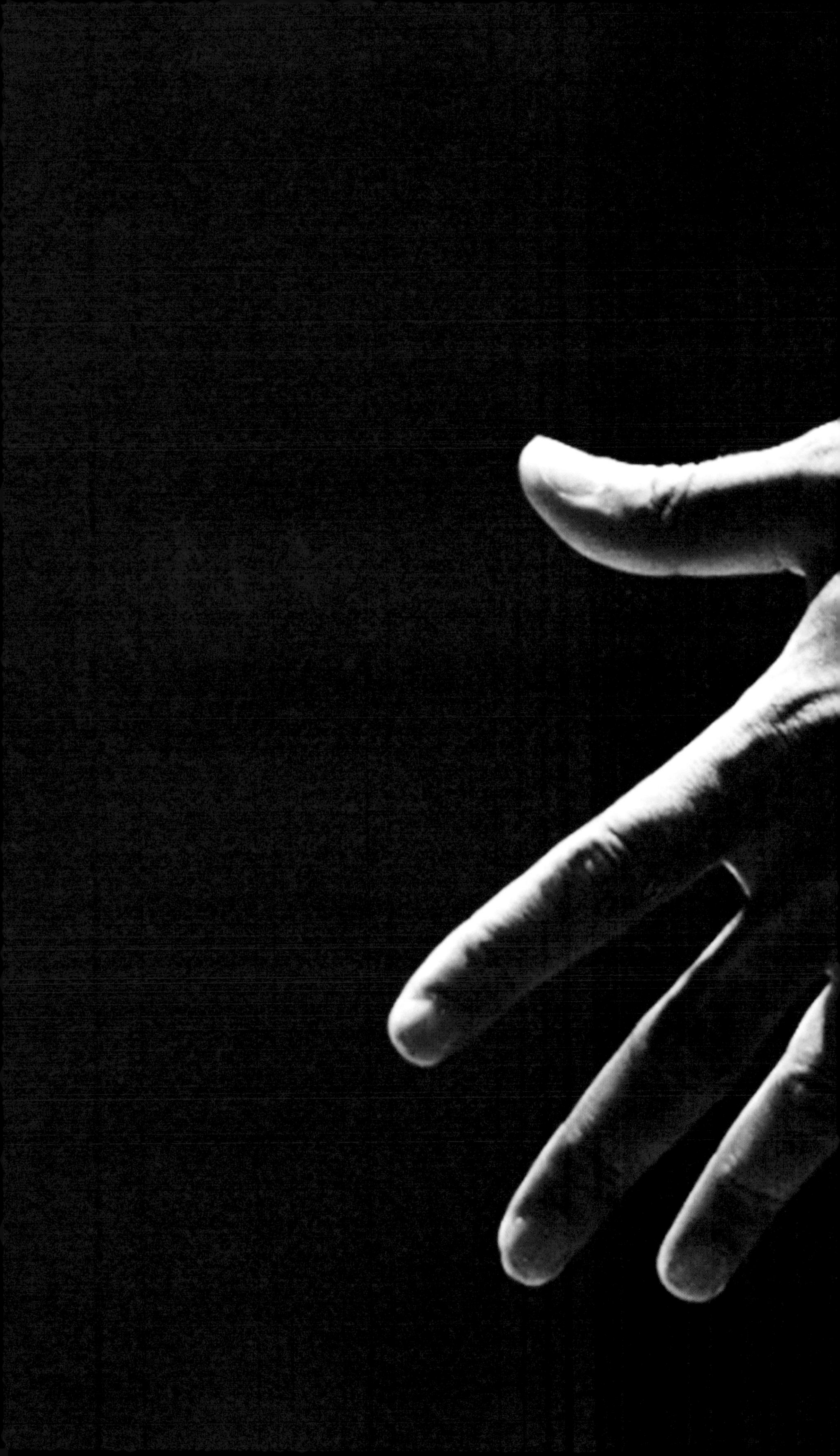

How to use 6 the Conduction Lexicon

Daniela Veronesi and J.A. Deane

Suggested Teaching Order

J.A. Deane

The following teaching order is suggested in the context of an intensive workshop with a new ensemble.

As new directives are introduced and practiced, new sequences and combinations of directives – from simple to more complex – can be explored by conductor and ensemble. In the course of a whole workshop, returning to each of the directives both in isolation and in different contexts will be crucial for gaining deeper clarity and understanding of how the Conduction Lexicon can be used, and will reveal new possibilities for the interpretation and the evolution of directives.

Rather than introducing and practicing the entire Conduction Lexicon, the conductor may decide to focus on certain directives only, depending on how the ensemble progresses.

SIGHT LINES (FIELD OF CLARITY) • DIVISION OF ENSEMBLE • DISCRETIONARY SUSTAIN • UPBEAT/DOWNBEAT • ALL STOP/CUT OFF • REAL-TIME DYNAMICS • NEXT DIRECTIVE DYNAMICS • STACCATO • EVENT • DISCRETIONARY ENDING • MELODIC MOVEMENT (MELODIC INFORMATION-CANTILENA)
HARMONICS • REPEAT: CREATE/CONSTRUCT • REPEAT: IMITATE/EMULATE • REPEAT: ECHO/REPRODUCE • MEMORY • PEDESTRIAN • CAPTURE-CONTINUE • REPEAT: SHADOW/PURSUE/FOLLOW • ACCOMPANY • DEVELOP-RECONSTRUCT (HORIZONTAL) • DEVELOP-RECONSTRUCT (VERTICAL)
PANORAMA • PANORAMA FRAGMENT/EXCERPT • PANORAMA HOCKET/BRIEF CONTRIBUTIONS • GRAPHIC INFORMATION (LITERAL MOVEMENT) • ACCOMPANY ME/IMAGING/SHAPING • DISTILL • SPIN • TRILL • PEDAL/SPLASH-CRASH • GROUND/TRAP-SAMPLE-LOOP • BRIDGE
YIELD • TEMPO DESIGNATION (PULSE-TEMPO/METER) • RHYTHM (INITIATING) • DOWNBEATS AND UPBEATS (INDICATING TEMPO/RHYTHM) • SPAR/PHRASE IN TIME • DOUBLETIME • HALFTIME • ACCELERANDO-RITARDANDO (WITH BATON) • ACCELERANDO-RITARDANDO (WITH HAND) • CHANGE IN TONALITY/PITCH • CHANGE BY OCTAVE • HARMODULATION/TRANSPOSITION • RESOLVE
WHISPER • TENSION • PITCHED SUSTAIN • PLACE IN TIME/FREE OF TIME • CALL AND RESPONSE • PROPORTIONAL TEMPO/TIME • NOTES TO THE BEAT • ACCENT • GLISSANDO • ARPEGGIO • BREATH • TONAL CENTER/KEY

6 How to use the Conduction Lexicon

Nota bene 1 | *Effects/Instrument-Specific Directives* and *Score-Related Directives* may be introduced at any time, as needed:

EFFECTS/INSTRUMENT-SPECIFIC DIRECTIVES	SCORE-RELATED DIRECTIVES
• STOPS • HARMONICS • VIBRATO • TREMOLO • PIZZICATO • ARCO • STRUM • TRILL • WITH MUTE/WITHOUT MUTE	• GO FORWARD • GO BACK • SECTION DESIGNATION • TOP • CODA

Nota bene 2 | Until the ensemble gets used to the lexicon, they will be operating too cerebrally, but as soon as they become comfortable executing the directives, it will immediately be reflected in the music. This "learning curve" is also true for the conductor.

Exercises

J.A. Deane and Daniela Veronesi

In the following, a few exercises are provided for the purpose of illustrating how a conductor can use the Conduction Lexicon by practicing simple to more complex sequences and combinations of directives, with the ensemble.

Since in Conduction the conductor is responsible for providing "structure," s/he must be able to track the through line of each member of the ensemble as the Conduction unfolds in real time; using simple structured exercises can be helpful in the beginning to enhance such ability. Also, articulating to the ensemble the sequence of events *backward* (from the end to the start) after a given sequence is finished will help clarify for everyone the logic of Conduction in terms of how directives can be layered both simultaneously and over time, by being in the moment and with no preconceived plan.

Discretionary Sustain – Develop-Reconstruct (Horizontal)

Designate a section (section 1) and give them the DISCRETIONARY SUSTAIN sign; execute a series of SUSTAIN. Add more instrumentalists to the SUSTAIN sequence, so as to progressively comprise the whole ensemble. Have the whole ensemble DEVELOP the last SUSTAIN, and then RECONSTRUCT it. Start a new series of SUSTAIN with the whole ensemble.

WHO	section 1	enlarged section/ group/whole ensemble	whole ensemble	whole ensemble	whole ensemble
WHAT	Discretionary SUSTAIN	Discretionary SUSTAIN	DEVELOP (SUSTAIN)	RECONSTRUCT (SUSTAIN)	Discretionary SUSTAIN

Repeat – Memory

Designate one instrumentalist (instrumentalist 1) and give her/him the REPEAT sign; have her/him execute the REPEAT several times. Designate the whole ensemble to REPEAT ("Imitate/Emulate") the pattern created by instrumentalist 1; execute the REPEAT with the whole ensemble (including instrumentalist 1) several times. Designate the REPEAT as MEMORY 1 and execute MEMORY 1 several times. Move to something new, and then go back to MEMORY 1 with the whole ensemble or with selected instrumentalists.

WHO	instrumentalist 1	whole ensemble	whole ensemble		whole ensemble
WHAT	REPEAT (Create/Construct)	REPEAT (Imitate/Emulate)	MEMORY 1	*new sequence*	MEMORY 1

Rhythm (Initiating)

Designate the rhythm section and define a rhythm to be performed (RHYTHM "initiating"), then give the REPEAT sign for that rhythm to be repeated. Designate the whole ensemble and have it REPEAT the established rhythm. Give the ensemble the DEVELOP (Horizontal) gesture, followed by the RECONSTRUCT (Horizontal) gesture. Once the initial rhythm is re-established, CUT OFF single sections. Individual instrumentalists can now be given DYNAMICS indications. Proceed with CUT OFF addressed to individual instrumentalists and/or to single sections until a single instrumentalist/section is the only one playing. Close with CUT OFF.

WHO	rhythm section	whole ensemble	whole ensemble	whole ensemble
WHAT	RHYTHM (initiating) + REPEAT (Echo/Reproduce)	REPEAT (Imitate/Emulate)	DEVELOP (Horizontal)	RECONSTRUCT (Horizontal)

WHO	single sections	individual instrumentalists	individual instrumentalists; single sections	remaining instrumentalist/ section
WHAT	CUT OFF	DYNAMICS	CUT OFF	CUT OFF

Panorama

Execute a PANORAMA wave (sequence) using half the ensemble; lock it into a REPEAT while designating the "one." Execute another PANORAMA wave using the other half of the ensemble; lock it into a REPEAT while designating the "one." Designate the REPEAT of each ensemble part as MEMORY 1; execute MEMORY 1 with the two parts of the ensemble, alternatively and together. Repeat all preceding steps and establish a new MEMORY (MEMORY 2); then execute MEMORY 1, alternating it with MEMORY 2. Add new memories, taking this as far as you can go.

WHO	half the ensemble 1	half the ensemble 1	half the ensemble 2	half the ensemble 2
WHAT	PANORAMA	REPEAT (Echo/Reproduce) + designation of the "one"	PANORAMA	REPEAT (Echo/Reproduce) + designation of the "one"

WHO	half the ensemble 1	half the ensemble 2	whole ensemble
WHAT	MEMORY 1	MEMORY 1	MEMORY 1

Types of Downbeats

Daniela Veronesi

In Conduction, several kinds of downbeats – ways of activating a preparatory directive – are given, as shown in the following table:

Downward stroke of baton/right hand/both hands	• NEXT DIRECTIVE DYNAMICS • DISCRETIONARY SUSTAIN; PITCHED SUSTAIN • REPEAT; MEMORY • TEMPO DESIGNATION; RHYTHM (INITIATING); PROPORTIONAL TEMPO/TIME • SPAR/PHRASE IN TIME; NOTES TO THE BEAT • DOUBLETIME; HALFTIME; PLACE IN TIME/FREE OF TIME • CHANGE IN TONALITY/PITCH; CHANGE BY OCTAVE • RESOLVE • BRIDGE • GROUND (ACOUSTIC INSTRUMENTS); EVENT • ARPEGGIO; PEDAL/SPLASH-CRASH; CALL AND RESPONSE
Large(r) downward stroke of baton/right hand	• STACCATO
Opening of left hand fingers	• TRAP-SAMPLE-LOOP (ELECTRONIC INSTRUMENTS)
First movement of baton/hand(s) after preparatory sign has been shown	• MELODIC MOVEMENT • PANORAMA; PANORAMA FRAGMENT/EXCERPT; PANORAMA HOCKET/BRIEF CONTRIBUTIONS • GRAPHIC INFORMATION (LITERAL MOVEMENT)
Beginning of a hand or arm movement	• HARMODULATION/TRANSPOSITION • DEVELOP-RECONSTRUCT (HORIZONTAL AND VERTICAL); DISTILL

Downward stroke of baton/right hand/both hands (optional downbeat)	• WHISPER • GLISSANDO • ACCENT

6 How to use the Conduction Lexicon

Real-time or immediate response; no downbeat requirement	• REAL-TIME DYNAMICS • TENSION • CAPTURE-CONTINUE • ACCELERANDO-RITARDANDO (WITH BATON); ACCELERANDO-RITARDANDO (WITH HAND) • TONAL CENTER/KEY (ESTABLISHING) • SPIN • BREATH
No downbeat (entrance at the i entalist's discretion)	• PEDESTRIAN • DISCRETIONARY ENDING • ACCOMPANY

Nota bene	In most cases when the baton is used, the downbeat may also be given through a nod of the head or a gaze, and with body movement in general, as the relationship between the conductor and the ensemble develops.

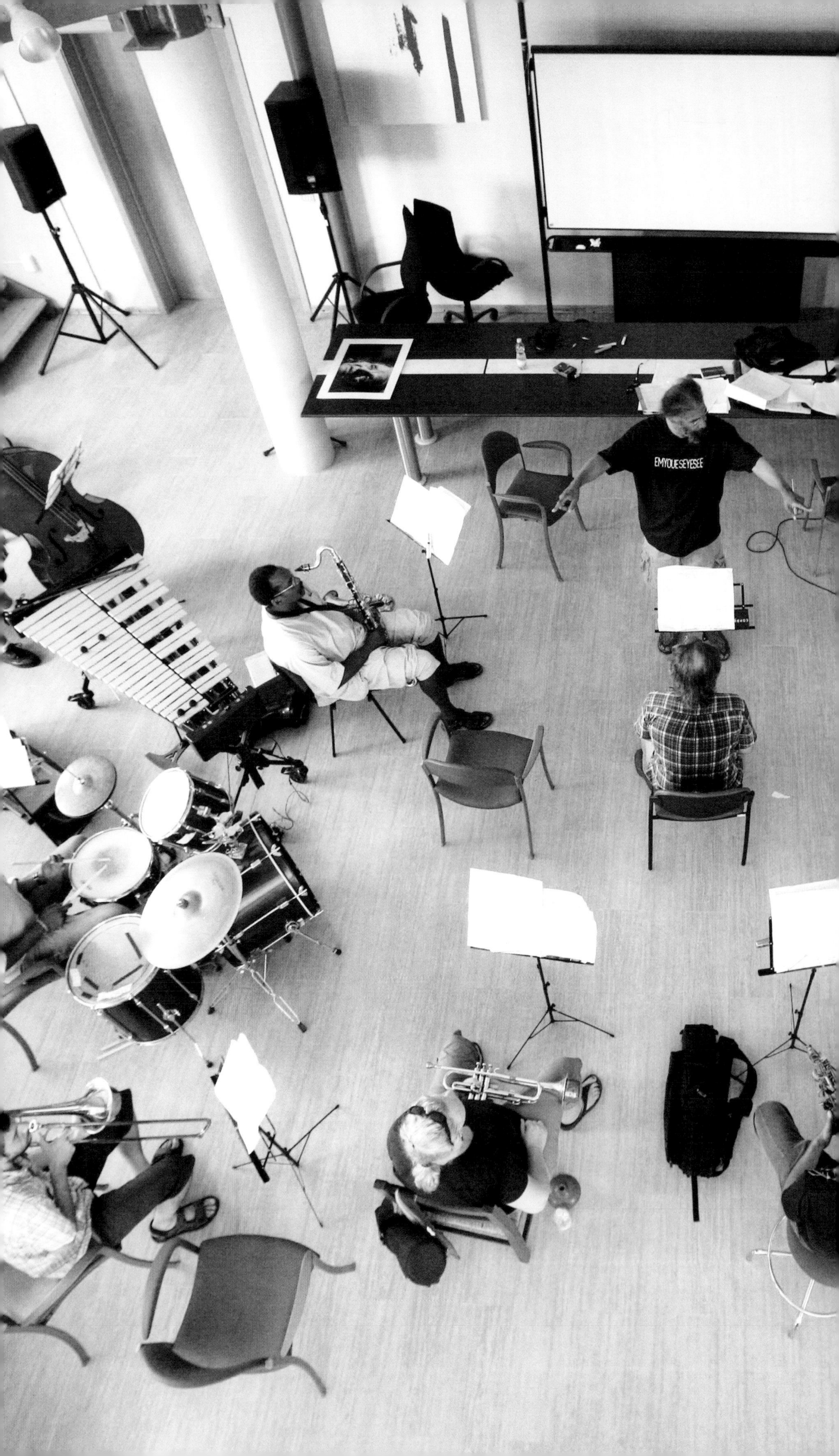
EMYOUESEYESEE

//
"Butch" Morris and the Evolution of Conduction®

Daniela Veronesi

THE ART OF CONDUCTION 7

A Biography[1]

Born in Long Beach, California, in 1947, Lawrence Douglas "Butch" Morris grew up in a household where music was played and appreciated, and a constant presence. His oldest and youngest brothers, Joe and Michael respectively, took up the clarinet; his sister Marceline studied piano; and his older brother, Wilber (1937-2002), played the drums, and later bass. Along with classical music, jazz was a given in the Morris home.

By the time he was fourteen, "Butch" owned a trumpet, and was off on his journey with brass. Throughout his public school years he studied music theory, harmony, and composition, and played in the school orchestra, and the marching and studio bands. During this time, Morris also taught himself to play French horn, flute, trombone, baritone-horn, and piano. Among his distinguished teachers were Walter Lowe, Donald Dustin, and Charles Lloyd.

After graduating, Morris enhanced his musical abilities. He often sat in with bassist George Morrow and saxophonist J. R. Montrose at Los Angeles jam sessions, playing standards and compositions by all the great jazz masters. It's significant, too, that at this point he also worked for a recording studio, transcribing and transposing big band and song arrangements. As he put it: "Sometimes I'd see three different arrangements of the same song, so I began to see the concepts of composing and arranging from various points of view."

In 1966, Morris's life took a decisive turn. Conscripted into the US army as a clerk typist, he served as a truck driver in Germany, a medic in Vietnam, and a postal clerk in Okinawa. "I used to practice the horn and write music in an ambulance," he wrote. "It's where I first started to think about music from a completely different perspective."

With his tour of duty over, Morris studied prosthetics and orthotics, with a view to pursuing a career in health science. But all that changed when he encountered the vibrant "new jazz" scene of 1960s Los Angeles. Through his brother Wilber he met Arthur Blythe, Bobby Bradford, John Carter, and pianist Horace Tapscott's Pan-Afrikan Peoples Arkestra, the leading community for innovative musicians. Morris then played with David Murray, James Newton, Diamanda Galas, and Mark Dresser. While working with master trumpet-maker Dominic Callicchio, Morris also discovered that the cornet possessed the sound he was seeking.

In 1971, drawn by its exceptional music and literary scene, Morris moved to the Bay Area of San Francisco, where he soon met musicians

[1] The section "A Biography" is partly based on Palmer, D., "Biographies", (programme notes to "Lawrence 'Butch' Morris, Artist in Residence, November 11-16, 1989, Whitney Museum of American Art at Philip Morris"), as well as Morris' biographical details on www.conduction.us, which are revised and updated here. Unless otherwise noted, all quotes in this chapter are taken from the following text: Morris, L.D. 1995. *Testament: A Conduction Collection* (Notes to the 10-CD box set *Testament*), New York: New World Records (Recorded Anthology of American Music), 3-12.

7 "Butch" Morris and the Evolution of Conduction®

Charles Moffett, Charles Tyler, Frank Lowe, Ray Anderson, Curtis Clark, Keshavan Maslak, and writer Ntozake Shange. He also studied cornet and composition with "Little" Benny Harris (composer of the jazz standard "Ornithology"), and conducting with Jacqueline Hairston. Morris's first interest in conducted improvisation also dates back from this period; he credits Charles Moffett with exposing him to a new way of conducting, which he later developed in his own terms under the name "Conduction®." As Morris recalls:

> Charles Moffett had a rehearsal band at what was called Club 7; we played compositions, but from time to time Charles would literally conduct the compositions and ensemble improvisations; I say literally, because he would slow them down or speed them up or give accents for the band to play. I had never seen anyone conduct this way before [...]. The sign I now use for "sustain" and the gesture I use for "literal movement" come from Moffett's vocabulary.

In 1976, Morris moved to New York, joining former collaborators Tyler, Lowe, and Murray, now established there. That fall, Morris and Lowe toured Europe, which introduced Morris to an international milieu that was to influence his entire career. He settled in Paris, then later in the south of France, and would, from 1977 on, teach workshops in France, Holland, and at the Conservatoire royale de Liège in Belgium, beginning to explore the use of his vocabulary of signs and gestures for ensemble creation. During that period he was also active as a cornetist, playing with musicians such as "Philly Joe" Jones, Steve Lacy, and Gil Evans.

But New York was still there, and Morris often returned to collaborate with writers, visual artists, dancers, and musicians on multidisciplinary performance events, finally moving back to live in Manhattan in 1981. In the years that followed, he was a regular contributor to the contemporary arts scene, conducting workshops for the Alvin Ailey American Dance Theater, collaborating with The Wooster Group, and serving as a musical director for an ABC TV action series called *A Man Called Hawk.* At the same time, Morris steadily broadened his musical circles as cornetist, composer, arranger, and, increasingly, as conductor – most notably with trios featuring Wayne Horvitz, Bobby Previte, and J.A. Deane; in his collaborations with Billy Bang and David Murray; and, starting with *Current Trends in Racism in Modern America* in 1985 (Conduction no. 1), in Conductions under his own name.

Around the mid-1990s, "Butch" Morris gradually reduced his musical commitments as cornet player to fully devote himself to the evolution of Conduction, introducing it to national and international audiences, through – among other projects – his Skyscraper orchestras: site-specific ensembles, consisting of local musicians, trained in Conduction, gathered in cities all over the world, including Berlin, London, New York, Verona, Minneapolis, Tokyo, and Marseille, among many others.

From 1998 to 2001, Morris was a resident teacher at Bilgi University in Istanbul, and his involvement in music education would later continue in the US, Europe and Southeast Asia, where he frequently led Conduction workshops at conservatories, universities, music schools, festivals, and assorted cultural institutions.

Throughout his extensive musical career, Morris has created and produced more than 200 Conductions worldwide, encompassing both improvisatory and interpretative musical cultures – from jazz ensembles, symphonic orchestras, electro-acoustic, and pop, to traditional music and instrumentation from North America, Europe, Asia, Africa and the Middle East. He has also expanded the use of Conduction to spoken word, applying his lexicon of signs and gestures to "orchestrate" written poetry and prose texts in what he called "A Chorus of Poets" – an idea that he developed with New York poet Steve Cannon in the early 1990s, and one well documented here, in several languages, in the Conduction Chronology.

Conduction, as Morris puts it, "is process and product, ensemble music, teamwork. It is a music of personal histories and individuals. It is not limited to style or category." Inspired by Morris's musical concept, a number of conductors and ensembles are now practicing the art of Conduction, or some form of conducted improvisation patterned after it, while scholars have similarly started to investigate in depth how such teamwork unfolds in workshop and performance.

Lawrence D. "Butch" Morris died in 2013, and he is a presence deeply missed in the music community. His legacy is carried on by all those who care for the evolution of music, musicianship, and music pedagogy.

A Name, a Lexicon, a Practice: Some Notes on the Evolution of Conduction

While Morris was developing and applying his new conducting method in the mid-1980s, the name he found for it was "Conduction:" not only because, by putting together "conducting" and "improvisation," it related to the act of "conducted improvisation," but also because in physics the same term refers to a process of transmission – the transfer of heat through the communication of energy from particle to particle – which seemed to capture what was taking place in the music he was making. As Morris remembered:

> It was at this time that I started thinking more about the combustion, or heat, that this system creates. The communication between eye, mind, and ear, between people – the psychology and imagination. I started to read physics books, primarily to create a rationalization for what I was doing and thinking. Here I found "conduction." It served dual purposes. One, it served the music – conducted improvisation. Two, it served the physical aspect of communication and heat […], the electric charge and response from body to body – the immediate transmission of information and result.

As a musical praxis in which theory, practice, and performance constantly nourished one another, Conduction was bound to naturally evolve over time; so did its definition, as well as the gestural lexicon it is based upon.

Conduction no. 1, for instance, was performed with five hand signals only: "sustain, repeat, dynamics, come in or feature improvisation, and a sign that I no longer use that meant for all to play (improvise)." Across nearly thirty years, this initial core of the Conduction Lexicon progressively grew to comprise more than sixty signs and gestures, now documented in this book.

As existing signs were refined and new signs entered the lexicon, others were abandoned or modified. Examples of this process are the instructions revolving explicitly around the idea of "improvisation." As used by Morris in Conduction no. 1 without written score, the sign asking everybody to play soon disappeared from his conducting vocabulary; the instruction to improvise was, rather, given to individual musicians through the directive "Entry (Come in or Feature)." Then later it was renamed "Feature (Solo)," and after the mid 1990s the gesture used for it – a wave of the hand, as if to beckon – became the cue for a new directive called "Pedestrian." These two directives coexisted for some time. In the late 2000s, however, it was "Pedestrian" – whose quite elaborate explanation (see p. 59), although suggesting ways in which musicians can contribute to the music of the ensemble, does not, in fact, draw on concepts like "improvisation" or "soloist" – that was kept.

Directives such as "Accompany," "Shadow," "Call and Response," and "Ground" – all developed after 1995, along with many others – might similarly shed light on how Morris conceived the collective dimension of ensemble music. It's worth noting that in his later years, as he stated in a 2012 interview,[2] Morris had come to consider the original meaning of Conduction, as *conducted improvisation*, no longer useful – "I found that using the term improvisation limited the concept and the community I was after"– and had thus started to refer to Conduction as *conducted interpretation*.

Indeed, Morris never ceased to refine his musical concept, and the way it could be employed in the service of music. A significant aspect of such process is the use of Conduction with notation, which he engaged with very early on in the development of his conducting lexicon:

> In 1984 I decided to use this Conduction method in concert but not to use my notation (music). I had already decided for a string quartet. I was standing in a store and I heard a Beethoven string quartet, so I bought the manuscript – Opus 130 Presto. Without changing a note on the page, four string improvisers and myself gave a lovely rendition. I only added rehearsal numbers 1, 2, 3, 4, 5. I used three signs/gestures: repeat, sustain, and improvise. I could send any of the players to any of the rehearsal numbers at any given time – I could also change the speed of what was being played. I don't think I was the only one to enjoy this concert on June 15, 1984, at the Manhattan Healing Arts Center.

In the years that followed, Morris focused more and more on the development of the lexicon itself, and on employing it without notation, although he never abandoned his idea that Conduction could serve as a means "by which a conductor may compose, (re)orchestrate, (re)arrange, and sculpt with notated and non-notated music."

Examples of how the Conduction Lexicon has been used with written materials, to be interpreted and modified in performance, are not rare in Morris's career; from his early engagement as a conductor with David Murray and Billy Bang (see, for instance, Bang's *Outline no. 12*), to a number of works documented in his Conduction Chronology, such as Conduction nos. 7 and no. 8 based on Misha Megelberg score "Impromptu 5," written for the occasion (Amsterdam, 1987). LPs like *Dust to Dust* (1990) and Burnt Sugar's adaptation of Stravinsky "Rite of Spring," *The Rite* (2003) – among many others – also document Morris' work with Conduction and scored music.

In a 2005 interview,[3] Morris expressed his wish to reintroduce notation his work, and thus move to what he called "Induction;" traces of this can be found in Conductions performed in Italy between 2006 and 2011 (Induction no. 2/1 *Emyoueseyesee.it*, Conductions nos. 180, 188, 192s and 195), in which Morris incorporated, to varying degrees, original compositions, such as "Otello-Cherry Suite," "Bosphorous Gail," and "Crucifix Key." Pieces like "Nowhere Ever After" and "The Long Goodbye," on the other hand, resonate like a common thread through Morris's entire body of work, interpreted and rearranged in real time in several performed and recorded Conductions.

[2] "Butch Morris e la scienza del trovare" ("Butch Morris and the Art of Finding"), interview by Luca Perciballi, May 7, 2012 (http://www.andymag.com/buzz/2030-butch-morris.html). Quote from the English original.

[3] "Interview with Lawrence "Butch" Morris" by Alessandro Cassin, The Symptom. On-line journal for Lacan.com, January 2005 (www.lacan.com/symptom6_articles/butch.html).

7 "Butch" Morris and the Evolution of Conduction®

Morris's collaborations with symphonic orchestras, too, are characterized by his use of Conduction, with or without notated music: Conduction nos. 57, 58, and 59 (*Holy Sea*, 1996), for instance, were performed with the Orchestra della Toscana without any written score. For his Conduction no. 146 (*Relative Sea*, 2005) with the Swiss Hochschule der Künste Bern, Morris, instead, took inspiration from Debussy's "La Mer." Similarly, in 2009 he developed "Folding Space: Modette & Other Songs," for the Filarmonica Arturo Toscanini, a special project merging sections of "Modette" (a chamber opera with texts and lyrics by Allan Graubard, first performed in 1985) with new songs and original compositions.

His commitment to exploring the potential of Conduction to make music "on paper" and "off the paper," and most of all between the two musical practices within the same work, continued up to his later performances: for example, his sessions with the Lucky Cheng Orchestra in New York between September 2011 and January 2012.

Morris's is a musical vision that resonates in any of the various characterizations he gave to Conduction over the years; from what he wrote back in 1985 in the liner notes of *Current Trends in Racism in America* – "in essence, [a Conduction] is an improvised duet for ensemble and conductor" – to his latest definition of Conduction, included in this book:

> Conduction®: The practice of conveying and interpreting a lexicon of directives to construct or modify sonic arrangement or composition; a structure-content exchange between composer/conductor and instrumentalists that provides the immediate possibility of initiating or altering harmony, melody, rhythm, tempo, progression, articulation, phrasing, or form through the manipulation of pitch, dynamics (volume/intensity/density), timbre, duration, silence, and organization in real time.

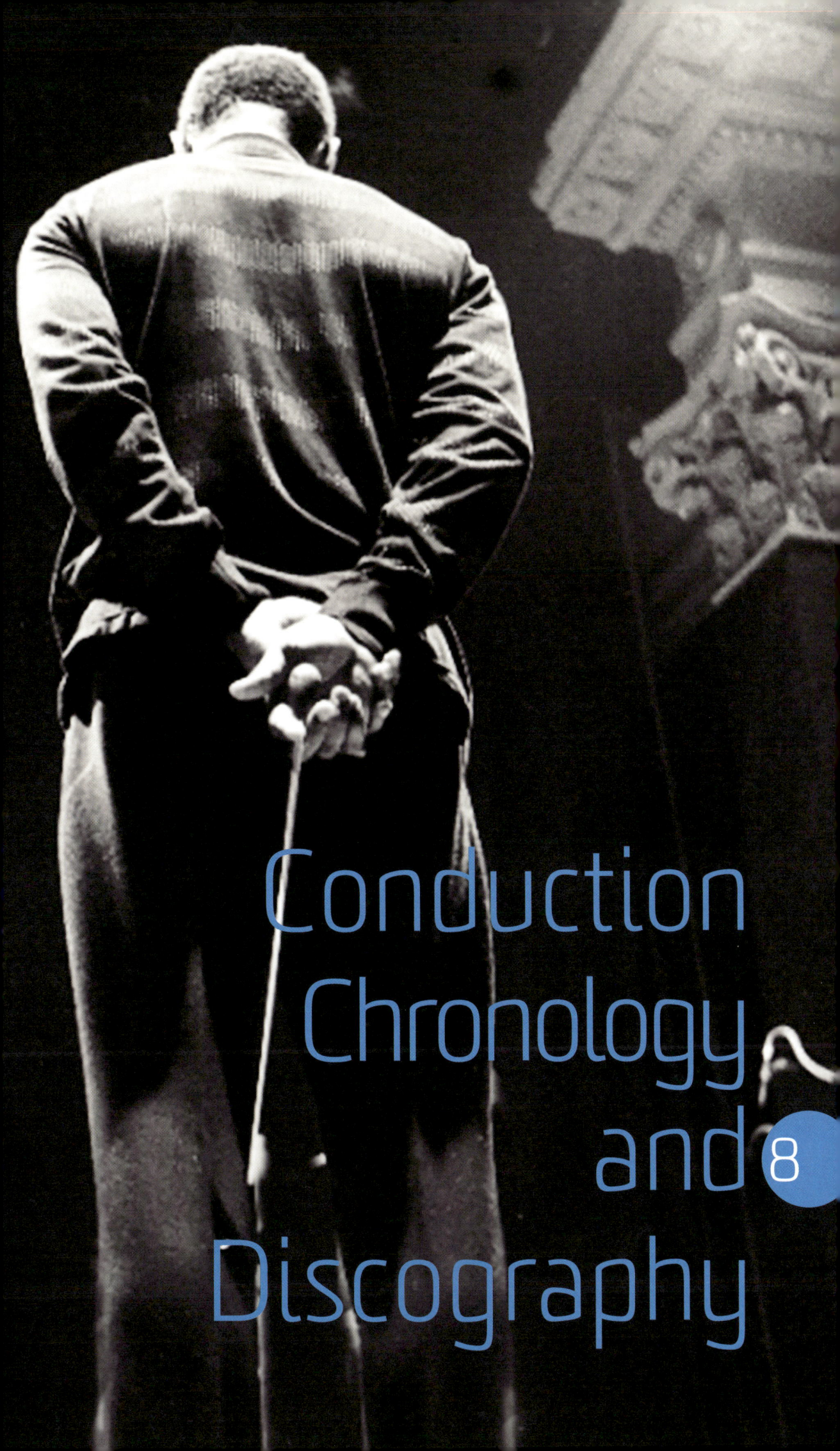

Conduction Chronology and Discography

8

Conduction® Chronology

19 Countries, 84 Cities

Conduction® No. 199, Nublu 16
Sala Kongresowa, Warsaw, Poland, June 20, 2011

> **Nublu Orchestra:** Graham Haynes (cornet), Ilhan Ersahin (tenor sax), Jonathon Haffner (alto sax), Doug Wieselman, Brandon Ross (guitar), Michael Kiaer (bass), Kenny Wollesen (drums), Joe Hertenstein (percussion), William Macintyre (vibes).

Conduction® No. 198/2
LIG Art Hall, Seoul, Korea, June 4, 2011

> **Ensemble TIMF:** Hyunjoo Jin, Sahran Kim (violin), Haejin Im, Kyoungbin Jung (viola), Kyoungran Kim, Heejung Keal (cello), Donghyuk Lee, Dongshik Shin (contrabass), Minhee Park (vocals).

Conduction® No. 198/1
LIG Art Hall, Seoul, Korea, June 3, 2011

> **Ensemble TIMF:** Hyunjoo Jin, Sahran Kim (violin), Haejin Im, Kyoungbin Jung (viola), Kyoungran Kim, Heejung Keal (cello), Donghyuk Lee, Dongshik Shin (contrabass), Minhee Park (vocals).

Conduction® No. 197, Nublu 14 & 15
Cemal Reşit Rey Konser Salonu, Istanbul, Turkey, April 29 & 30, 2011

> **Nublu Orchestra Istanbul:** Ilhan Ersahin (tenor sax), Serhan Erkol (alto sax), Eddie Henderson, Imer Demirer (trumpet), Ersin Özer (trombone), Juini Booth, Ozan Musluoglu (bass), Bilal Karaman, Sarp Maden (electric guitar), Nasheet Waits, Ediz Hafizoglu (drums), Izzet Kizil (percussion), Selen Gulun (keyboard).

Conduction® No. 196, Huseyin Alptekin: Chewing Hair
SALT Gallery, Istanbul, Turkey, April 21, 2011

> **Chorus:** Ayse Draz, Kivilcim Yavuz, Melis Altin, Ceren Tosun, Efe Demiral, Duygu Sezgin, Emre Savci (voice).

Conduction® No. 195
Catania Jazz XXVIII, Teatro Metropolitan, Catania, Italy, April 14, 2011

> **Catania Jazz Orchestra:** Seby Burgio (piano), Carmelo Venuto, Alberto Amato (bass), Alessandro Borgia, Emanuele Primavera (drums), Giuseppe Risiglione, Enzo Pafumi (electric guitar), Giuseppe Asero (alto sax), Cristiano Giardini, Nino Sortino (tenor sax), Ivan Cammarata (trumpet).

Conduction® No. 194, Macerata
XXIX Rassegna di Nuova Musica, Teatro Lauro Rossi, Macerata, Italy, March 31, 2011

> **Macerata Ensemble:** Gianpaolo Antongirolami (sax), Serena Cavalletti (violin), Giorgio Casati (cello), Paolo Casiraghi (clarinet), Luca Leracitano (piano), Gianluca Gentili (guitar), Laura Mancini (vibes), Daniele Roccato, Giacomo Piermatti (bass), Ladislao Vieni (viola).

Conduction® No. 193, Anyang Skyscraper
Anyang, Korea, October 1 & 2, 2010

> **Anyang Skyscraper:** Chung Hye Yun, Lee Su Yeon (gayagum), Kim Hwa Bok, Kang Hye Jin (kumoongo), Chang Eun Jung, Shin Kyung Hyun (hagum), Lee Pil Chun (percussion), Kim Sah Ran, Jin Hyeon (violin), Lim Hae Jin, Rah Se Won (viola), Kim Da Hye, Keal Hee Jung (cello), Kim Eun Jin, Yong Ye Rang (bass).

8 Conduction Chronology

Conduction® No. 192, Possible Universe Ai Confini tra Sardegna e Jazz, Sant'Anna Arresi Jazz Festival, Sant'Anna Arresi, Italy, August 29, 2010	
	Sant'Anna Arresi Festival Orchestra: David Murray (tenor sax, bass clarinet), Evan Parker (tenor, soprano sax), Pasquale Innarella, Greg Ward (alto sax), Joe Bowie, Tony Cattano (trombone), Meg Montgomery, Riccardo Pittau (trumpet), J. Paul Bourelly, On Ka'a Davis (acoustic/electric guitar), Hamid Drake (drums), Chad Taylor (drums, vibes), Harrison Bankhead, Silvia Bolognesi (acoustic bass), Alan Silva (synth, bass, piano).
Conduction® No. 191, Vivaldi Südtirol Jazz Festival Alto Adige, Conservatorio "C. Monteverdi", Bolzano, Italy, June 26, 2010	
	South Tyrol Jazz Festival Orchestra: Susy Lughezzani (piano), Gagliano Sabrina, Petra Langheinrich (vocals), Luca Pignata (accordion), Annamaria Quinzio, Torbjörn Ericson (violin), Katia Duregon (cello), Antonio Slam Rossetti (double bass), Tomas Schön (trumpet), Paolo Bergamaschi (tenor sax), Sarah Zanarotti (soprano sax), Phillip Balunovic (alto sax), Fabio Raffaelli, Daniele Endrizzi (electric guitar), Marco Buzzoni (acoustic guitar), Massimo Andreasi (electric bass), Lorenzo Bianchi, Sergio Pircali (self-made and mutant percussion), Carlo Benzi (keyboards, electronics), Marco Giuliani (keyboards), Michele Pedrazzi (toy organ/Rhodes), Ermanno Zanella (ukulele).
Conduction® No. 190, Tête-à-Tête, Nublu 13 Festival Banlieues Bleues, Jazz en Seine-Saint Denis 27, Paris, France, March 12, 2010	
	Nublu Orchestra: Graham Haynes (cornet), Ilhan Ersahin (tenor sax), Jonathon Haffner (alto sax), Denis Colin (bass clarinet), Doug Wieselman, Rubin Steiner (guitar), Juini Booth (acoustic bass), Alp Ersönmez (electric bass), Aaron Johnston, Turgut Alp Bekoglu (drums), Izzet Kizil (Eastern percussion).
Conduction® No. 189, S&P Part II PONCHO Concert Hall, Cornish College of the Arts, Seattle, Washington, March 6, 2010	
	Master Artists Ensemble: Brianna Atwell (viola), Heather Bentley (violin), Samantha Boshnack (trumpet), Greg Cambell (percussion), Lesli Dalaba (trumpet), Beth Fleenor (clarinet), Craig Flory (woodwinds), Wayne Horvitz (electronics), Paris Hurley (violin), Paul Kukichu (percussion), Joanne de Mars (cello), Lisa Miller (piano), Steve Moore (keyboards), Katie Rife (vibes), Monica Schley (harp), Tom Varner (French horn).
Conduction® No. 189, S&P Part I PONCHO Concert Hall, Cornish College of the Arts, Seattle, Washington, March 6, 2010	
	Associate Artists Ensemble: Darian Asplund (soprano sax), Jacob Brady (drums), Colin Field (cello), Jacob Herring (trombone), Jamie Maschler (accordion), Evan McPherson (guitar), Steven O'Brien (trumpet), James Pfeffer (percussion), Matthew Reed (clarinet), Dick Robinson (flute), Sydney Robinson (vocals), Jacob Stickney (tenor sax), Martin Strand (bass), Brent Vaartstra (guitar), Colby White (alto sax).
Conduction® No. 188 Ai Confini tra Sardegna e Jazz, Sant'Anna Arresi Jazz Festival, Sant'Anna Arresi, Italy, September 3, 2009	
	Sant'Anna Arresi Festival Orchestra: Giorgio Deidda, Claudio Rainò, Andrea Massaria (guitar), Giovanni Perri (bass), Mauro Medda, John Waters, Cousin John Heyenga (trumpet), Jason Candler, Achille Succi (alto sax), Emily Fairey (tenor sax), Tom Abbs (tuba), Sebastian Isler, Cecil Scheib (trombone), Kris Anton (timpani), Samantha Tsistinas (cymbals), Adam Loudermilk, Enzo Carpentieri (drums), Kevin Raczka (bass drum), Titta Nesti (vocals).
Conduction® No. 187, Erotic Eulogy Vision Festival, New York, NY, June 9, 2009	
	String Ensemble: Nicole Federici, Jason Kao Hwang (viola), Shawn McGloin, Jane Wang (bass), Skye Steele, Charlie Burnham (violin), Greg Heffernan, Alisa Horn (cello). **A Chorus of Poets:** Yasha Bilan, Mark Gerring, Chavisa Woods, Nora McCarthy, Justin Carter, Alex Bilu, Helga Davis, David Devoe (voice). **Text:** Allan Graubard.
Conduction® No. 186, Nublu 12 Jazz em Agosto, Lisbon, Portugal, August 2, 2009	
	Nublu Orchestra: Fabio Morgera (trumpet), Ilhan Ersahin (tenor sax), Jonathon Haffner (alto sax), Doug Wieselman, Ava Mendoza, Thor Madsen (guitar), Kenny Wollesen (drums), J. A. Deane (electronics), Juini Booth, Michael Kiaer (bass).
Conduction® No. 185/II, Lo Spirito Perfetto Parma Teatro Due, Parma, Italy, July 10, 2009	
	Coro di Poeti (A Chorus of Poets): Michele Andrei, Michele Bandini, Valentina Capone, Valentina Carnelutti, Marco Cavalcoli, Ambra D'Amico, Andrea de Luca, Riccardo Festa, Sara Masotti, Silvia Pasello, Graziella Rossi, Giulia Weber (voice).
Conduction® No. 185/I, Lo Spirito Perfetto Santarcangelo Festival Internazionale del Teatro in Piazza, Santarcangelo, Italy, July 9, 2009	
	Coro di Poeti (A Chorus of Poets): Michele Andrei, Michele Bandini, Valentina Capone, Valentina Carnelutti, Marco Cavalcoli, Ambra D'Amico, Andrea de Luca, Riccardo Festa, Sara Masotti, Silvia Pasello, Graziella Rossi, Giulia Weber (voice).

THE ART OF CONDUCTION 8

Conduction® No. 184, BangBoom Jazz in'It Festival, Vignola, Italy, June 21, 2009	
	Ensemble: Ramon Moro (trumpet), Gaspare De Vito (alto sax), Dario Fariello (tenor sax), Alberto Capelli, Filippo Giuffrè (electric guitar, electronics), Federico Marchesano, Antonio d'Intino (electric bass), Dario Bruna, Francesco Cusa (drums), Fabrizio "Abi" Rota, Davide Tidoni (electronics, live sampling).
CONDUCTION® No. 183, The Bible of Wall Street Part II The Stone, New York, NY, December 2, 2008	
	A Chorus of Poets: Nora McCarthy, Helga Davis, David Devoe, Alex Bilu, Barbara Duchow, Susan Kramer, Alva Rogers, Yasha Bilan, Jessica Eubanks, Justin Carter, Mark Gerring, Chavisa Woods (voice), Eri Yamamoto (piano).
CONDUCTION® No. 183, The Bible of Wall Street Part I The Stone, New York, NY, November 30, 2008	
	A Chorus of Poets: Nora McCarthy, Helga Davis, David Devoe, Alex Bilu, Barbara Duchow, Susan Kramer, Alva Rogers, Yasha Bilan, Jessica Eubanks, Justin Carter, Mark Gerring, Chavisa Woods (voice).
CONDUCTION® No. 182, Nublu 11 Teatro Sesc Pompeia, São PaUlo, Brazil, October 18, 2008	
	Nublu Orchestra: Graham Haynes (cornet), Ilhan Ersahin (tenor sax), Juini Booth (acoustic bass), Otto Catatau (percussion and vocals), Pedro Sá (guitar), Sylvia Gordon, Nina Becker, Thalma de Freitas (vocals), Marcello Callado, Aaron Johnston (drums), Ricardo Dias (keyboards), Gabriel Mayall (electric bass).
CONDUCTION® No. 181, Trumpet Nation BricStudio, Brooklyn, NY, September 23, 2008	
	Trumpet Nation: Paolo Fresu, Rich Johnson, Wilmer Wise, Amir El Saffar, Reut Regev, Stephen Haynes, Jaime Branch, Errol Tamerman, Kenny Warren, Chris DiMeglio, Lewis Barnes, Frank London, Taylor Ho Bynum, Dave Douglas (trumpet).
CONDUCTION® No. 180 Ai Confini tra Sardegna e Jazz, Sant'Anna Arresi Jazz Festival, Sant'Anna Arresi, Italy, September 3, 2008	
	Sant'Anna Arresi Festival Orchestra: Noemi Loi, Sara Aretino (violin), Giorgio Musiu (viola), Marco Ravasio (cello), Luigi Ciaffaglione, Mauro Medda, Claudio Comandini (trumpet), Luca Nocerino (electric bass), Alessio Bruno, Michele Staino (contrabass), Juri Deidda, Andrea Morelli (tenor sax), Alessandro Medici, Mauro Perrotta, Federico Eterno (alto sax), Giorgio Deidda, Gian Luca Locci, Roberto Boi (guitar), Andrea Turi (piano), Stefano Cortese (keyboards), Fabrizio Pisu (flute), Simone Floris (clarinet), Mauro Rolfini (bass clarinet), De Liso Paolo, Matteo Parlanti (drums, percussion), Antonello Gallo (trombone), Enrico Zara, Adele Grandulli, Simona Bandino, Carla Genchi (vocals).
CONDUCTION® No. 179, Nublu 10 Pomigliano Jazz Festival, Pomigliano, Italy, July 12, 2008	
	Nublu Orchestra: Kirk Knuffke (trumpet), Mike Williams (bass trumpet), Ilhan Ersahin (tenor sax), Jonathon Haffner (alto sax), Doug Wieselman, Zeke Zima (guitar), Jochen Rueckert (drums), Juini Booth (acoustic bass).
CONDUCTION® No. 178, Nublu 9 North Sea Jazz Festival, Rotterdam, Holland, July 11, 2008	
	Nublu Orchestra: Kirk Knuffke (trumpet), Mike Williams (bass trumpet), Ilhan Ersahin (tenor sax), Jonathon Haffner (alto sax), Doug Wieselman, Zeke Zima (guitar), Kenny Wollesen, Jochen Rueckert (drums), J. A. Deane (electronics), Juini Booth (acoustic bass).
CONDUCTION® No. 177, Nublu 8 Bordeaux, France, July 8, 2008	
	Nublu Orchestra: Kirk Knuffke (trumpet), Mike Williams (bass trumpet), Ilhan Ersahin (tenor sax), Jonathon Haffner (alto sax), Doug Wieselman, Zeke Zima (guitar), Kenny Wollesen, Jochen Rueckert (drums), J. A. Deane (electronics), Juini Booth (acoustic bass).
CONDUCTION® No. 176, Due cose amare e una dolce MAT, Rome, Italy, March 19, 2008	
	Chorus of Poets.IT: Iris Peynado, Adalgisa Fiorillo, Gabriele Vitali, Ludovica Manfredini, Cara Kavanaugh, Daniela Zanchini, Rita Del Piano, Vito Mancusi, Camillo Ventola, Carlo Fineschi, Silvana Pedrini (voice). **Text:** Tiziana Rinaldi Castro.
CONDUCTION® No. 175, Nublu 7 Bergamo Jazz, Teatro Donizetti, Bergamo, Italy, March 15, 2008	
	Nublu Orchestra: Graham Haynes (cornet), Mike Williams (bass trumpet), Ilhan Ersahin (tenor sax), Jonathon Haffner (alto sax), Doug Wieselman, Zeke Zima (guitar), Kenny Wollesen, Aaron Johnston (drums), J. A. Deane (electronics), Juini Booth (acoustic bass).

8 Conduction Chronology

CONDUCTION® No. 174, Nublu 6 Auditorium Parco della Musica di Roma, Rome, Italy, March 12, 2008	
	Nublu Orchestra: Graham Haynes (cornet), Mike Williams (bass trumpet), Ilhan Ersahin (tenor sax), Jonathon Haffner (alto sax), Doug Wieselman, Zeke Zima (guitar), Kenny Wollesen, Aaron Johnston (drums), J. A. Deane (electronics), Juini Booth (acoustic bass).
CONDUCTION® No. 173, Gregorian Leap Asbury Hall, Buffalo, NY, February 29, 2008	
	Buffalo Improvisers Orchestra: Jenece Gerber (vocals), Geoff Perry (violin), Mary Ramsey (viola), Jonathan Golove (cello), Greg Piontek (contrabass), Stuart Fuchs (acoustic guitar), Joe Rozler (piano, synthesizer), Michael Colquhoun (flutes), Mike Allard (alto sax), Steve Baczkowski (tenor sax, bass clarinet), Rey Scott (baritone, soprano sax, oboe), Bill Sack (electric guitar, prepared lap steel guitar), J.T. Rinker (laptop, live sampling), Ray Stewart (tuba), Andrew Peruzzini (trumpet), Jim Whitefield (trombone), Ravi Padmanabha (tabla, percussion), John Bacon (vibes, percussion), Ringo Brill (djembe, congas, percussion).
CONDUCTION® No. 172, Where Is Peace The Living Theatre, New York, NY, October 15, 2007	
	A Chorus of Poets: Nora McCarthy, Justin Carter, Chavisa Woods, Yasha Bilan, Alexander Bilu, Mark Gerring, David Devoe, Barbara Duchow, Alva Rogers, Eric Mingus, Elliot Levin, Fay Victor (voice).
CONDUCTION® No. 171, (The) Dessicate Ablution Klean & Kleaner, New York, NY, September 7, 2007	
	A Chorus of Poets: Nora McCarthy, Jessica Eubanks, Helga Davis, Chavisa Woods, Jameel Hobbins, David Devoe, Alexander Bilu (voice).
CONDUCTION® No. 170, Nublu 3 Nancy Jazz Pulsations, Nancy, France, October 18, 2007	
	Nublu Orchestra: Graham Haynes (cornet), Clark Gayton (trombone), Ilhan Ersahin (tenor sax), Jonathon Haffner (alto sax), Thor Madsen, Jessie Murphy (guitar), Kenny Wollesen, Aaron Johnston (drums), Didi Gutman (keyboards), Cavassa Nickens (electric bass).
CONDUCTION® No. 169, Nublu 2 Ai Confini tra Sardegna e Jazz, Sant'Anna Arresi Jazz Festival, Sant'Anna Arresi, Italy, August 27, 2007	
	Nublu Orchestra: Graham Haynes (cornet), Fabio Morgera, Kirk Knuffke (trumpet), Ilhan Ersahin (tenor sax), Jonathon Haffner (alto sax), Zeke Zima, Thor Madsen (guitar), Kenny Wollesen (drums), Mauro Rofosco (percussion).
CONDUCTION® No. 168 Festiwal Ad Libitum 2, Warsaw, Poland, November 10, 2007	
	The Odyssey Chamber Orchestra of Kracow: Konrad Oklejewicz (flute), Justyna Komorowska (oboe), Marek Nemtusiak, Grzegorz Wierus, Pawel Miskowicz, (clarinet), Paulina Strzegowska (alto sax), Wiktor Krzak (contra-bassoon), Weronika Krowka (piano), Kaja Cyganek (harp), Dominik Przywara, Paulina Tarnawska (violin), Zuzanna Iwanska (viola), Piotr Nowak, Magdalena Sas, Maciej Lisowski (cello), Duszan Korczakowski (double bass), Michal Gorczynski (bass clarinet, clarinet, tenor sax), Tomasz Duda (alto, baritone and tenor sax), Rafal Mazur (acoustic bass guitar), Tomasz Choloniewski, Dariusz Bury (percussion), Raymond Strid (drums, percussion instruments, objects).
CONDUCTION® No. 167, Samson Occom Dartmouth College, Hanover, New Hampshire, November 2, 2007	
	Barbary Coast Jazz Orchestra: Don Glasgo (director, valve trombone), Elyse George (flute), Kimia Shahi (oboe), Steven Weber (clarinet), Kyle Polite (bassoon), Derek Stenquist, Brevan D'Anglelo, Kelley Weed (alto saxes), Raj Majumder, Katie Pine (tenor sax), Greg Hart (baritone sax), Tom McDermott, Nate Caron, Kersti Spjut, Joe Pearl (trumpet, flugelhorn), Evan Carlson, Christopher Martin, (trombone), Jimmy Kircher, (bass trombone), Ellen Pettigrew (harp), Evan Lamont (piano), Jack Sisson, Joseph Ornstein (guitar), Theresa Flanagan, Tucker Hanson, Emily Eberle, Hannah Payne, Emily Chang (violin), Laura Little (viola), Emmett Knox, Joe Naeem (string bass), Andrew Lebovich (drums), Beau Sievers (live sampling, electronics).
CONDUCTION® No. 166, Nublu 5 Cemal Reşit Rey Konser Salonu, Istanbul, Turkey, October 24, 2007	
	Nublu Orchestra: Graham Haynes (cornet), Clark Gayton (trombone), Ilhan Ersahin (tenor sax), Jonathon Haffner (alto sax), Thor Madsen, Jessie Murphy (guitar), Kenny Wollesen, Aaron Johnston (drums), Didi Gutman (keyboards), Cavassa Nickens (electric bass).
CONDUCTION® No. 165, Nublu 4 Skopje Jazz Festival, Skopje, Macedonia, October 21, 2007	
	Nublu Orchestra: Graham Haynes (cornet), Clark Gayton (trombone), Ilhan Ersahin (tenor sax), Jonathon Haffner (alto sax), Thor Madsen, Jessie Murphy (guitar), Kenny Wollesen, Aaron Johnston (drums), Didi Gutman (keyboards), Cavassa Nickens (electric bass).

CONDUCTION® No. 164, When the Bough Breaks Rose Live Music, Brooklyn, NY, September 23, 2007	
	Ensemble: Charles Burnham (violin), Stomu Takeishi (acoustic bass guitar), Timothy Hill (harmonic, overtone vocals), JT Lewis (drums), Carlo Vutera (tenor vocals), Melvin Gibbs (electric bass), Brandon Ross (acoustic guitar).
CONDUCTION® No. 163, Nublu 1 Internationales Jazzfestival Saalfelden, Saalfelden, Austria, August 25, 2007	
	Nublu Orchestra: Graham Haynes (cornet), Fabio Morgera, Kirk Knuffke (trumpet), Ilhan Ersahin (tenor sax), Jonathon Haffner (alto sax), Zeke Zima, Thor Madsen (guitar), Kenny Wollesen (drums), Mauro Rofosco (percussion).
CONDUCTION® No. 162 Barbès, Brooklyn, NY, June 6, 2007	
	Ensemble: Kirk Knuffke (trumpet), Tony Barba (clarinet), Christof Knoche (bass clarinet), Eivind Opsvik, Reuben Radding (double bass).
CONDUCTION® No. 161, Unpaved Road The Putney School, Putney, Vermont, May 4, 2007	
	The Putney School Orchestra: Asako Nomoto, Chun Cao, Ruth E. Carter, Lucille B. Cochran, Swan Lee, Jeong Eun So, Julie Marden, Amy Cann (violin), James G. Southcott, Elena Ramón, Iymaani Abdul-Hamid (viola), Chloe A. Civin, Annika Amstutz (cello), Shawn Brewer (bass), Juhyeong Chung Jun Lee, Won Jun Lee (flute), Dong Chul Rhue, Tae Yong Yoon (clarinet), Robert E. McGinness, Rachel Axtell, Gryphon Rower-Upjohn, Benjamin L. Russell (voice), Adam Keil (electric guitar), Malcolm Donaldson (bass guitar), Harry Bauld, Leslie Wilson (piano), Inés Gómez-Ochoa (harpsichord), Oliver Dobrian (drums).
CONDUCTION® No. 160 Creative Music Festival, REDCAT Theater, Los Angeles, California, February 3, 2007	
	Creative Music Festival Orchestra: Josh Aguiar, Kyle Ballarta, Stephanie Richards (trumpet), Jon Armstrong (baritone sax), Ori Barel (tenor sax), Lance Peterson (soprano sax), Mercedes Smith, Gavin Templeton (alto sax), Erin Breen (clarinet), Vinny Golia (bass clarinet), Leticia Callela, Leonard Lee, Andrew Tholl (violin), Chris Votek, Ashley Walters (cello), Daren Burns, Wylie Cable, David Tranchina (bass), Scott Collins (guitar), Ingo Deul, Kevin Su Fukugawa, Qasim Naqvi (percussion), Robin Sukhadia (tabla), Antony DiGennaro (guitar, electronics), Clay Chaplin (live sampling), Lorna Kohler (oboe), Blake Layman (flute), Kathryn Nockels (bassoon), Sarah Phillips, Sarah Seelig (piano).
CONDUCTION® NO. 159, Marseille Skyscraper Théâtre National de Marseille, Marseille, France, December 14, 2006	
	Marseille Skyscraper: Alexandre de Waure, Christophe Rodomisto, Gérard Cazali, Mathieu Ruillet, Rémi Savignat, Alexis Chevrier, Mathieu Barthet, Félix Hunot, Lionel Burési (guitar), Julia Suero, Nicolas Malik Saadane (piano), Dominique Viger (voice), Emanuel Vidal (viola), Laure Bonomo (electric violin), Claude-Chantal Hess and Balthazar Montanaro (violin), Alexandre Lezy (bass), Pierre-Marc Martelli, Marc-Antoine Dagenais (sax), Erik Billabert (billotron), Guilhem Fontes (clarinet), Margaux Bidault and Adèle Ropars (flute), Geneviève Berjaud (bass), Aurélie Lombard (accordion), Ahmad Compaoré (drums).
CONDUCTION® No. 158, Trumpet Nation Font Festival, Cornelia Street Cafe, New York, NY, October 14, 2006	
	Trumpet Nation: Steven Bernstein, Taylor Ho Bynum, Ted Daniel, Dave Douglas, Sarah Ferholt, Jonathan Finlayson, Graham Haynes, Thomas Heberer, Nabate Isles, Ingrid Jensen, Kirk Knuffke, Reut Regev, Jesse Selengut, Matt Shulman (trumpet).
CONDUCTION® No. 157/2, Freedom Club Brecht Forum, New York, NY, October 8, 2006	
	A Chorus of Poets: Yasha Bilan, Alexander Bilu, Justin Carter, David Devoe, Merry Fortune, Mark Gering, Jameel Hobbins, Anyssa Kim, Nora McCarthy, Golda Solomon, Chantal Ughi, Fay Victor, Chavisa Woods (voice).
CONDUCTION® No. 157/1, Freedom Club Brecht Forum, New York, NY, October 7, 2006	
	A Chorus of Poets: Yasha Bilan, Alexander Bilu, Justin Carter, David Devoe, Merry Fortune, Mark Gering, Jameel Hobbins, Anyssa Kim, Nora McCarthy, Golda Solomon, Chantal Ughi, Fay Victor, Chavisa Woods (voice).
CONDUCTION® No. 156, New Haven Firehouse 12, New Haven, Connecticut, October 29, 2005	
	New Haven Improvisers Collective: Jeff Cedrone (guitar), David Chevan (bass), Stephen Haynes, Louis Guarino, Jr. (trumpets), Bob Gorry (guitar), Brian Slattery (violin), Paul McGuire (soprano sax), Chris Oleskey (alto sax), Albert Rivera (tenor sax), John O'Reilly (electric bass), Steve Zieminski (drums, percussion).

8 Conduction Chronology

CONDUCTION® No. 155, Central Square Central Square, Cambridge, Massachusetts, September 25, 2005	
	New England Skyscraper®: Joe Albano (bass), Kaethe Hostetter, Haruka Horii (violin), Neil Leonard (bass, alto clarinet), Dave Zox (string bass), Jonathan LaMaster (violin, erhu), Paul Dilley (guitar), Gary Fieldman (percussion), Ara Sarkissian (piano), Junko Simons (cello), Todd Brunel (clarinet).
CONDUCTION® No. 154 Barbès, Brooklyn, NY, August 16, 2005	
	Barbès String Orchestra: Jenny Scheinman, Carla Kihlstedt, Beth Cohen, Sam Bardfeld, Eric Clark (violin), David Gold, Ron Lawrence (viola), Catherine Bent, Greg Heffernan, Tomas Ulrich (cello), Todd Sickafoose, Greg Cohen, Lisle Ellis (bass).
CONDUCTION® No. 153 Green Street Grill, Cambridge, Massachusetts, June 17, 2005	
	New England Skyscraper®: Haruka Horii (violin), Bennett Miller (bass), David Bailis (guitar), Todd Brunel (clarinet), Joe Caputo (electronics, sampling), Julee Avallone (flute), Philip E. Paré Jr. (viola), Andrea Parkins (accordion), Shelley Burgon (harp), Sylvia Ryerson (violin), Joe Albano (bass clarinet), Junko Simons (cello).
CONDUCTION® No. 152 Green Street Grill, Cambridge, Massachusetts, June 16, 2005	
	New England Skyscraper®: Haruka Horii (violin), Bennett Miller (bass), David Bailis (guitar), Todd Brunel (clarinet), Joe Caputo (electronics, sampling), Julee Avallone (flute), Philip E. Paré Jr. (viola), Andrea Parkins (accordion), Shelley Burgon (harp), Sylvia Ryerson (violin), Joe Albano (bass clarinet), Junko Simons (cello).
CONDUCTION® No. 151 Green Street Grill, Cambridge, Massachusetts, June 15, 2005	
	New England Skyscraper®: Haruka Horii (violin), Bennett Miller (bass), David Bailis (guitar), Todd Brunel (clarinet), Joe Caputo (electronics, sampling), Julee Avallone (flute), Philip E. Paré Jr. (viola), Andrea Parkins (accordion), Shelley Burgon (harp), Sylvia Ryerson (violin), Joe Albano (bass clarinet), Junko Simons (cello).
CONDUCTION® No. 150, Stone String The Stone, New York, NY, August 19, 2005	
	Ensemble: Todd Sickafoose, Trevor Dunn, Lisle Ellis (bass), Marika Huhes, Okkyung Lee, Greg Heffernan (cello), Jessica Troy (viola), Jenny Scheinman, Jennifer Choi, Carla Kihlstedt, Meredith Yayanos (violin), Sylvie Courvoisier (piano), Shelley Burgon (harp).
CONDUCTION® No. 149, Tribes Nuyorican Poets Café, New York, NY, June 28, 2005	
	A Chorus Of Poets: Melanie Goodreaux, Jessica Eubanks, Nora McCarthy, Merry Fortune, Anyssa Kim, Connie MacNamee, Fay Victor, Chantal Ughi, Mark Gering, Kimberly Amante, Alexander Bilu (voice).
CONDUCTION® No. 148, Charlie Parker Tribes Gallery, New York, NY, August 27, 2005	
	A Chorus Of Poets: Amy Ouzoonian, Merry Fortune, Anyssa Kim, Fay Victor, Justin Carter, Chantal Ughi, Mark Gering, Yascha Janet Bilan, Kimberly Amante, Alexander Bilu, Nora McCarthy (voice).
CONDUCTION® No. 147, Trumpet Nation Yamaha Artist Services Center, New York, NY, August 27, 2005	
	Trumpet Nation: Ahmed Abdulla, C.J. Camerieri, Ted Daniel, Chris DiMeglio, Dave Douglas, Peter Evans, Mac Gollehon, Nabate Isles, Glenn Makos, Bart C. J. Miltenberger, Jon Nelson, Jesse Selengut, Matt Shulman, Sarah Wilson, Wilmer Wise (trumpet).
CONDUCTION® No.146, Relative Sea Hochschule der Künste, Bern, Switzerland, October 7, 2005	
	HKB Orchestra: Christian Bauer, Vanya Hristova, Irene Arametti, Romain Hurzeler, Yelizavetas Kozlova, Nagano Mariko, Simone Roggen, Christian Stejskal, Sabine Stoffer, Mate Visky, Gwen Heming (first violins), Maciej Chodziakiewicz, Vladimir Tchinovsky, Rachel Wieser, Tabea Kämpf, Erika Yamazaki, Katrin Hasler, Muriel Gabathurler, Johanna Egloff, Jerome Faller (second violins), M. Locher (viola), Tomasz Slowikowski, Diego Liberati, Ionut Plamada, Solme Hong, Luise Bammes, Silvia Halter, Valentina Velkova, Miriam Erig (cello), Attila Antal, Simone Schranz, Ivan Nestic, Simone Sturzenegger, Kaspar Wirz, Christian Schmid (bass), Catalin Palaghia, Jin-Young Back, Ksenija Radosavljevic (flute), Adrian Cioban, Benjamin Fischer, Stefan Arni (oboe), Dimitar Tsandev (clarinet), Takashi Sugimoto, Diego Barone, Gorjan Slokar, Severin Zoll (French horn), Gregor Krtschek, Peter Schwegler, Julian Zimmermann (trumpet), Simon Röthlisberger, Dimo Pishtyalov, Mihael Suler (trombone), Pascal Schafer (tuba), Didier Vogel, Emil Bolli (percussion), Blathnaid Fischer-Fuhrer (harp), Jonas Tschanz (soprano sax), Michelle Hess (alto sax), Remo Schnyder (tenor sax), Stefan Rolli (baritone sax), Simon Bucher, Alexander Ruef (piano).

THE ART OF CONDUCTION 8

CONDUCTION® No. 145, In The Upper Room River to River Festival, New York, NY, June 2 & 3, 2005
A Chorus Of Poets: Amy Ouzoonian, Melanie Goodreaux, Jessica Eubanks, Nora McCarthy, Merry Fortune, Anyssa Kim, Connie MacNamee, Fay Victor, Lindsay Campbell, Justin Carter, Chantal Ughi, Mark Gering, Jascha Janet Bilan, Makeda Christodoulos, Kimberly Amante, Tracie Morris, Alexander Bilu (voice).
CONDUCTION® No. 144, Floating Stone The Stone, New York, NY, June 5, 2005
Ensemble: Steve Smithie (guitar), Dylan Willemsa (viola), Aki Onda (electronics), Chantal Ughi, Justin Carter, Fay Victor, Nora McCarthy (vocals).
CONDUCTION® No. 143/2, Novamusica Total Music Meeting, Berlinische Galerie, Berlin, Germany, November 5, 2004
Ensemble Laboratorio Novamusica: Armand Angster, Wolfgang Fuchs, Hans Koch, Peter Van Bergen (bass clarinet), Cecilia Vendrasco (flutes), Ilich Fenzi (trumpet), Umberto de Nigris (trombone), Piergabriele Mancuso (viola), Carlo Carratelli (piano, harpsichord), Giovanni Mancuso (piano), Andrea Carlon (double bass), Peter Gallo (drums, percussion).
CONDUCTION® No. 143/1, Novamusica Teatrino Groggia, Venice, Italy, November 2, 2004
Laboratorio Novamusica: Cecilia Vendrasco (flutes), Ilich Fenzi (trumpet), Umberto de Nigris (trombone), Piergabriele Mancuso (viola), Carlo Carratelli (piano), Giovanni Mancuso (piano), Andrea Carlon (double bass), Peter Gallo (drums, percussion).
CONDUCTION® No. 142, Trumpet Nation Tonic, New York, NY, August 4, 2004
Trumpet Nation: Ted Daniel, Matt Lavelle, Dave Douglas, Graham Haynes, Bart Miltenberger, Nate Wooley, Jesse Neuman, John McNeil, C.J. Camerieri, Ron Horton, Roy Campbell, Sycil Mathai, Matt Shulman, Jon Finlayson, Sarah Wilson, Flip Barnes, Steven Bernstein, J. P. Carter, Jon Nelson, Glenn Makos, Peter Evans, Wilmer Wise (trumpet).
CONDUCTION® No. 141/2, Emyoueseyesee Bowery Poetry Club, New York, NY, October 17, 2004
Sound Infusion Orchestra: Jay Rozen (tuba), Jeremiah Cymerman (clarinet), Lukas Ligeti (drums), James Ilgenfritz, Adam Lane (bass), Kelly Pratt, Nate Wooley (trumpet), Skye Steele (violin), Ursel Schlicht (piano), Diana Wayburn (flute), Chris Hoffman (cello), Ras Moshe (tenor sax), Jonathon Moritz (soprano sax), Matt Mottel (synthesizer), Eddy Rollin (oboe), Nick Mancini (vibes), Reut Regev (trombone), Ty Cumbie (guitar).
CONDUCTION® No. 141/1, Emyoueseyesee The Tank Theatre, New York, NY, October 12, 2004
Sound Infusion Orchestra: Jay Rozen (tuba), Jeremiah Cymerman (clarinet), Lukas Ligeti (drums), James Ilgenfritz, Adam Lane (bass), Kelly Pratt, Nate Wooley (trumpet), Skye Steele (violin), Ursel Schlicht (piano), Diana Wayburn (flute), Chris Hoffman (cello), Ras Moshe (tenor sax), Jonathon Moritz (soprano sax), Matt Mottel (synthesizer), Eddy Rollin (oboe), Nick Mancini (vibes), Reut Regev (trombone), Ty Cumbie (guitar).
CONDUCTION® No. 140, Controversy Konfrontationen, Nickelsdorf, Austria, July 25, 2004
Nickelsdorf Konfrontationen Festival Orchestra: Tobias Delius, Marco Eneidi (sax), Tony Buck, Paul Lovens (drums, percussion), Andy Moor, Terrie Ex (guitar), John Norman (bass), Martin Schütz (cello), Cordula Bösze (flute), Saadet Türköz (vocals), Christof Kurzmann (computer), Hans Falb (turntables).
CONDUCTION® No. 139, Brother to Brother Vision Festival, New York, NY, May 31, 2004
New York Skyscraper®: Cornelius Dufallo, Rose Bartu (violin), Steffany Griffin (viola), Okkyung Lee (cello), Andrew Gross (soprano sax), Mia Theodorakis (harp), Andrea Parkins (accordion), Helga Davis (voice), Shahzad Ismaily, Miguel Frasconi (electronics), Matt Moran (vibes, percussion), Salim Washington (oboe), Reut Regev (trombone), Abraham Burton (tenor sax), Nabate S. Isles (trumpet), Tom Abbs (tuba), Michael Marcus (clarinet), Tim Price (bassoon), Kahil Smith (flute), Mark Taylor (French horn), Tyshawn Sorey (drums), Ron Kozak (soprano sax), Andrew Bemkey (piano).
CONDUCTION® No. 138 VIII Festival Internacional de Improvisación Hurta Cordel, Casa Encendida, Madrid, Spain, February 1, 2004
Orquesta Foco: Baldo Martinez (bass), Rodrigo Campaña (electric bass), Javier Carmona, Nilo Gallego (drums), Pablo Rega, Antonio Bravo (electric guitar), Merran Laginestra (piano), Ute Voelker (accordion), Belen Lopez (marimba), Carl-Ludwig Hubsch (tuba), Gregorio Kazaroff (sampler), Barbara Meyer (cello), Marcos Monge (tenor sax), Ricardo Tejero, Javier Escaned, Noemi Olmos (alto sax), Mark Sefton, Chefa Alonso (soprano sax), Javier Paxariño (sopranino sax), Ildefonso Rodriguez (clarinet), Alessandra Rombola, Cristina Fernandez, Ernesto Santana (flute), Cova Villegas (voice), Victor M. Diez (poet).

Conduction Chronology

CONDUCTION® No. 137, Golden Age
Schauspielhaus Zürich/Schiffbau, Zürich, Switzerland, December 8, 2003

> **Ensemble:** Raphael Clamer, Corin Curschellas, Olivia Grigolli, Robert Hunger-Buhler, Ueli Jaggi, Katja Kolm, Bettina Stucky, Graham F. Valentine, Melanie Wandel (vocals), Monika Baer, Renate Steinmann, Mathias Weibel, Martin Zeller (string quartet), Martin Schütz (live sampling).

CONDUCTION® No. 136
VIII Festival Internacional de Improvasación Hurta Cordel, Casa Encendida, Madrid, Spain, January 31, 2004

> **Orquesta Foco:** Baldo Martinez (bass), Rodrigo Campaña (electric bass), Javier Carmona, Nilo Gallego (drums), Pablo Rega, Antonio Bravo (electric guitar), Merran Laginestra (piano), Ute Voelker (accordion), Belen Lopez (marimba), Carl-Ludwig Hubsch (tuba), Gregorio Kazaroff (sampler), Barbara Meyer (cello), Marcos Monge (tenor sax), Ricardo Tejero, Javier Escaned, Noemi Olmos (alto sax), Ildefonso Rodriguez (clarinet), Chefa Alonso, Mark Sefton (soprano saxes), Javier Paxariño (sopranino sax), Alessandra Rombola, Cristina Fernandez, Ernesto Santana (flute), Cova Villegas (voice), Victor M. Diez (poet).

CONDUCTION® No. 135, Sheng/Skyscraper®
Festival Internazionale di Musica Contemporanea, *Remix, Structures and Improvisations,* Teatro alle Tese, Venice, Italy, September 21, 2003

> **Sheng Skyscraper®:** Thomas E. Chess (oud), Jason Kao Hwang (violin), J. A. Deane (live sampling, drum machine), Shahzad Ismaily (keyboards, drum machine), Okkyung Lee (cello), Cooper-Moore (tese, homemade thunder), Matt Moran (vibes), Jesse Murphy (electric bass), Brandon Ross (electric guitar), Tyshawn Sorey (drums), Abou Sylla (balafon), Dalla Tounkara (kora), Shu-ni Tsou (dizi), Guowei Wang (erhu), Junling Wang (guzheng).

CONDUCTION® No. 134, Trumpet Nation
Tonic, New York, NY, August 1, 2003

> **Trumpet Nation:** Dave Ballou, Lewis Barnes, Steven Bernstein, Eric Biondo, Colin Brigstocke, David Buchbinder, Dave Douglas, Franz Hautzinger, Nabate Isles, Ingrid Jensen, Matt Lavelle, John McNeil, Jesse Neuman, Nils Ostendorf, Eric Shanfield (trumpet).

CONDUCTION® No. 133, Swissmix
Tonic, New York, NY, March 29, 2003

> **Ensemble:** Jacques Demierre (piano), Hans Kenel with Mytha Alp Horn Quartet: Marcel Huonder, Philip Powell, Marc Unternährer, Hans Koch (bass clarinet), Tomas Korber, Norbert Moeslang, Guenter Mueller, Ralph Steinbruechel (electronics), Dorthea Schuerch (vocals), Daniel Schneider (sounds), Fredy Studer (drums), Andrea Parkins (accordion), Martin Schuetz, Okkyung Lee (cello).

CONDUCTION® No. 132
Bowery Poetry Club, New York, NY, February 7-10, 2003

> **New York Skyscraper®:** Tyshawn Sorey (drums), Brandon Ross (guitar), Vijay Iyer (keyboards), Cooper-Moore (electric harp), Stomu Takeishi (bass), Matt Moran (vibes), Omar Kabir (trumpet), Ilhan Ersahin (soprano sax), Patience Higgins (tenor sax), Abdoulaye N'Diaye (alto sax), Kahil Smith (flute), Vincent Chancey (French horn), Doug Wieselman (bass clarinet), Art Baron (trombone), David Hofstra (tuba), Okkyung Lee (cello), Billy Bang, Cornelius Duffallo (violin), Stephany Griffin (viola).

CONDUCTION® No. 131/4701, The Year of the Ram
Columbus Park, New York, NY, February 1 & 2, 2003

> **Sheng Skyscraper®:** Tarik Bendrahim (oud), Balla Kouyate (balafon), Xiao-Fen Min (pipa), Zhipeng Shen (gaohu), Yacouba Sissoko (kora), Ibrahim Fall, Diagne Tchokoo (m'balak/talking drum), Shu-ni Tsou (dizi), Thomas Thuân Dang Vu (guzheng).

CONDUCTION® No. 130, Bertolt
Brecht Forum, New York, NY, December 15, 2002

> **Jump Arts Orchestra:** Cornelius Duffallo (violin), Jessica Pavone (viola), Okkyung Lee (cello), Terence Murren (bass), Gamiel Lyons (flute), Patrick Holmes (clarinet), Matt LaVelle (bass clarinet), Stuart Bogie (contra alto clarinet), Susanne Chen (bassoon), Jordan McLean (trumpet), Vincent Chancey (French horn), Steve Swell (trombone), Dave Brandt (vibes), Yayoi Ikawa (piano), Warren Smith (percussion).

CONDUCTION® No. 129, Calligraphy
Bowery Poetry Club, New York, NY, November 19, 2002

> **Sheng Skyscraper®:** Bailo Bah (tambin), Tarik Benbrahim (oud), Famoro Dioubate (balafon), Lofti Gamal (qanoon), Xiao-fen Min (pipa), Seido Salifoski (dumbek), Zhipeng Shen (gaohu), Yacouba Sissoko (kora), Shu-ni Tsou (dizi).

CONDUCTION® No. 128, The Burnt Sugar Rite
Bowery Poetry Club, New York, NY, November 12, 2002

> **Burnt Sugar:** Vijay Iyer, Bruce Mack (synthesizer), Morgan Craft, René Akhan (guitar), DJ Mutamassik (turntables/kaos pad), Shazad Ismaily (drum machine), Qasim Naqui (drums), Jason Di Matteo (acoustic bass), Jared Nickerson (electric bass), Okkyung Lee (cello), Justice Dilla-X (vocals).

THE ART OF CONDUCTION

CONDUCTION® No. 127, A Chorus of Poets
Bowery Poetry Club, New York, NY, November 2, 2002

A Chorus of Poets: Bob Holman, Billy Martin, Edwin Torres, Tish Benson, Regie Cabico, Shappy, Taylor Mali, Shawn Randall, Elliott Levin, Todd Colby, Matthew Courtney, Celena Glenn, Max Blagg (poets).

CONDUCTION® No. 126, A Chorus of Poets
Bowery Poetry Club, New York, NY, September 25, 2002

A Chorus of Poets: LaTasha Natasha Diggs, Maggie Estep, David Henderson, Max Blagg, Jackie Sheeler, Edwin Torres, Steve Cannon, Suheir Hammad, Regie Cabico, Bob Holman, Roger Bonair-Agard, Dana Bryant, Sapphire (poets).

CONDUCTION® No. 125, LOL LOVE
Nuoro Jazz, Lollove (Nuoro), Italy, September 5, 2002

Ensemble: Valentina Picconi, Laura Mura, Silvana Porcu, Renato Dametti, Paola Luffarelli, Serena Oggiano, Musina, Clelia Tanda, Anna Frassetto, Francesca Putzu, Maria Pia De Vito, Carlo Porrà, Silvia Trezza, Antonella Uras, Barbara Carta, Giacinto Ricchetti, Fabrizia Migliarotti, Nicola Petrocchi, Paola Alessandrini, Chica Piazzolla, Alessia Obino, Marta Capponi, Daniela Di Gioia, Marta Loddo, Federica Zucchini (vocals), Massimiliano Tuveri, Roberta Musumeci, Antonio Sotgiu, Matteo Frau, Enrica Palla (trumpet), Davide Sezzi, Federico Eterno, Damiano Niccolini, Francesca Corrias, Alessandro Dell'Anna, Daniel Theissen, Andrea Mocci, Andrea Nulchis, Christian Ferlaino, Alessandro Medici, Mauro Perrotta, Gianfranco Faret, Luca De Vito, Morfini Luisa, Daniele Pasini, Letizia Sechi, Gianmario Corrias, Tino Tracanna (sax), Paolo Fresu (flugelhorn), Riccardo Parrucci (flute), Giulio Picasso (trombone), Luca Musumeci (bass tuba), Paola Agostino Sanna, Gavino Fonnesu, Francesco Albano, Alessandro Cadoni, Luca Gatta, Maurizio Sammicheli (guitar), Stefano Tedesco (vibes), Marcella Carboni (harp), Michele Francesconi (piano), Elisabetta La Corte, Stefano Delfini, Riccardo Barbera (bass), Matteo Carcassi, Lorenzo Capello, Francesco Santucci, Paolo Orlandi, Davide Marras, Andrea Ruggeri, Maurizio Vizilio, Fabrizio Saiu (drums).

CONDUCTION® No. 124
Klangbrücke, Aachen, Germany, November 30, 2002

Aachen Skyscraper®: Uwe Bottcher (violin), Lutz Felbick (piano), Johanna Futyma-Daske (flute), Andreas Herrlich-Volke (viola), Manou Liebert (harp), Regina Pastuszky (clarinet), Gitta Schafer (sax, clarinet), Luger Schmidt (cello), Sebastien Semal (trombone), Steffen Thormahlen (percussion).

CONDUCTION® No. 123, East Wind West Wind
CBGB, New York, NY, September 18, 2002

East Wind West Wind Orchestra: Baojie Gao (yang qin), Xiao-fen Min (pipa), Zhipeng Shen (gaohu), Yayoi Ikawa (piano), Hillard Green, Mark Deutsch (bass), Zane Massey (tenor sax), Billy Bang (violin), Roy Campbell Jr. (trumpet).

CONDUCTION® No. 122, Jumping in Context
Context Studio, Brooklyn, NY, April 13, 2002

Jump Arts Orchestra: Gamiel Lyons (flute), Charles Waters, Patrick Holmes, Stuart Bogie (clarinet), Ras Moshe, Andrew Lamb (tenor sax), Patrick Brennan (alto sax), Alex Harding (baritone sax), Jordan McLean (trumpet), Matt LaVelle (bass clarinet), Bethany Ryker (French horn), Steve Swell, Reut Regev (trombone), Tom Abbs (tuba), Dillian Willemsa (viola), Rosie Hertin (violin), Okkyung Lee (cello), Francois Grillot, Todd Nicholson, Terence Murren, Bernard Rosat (bass), Andrew Barker (drums), Andrew Bemkey (piano), David Brandt (vibes).

CONDUCTION® No. 121, Jumping in Context
Context Studio, Brooklyn, NY, April 12, 2002

Jump Arts Orchestra: Gamiel Lyons (flute), Charles Waters, Patrick Holmes, Stuart Bogie (clarinet), Ras Moshe, Andrew Lamb (tenor sax), Patrick Brennan (alto sax), Alex Harding (baritone sax), Susanne Chen (bassoon), Jordan McLean (trumpet), Matt LaVelle (bass clarinet), Bethany Ryker (French horn), Steve Swell, Reut Regev (trombone), Tom Abbs (tuba), Dillian Willemsa, Jessica Pavone (viola), Rosie Hertin (violin), Okkyung Lee (cello), Francois Grillot, Todd Nicholson, Terence Murren, Bernard Rosat (bass), Andrew Barker (drums), Andrew Bemkey (piano), David Brandt (vibes).

CONDUCTION® No. 120
Aaron Davis Hall, Harlem, New York, NY, October 27, 2001

New York Skyscraper®: Jana Andeuska, Billy Bang (violin), Stephanie Griffin, Shayshawn MacPherson (viola), Okkyung Lee (cello), Juini Booth, Brian Smith (bass), Liberty Ellman (guitar), Rolando Briceno (flute), Arnold Greenwich (oboe), Gamiel Lyons (flute), David Miller (basson), Doug Wieselman (bass clarinet), John Carlson (trumpet), Vincent Chancey (French horn), Ilhan Ersahin (soprano sax), Steve Swell (trombone), Louis Perdomo (piano), Warren Smith (vibes), Mia Theodorakis (harp).

CONDUCTION® No. 119
Aaron Davis Hall, Harlem, New York, NY, October 26, 2001

New York Skyscraper®: Jana Andeuska, Billy Bang (violin), Stephanie Griffin, Shayshawn MacPherson (viola), Okkyung Lee (cello), Juini Booth, Wilber Morris, Brian Smith (bass), Liberty Ellman (guitar), Rolando Briceno (flute), Arnold Greenwich (oboe), Gamiel Lyons (flute), David Miller (bassoon), Doug Wieselman (bass clarinet), John Carlson (trumpet), Vincent Chancey (French horn), Ilhan Ersahin (soprano sax), Steve Swell (trombone), Louis Perdomo (piano), Warren Smith (vibes), Mia Theodorakis (harp).

8 Conduction Chronology

CONDUCTION® No. 118
Tonic, New York, NY, April 21, 2001

Ensemble: J.A. Deane (drum machine, live sampling), Christian Marclay (turntables), Graham Haynes (cornet), Andrew Bemkey (piano), Billy Bang, Jana Andeuska (violin), Okkyung Lee (cello), Simon H. Fell (bass), Rhodri Davies (harp), Elliott Sharp, Morgan Craft (guitar).

CONDUCTION® No. 117, Good Friday the 13th
The Brecht Forum, New York, NY, April 13, 2001

Jump Arts Orchestra: Chris Jonas (soprano sax), Patrick Brennan (alto sax), Brian Settes, Assif Tsahar (tenor sax), Charles Waters (clarinet), Oscar Noriega (bass clarinet), Stewart Bogie (contra alto clarinet), Susanne Chen (bassoon), Gamiel Lyons (flute), Jessica Pavone, Dylan Willemsa (viola), Okkyung Lee (cello), Todd Nicholson, Bernard Rosat (bass), Jon Birdsong, Matt LaVelle (trumpet), Bethany Ryker (French horn), Reut Regev, Steve Swell (trombones), Tom Abbs (tuba), John Blum (piano), David Brandt (marimba), Andrew Barker (drums).

CONDUCTION® No. 116
Tonic, New York, NY, August 25, 2000

Jump Arts Orchestra: Michael Herbst (oboe), Chris Jonas (soprano sax), Ori Kaplan (alto sax), Susanne Chen (bassoon), Jordan Mclean (French horn), Aaron Johnson (trombone), Tom Abbs (tuba), Andrew Bemkey (piano), David Brandt (marimba), Andrew Barker (drums), Jeremy Wilms (guitar), Dylan Willemsa (viola), Shiau Shu Yu, Gil Selinger (cello), Jane Wong, Juini Booth (acoustic bass).

CONDUCTION® No. 115, E-Mission
Knitting Factory, New York, NY, December 1, 2000

Ensemble: Ilhan Ersahin, Frank Lowe (tenor sax), Jana Andeuska, Billy Bang Walker (violin), Eric Charlston (vibes), Andrew Bemkey (piano), Dave Reaboi (bass), Matt Mottel (synthesizer), Leslie Ross (bassoon), Okkyung Lee (cello), Mike Pride (clarinet), David Lindsey (concertina).

CONDUCTION® No. 114, The Catalan Project
7th Festival of Contemporary Music, L'Auditori, Barcelona, Spain, October 21, 2000

Barcelona Skyscraper®: Catalina Claro, Anna Subirana (vocals), Raphael Zweifel (cello), Ruth Barberan, Matt Davis (trumpet), Liba Villavecchia (tenor sax), Anuska Moratxo (alto sax), Chefa Alonso (soprano sax), Imma Udina (clarinet), Alfredo Costa Monteiro, Maddish Falzoni (accordion), Daniel Figueras (Spanish guitar), Ferran Fages, Pablo Svarzman (guitar, electronics), Mariano Martos (electric bass), Manolo Lopez (bass), Virginia Espin (piano), Joan Saura (sampler), Betelgeuse Martinez, Katia Riera (percussion).

CONDUCTION® No. 113, Interflight
Palacio de Cristal, Madrid, Spain, October 1, 2000

Ensemble: Graham Haynes (sampler, cornet, electronics), Joan Saura (sampler, computer), J.A. Deane (sampler, drum machine), Agusti Fernandez (piano), Lawrence D. "Butch" Morris (cornet, conductor).

CONDUCTION® No. 112, New Mehter Culture
Babylon Performance Center, Istanbul, Turkey, April 2, 2000

Istanbul Skyscraper®: Oguz Buyukberber (bass clarinet), Ali Perret (electric keyboard), Ozkan Alici (baglama), Husnu Senlendirici (clarinet), Pinar Baltacigil, Tolga Sevim, Tuba Ozkan, Ayse Bolukbasi (violin), Reyent Bolukbasi (cello), Mehmet Akatay (percussion), Nuri Lekesizgoz (kanun), Ilhan Ersahin (tenor sax), J.A. Deane (sampler), John Davis (piano).

CONDUCTION® No. 111, New Mehter Culture
Babylon Performance Center, Istanbul, Turkey, April 1, 2000

Istanbul Skyscraper®: Oguz Buyukberber (bass clarinet), Ali Perret (electric keyboard), Ozkan Alici (baglama), Husnu Senlendirici (clarinet), Pinar Baltacigil, Tolga Sevim, Tuba Ozkan, Ayse Bolukbasi (violin), Reyent Bolukbasi (cello), Mehmet Akatay (percussion), Nuri Lekesizgoz (kanun), Ilhan Ersahin (tenor sax), J. A. Deane (sampler), John Davis (piano).

CONDUCTION® No. 110
Brecht Forum, New York, NY, April 21, 2000

Jump Arts Orchestra: Edda Kristansdotter (flute), Michael Herbst (oboe), Charles Waters (clarinet), Chris Jonas (soprano sax), Ori Kaplan (alto sax), Assif Tsahar (bass clarinet), Susanne Chen (basson), Jordan Mclean (French horn), Todd Margasak (trumpet), Aaron Johnson, Reut Regev (trombone), Tom Abbs (tuba), Andrew Bemkey (piano), David Brandt (marimba), Andrew Barker (drums), Jessica Pavone (viola), Shiau Shu Yu, Gil Selinger (cello), Jane Wong, Matt Heyner, Juini Booth (acoustic bass).

CONDUCTION® No. 109, 9.9.99
Kryptonale Festival, Großer Wasserspeicher, Berlin, Germany, September 9, 1999

Berlin Skyscraper®: Johannes Bauer (trombone), Matthias Bauer, David de Bernardi (double bass), Elisabeth Böhm-Christl (bassoon), Johanne Braun (oboe), Nicholas Bussmann (cello), Axel Dorner (trumpet), Tobias Dutschke (vibes), Gregor Hotz (alto clarinet), Wolfgang Fuchs (bass clarinet), Michael Griener (percussion), Dietrich Petzold (viola), Kirsten Reese (flute), Olaf Rupp (guitar), Aleks Kolkowski (violin).

THE ART OF CONDUCTION 8

CONDUCTION® No. 108
Muzeum Książki Artystycznej, Lodz, Poland, October 1, 1999

Ensemble: Dorota Kowalczyk (violin), Dorota Stanistawska (viola), Matgorzata Sek (cello), Kinga Szmigulska (oboe), Maciej Flis (bassoon), Gnegorz Nowak (acoustic guitar), Dariusz Adryarizyk (electric guitar), Kamil Bilski (alto sax), Yakub Kawnik (vibes), Agata Dorota Fiecko (piano), Piotr Kozasa (percussion).

CONDUCTION® No. 107, The Bodensee Project
Kulturzentrum Kammgarn, Schaffhausen, Switzerland, August 21, 1999

Ensemble: Evaline Fink, Inge Hager, Achim Braun, Gregor Hubner (violin), Annette Nigsch, Karoline Pilz, Julia Kathen (viola), Egon Reitmann (trombone), Monika Furrer (English horn), Karl Schimke (tuba), Christoph Luchsinger, Stefan Wyler (trumpet), Marianne Knecht (flute), Urs Rollin (guitar), Desiree Senn, Bernard Gottert, Martin Schütz (cello), Wolfgang Lindner, Claus Furchtner, Marc Huber, Freddy Studer, Niklaus Keller (percussion), Gordula Dietrich (bassoon), Carles Peris (soprano sax), Peter Gossweiler (bass), Roberto Domeniconi (piano), Frank Strodel (clarinet), Ewald Hugle (tenor sax), Bernd Konrad (bass clarinet), Klaus Sell (French horn), Karl Friedrich Wenzel (oboe), Karoline Hofler (bass), Hans Koch (bass clarinet, sax).

CONDUCTION® No. 106
Teatro Central, Seville, Spain, January 24, 1999

Orquestra Joven de Andalucia: Jesus Sanchez Valladares, Maria Dolores Sanchez Lorca (flute), Jose Maria Benitez Ortiz, Wolfgang Puntas Robleda (clarinet), Francisco Cerpa Roman (bassoon), Maria Rosa Navas Perez (harp), Abdon Santos Lopez (sax), Teresa Maria Martinez Leon, Francisco Manuel Hurtado Sanchez, Jesus Andres Busto Barea, Juan Antonio Garcia Delgado, Antonio Moreno Saenz (percussion), Oscar Garcia Fernandez, Moises Romero Obrero, Belen Fernandez Gamez, Maria De La Lus Moreno Rojas, Anna Emilova Sivova, Modesto Berna Guisado, David Garcia Guglieti (violin), Faustino Pinero Arrabal, Maria Paz Dias Marques, Juan Carlos Rodrigues Romero (viola), Carmen Garcia Moreno (cello), Peter Kowald, Felix Gomez Gomex, Juan Miguel Guzman Pentinel (bass), Le Quan Ninh (percussion), Agustí Fernández (piano).

CONDUCTION® No. 105
Taller de Músics, Barcelona, Spain, September 26, 1998

Ensemble: Agustí Fernandez, Joan Pau Piqué (piano), Gorka Benitez, Xavier Maristany (sax), Chefa Alonso (soprano sax), Idelfonso Rodriguez (alto sax, clarinet), Assif Tsahar (tenor sax), Alfredo Costa (accordion), Mark Cunningham (trumpet), Eduard Altaba, Pere Lowe (basses), Barbara Meyer (cello), Isabel Lucio (vocals), Mat Maneri (violin).

CONDUCTION® No. 104, Experimenta
Teatro Sarmiento, Buenos Aires, Argentina, August 15, 1998

Ensemble: Arauco Yepes (percussion), Pablo Ledesme (soprano sax), Marcelo Moguilevsky (shofar, clarinet), Lucio Capece (bass clarinet, alto sax), Gregorio Kasaroff (turntables, tapes), Edgardo Cardozo (guitar), Hernan Vives (electric guitar, theorbo), Wenchi Lazo (electric guitar), Adriana de los Santos (piano), Patricia Martinez (synthesizer), Alejandro Franov (accordion), Alejandro Teran (viola), Martin Iannacone (cello), Damian Bolotin, Javier Casalla (violin), Diego Pojomovsky (bass, processors).

CONDUCTION® No. 103, Holy Ghost
Texaco Jazz Festival, New York, NY, June 12, 1998

Holy Ghost: Beth Coleman (turntables), Brandon Ross, James "Blood" Ulmer (guitar), J. T. Lewis (drums), Graham Haynes (cornet), Micha (alto sax), Ilhan Ersahin (tenor sax), Melvin Gibbs (bass), Charles Burnham, Jasmine Morris (violin), Rufus Capadocia (cello), Mark Baston (keyboards), J.A. Deane, Hahn Rowe (electronics), Helga Davis (vocals), Daniel Moreno (percussion).

CONDUCTION® No. 102, The Western Front
The Western Front Society, Vancouver, B.C., June 19, 1998

New Orchestra Workshop Society (NOW): Paul Plimley (piano), Kate Hammet-Vaughan (voice), Peggy Lee (cello), Dylan van der Schyff (drums, percussion), Paul Blaney, Clyde Reed (bass), Ralph Eppel (tenor trombone), Brad Muirhead (bass trombone), Bruce Freedman (soprano sax), Saul Berson (alto sax), Graham Ord, Coat Cooke (tenor sax), John Korsrud, Bill Clark (trumpet), Ron Samworth (guitar).

CONDUCTION® No. 101
Harwood Art Center, Albuquerque, New Mexico, April 10, 1998

Ensemble: Stephan Dill (acoustic guitar), Tom Zannes (violin), Alicia Ultan (viola), Katie Harlow (cello), David Parlato (bass), Courtney Smith (harp), Jon Baldwind (cornet), Mark Weaver (tuba), Ken Battat (vibes, percussion), J.A. Deane (electronics).

CONDUCTION® No. 100/2
Tribeca Performing Arts Center, New York, NY, April 5, 1998

Double Skyscraper (Tokyo & Istanbul): Tomomi Acachi (vocals), Kizan Daiyoshi (shakuhachi), Remi Fujimoto (sho), Hisami Hanaki (wa-daiko), Miki Maruta (koto), Sachika Nagata (percussion), Kenichi Takeda (taisho-koto), Yumiko Tanaka (gidayu-shamisen), Motoharu Yoshizawa (electric vertical bass), Suleyman Erguner (ney), Neva Ozgen (kermence), Mirsa Basara (tar), Hakan Gungor (kanun).

8 Conduction Chronology

CONDUCTION® No. 100/1
Tribeca Performing Arts Center, New York, NY, April 5 1998

Triple Skyscraper (Tokyo, Istanbul & New York): Tomomi Acachi (vocals), Kizan Daiyoshi (shakuhachi), Remi Fujimoto (sho), Hisami Hanaki (wa-daiko), Miki Maruta (koto), Kenichi Takeda (taisho koto), Yumiko Tanaka (gidayu shamisen), Motoharu Yoshizawa (electric vertical bass), Suleyman Erguner (ney), Neva Ozgen (kermence), Mirsa Basara (tar), Hakan Gungor (kanun), Ron Lawrence, Maryam Blacksher (viola), Marlene Rice, Charles Burnham (violin), Yuko Fujiyama (piano), Sachika Nagata, Diana Herold (percussion), Susie Ibarra (drums, percussion), Elizabeth Panzer (harp), Brandon Ross (guitar), Nioka Workman (cello).

CONDUCTION® No. 99
Tribeca Performing Arts Center, New York, NY, April 4, 1998

Triple Skyscraper (Tokyo, Istanbul & New York): Tomomi Acachi (vocals), Kizan Daiyoshi (shakuhachi), Remi Fujimoto (sho), Hisami Hanaki (wa-daiko), Miki Maruta (koto), Kenichi Takeda (taisho koto), Yumiko Tanaka (gidayu shamisen), Motoharu Yoshizawa (electric vertical bass), Suleyman Erguner (ney), Neva Ozgen (kermence), Mirsa Basara (tar), Hakan Gungor (kanun), Ron Lawrence, Maryam Blacksher (viola), Marlene Rice, Charles Burnham (violin), Yuko Fujiyama (piano), Sachika Nagata, Diana Herold (percussion), Susie Ibarra (drums, percussion), Elizabeth Panzer (harp), Brandon Ross (guitar), Nioka Workman (cello).

CONDUCTION® No. 98
Tribeca Performing Arts Center, New York, NY, April 3, 1998

Ensemble: Double Skyscraper (Tokyo & New York): Tomomi Acachi (vocals), Kizan Daiyoshi (shakuhachi), Remi Fujimoto (sho), Hisami Hanaki (wa-daiko), Miki Maruta (koto), Kenichi Takeda (taisho koto), Yumiko Tanaka (gidayu shamisen), Motoharu Yoshizawa (electric vertical bass), Ron Lawrence, Maryam Blacksher (viola), Marlene Rice, Charles Burnham (violin), Yuko Fujiyama (piano), Sachika Nagata, Diana Herold (percussion), Susie Ibarra (drums, percussion), Elizabeth Panzer (harp), Brandon Ross (guitar), Nioka Workman (cello).

CONDUCTION® No. 97
Tribeca Performing Arts Center, New York, NY, April 3, 1998

Triple Skyscraper (Tokyo, Istanbul & New York): Tomomi Acachi (vocals), Kizan Daiyoshi (shakuhachi), Remi Fujimoto (sho), Hisami Hanaki (wa-daiko), Miki Maruta (koto), Kenichi Takeda (taisho koto), Yumiko Tanaka (gidayu shamisen), Motoharu Yoshizawa (electric vertical bass), Suleyman Erguner (ney), Neva Ozgen (kermence), Mirsa Basara (tar), Hakan Gungor (kanun), Ron Lawrence, Maryam Blacksher (viola), Marlene Rice, Charles Burnham (violin), Yuko Fujiyama (piano), Sachika Nagata, Diana Herold (percussion), Susie Ibarra (drums, percussion), Elizabeth Panzer (harp), Brandon Ross (guitar), Nioka Workman (cello).

CONDUCTION® No. 96
Tribeca Performing Arts Center, New York, NY, April 3, 1998

Double Skyscraper (Istanbul & New York): Suleyman Erguner (ney), Neva Ozgen (kermence), Mirsa Basara (tar), Hakan Gungor (kanun), Ron Lawrence, Maryam Blacksher (viola), Marlene Rice, Charles Burnham (violin), Yuko Fujiyama (piano), Diana Herold (percussion), Susie Ibarra (drums, percussion), Elizabeth Panzer (harp), Brandon Ross (guitar), Nioka Workman (cello).

CONDUCTION® No. 95
Sun City Theater, Tempe, Arizona, March 27, 1998

Tokyo Skyscraper®: Tomomi Acachi (vocals), Kizan Daiyoshi (shakuhachi), Remi Fujimoto (sho), Hisami Hanaki (wa-daiko), Miki Maruta (koto), Sachika Nagata (percussion), Kenichi Takeda (taisho koto), Yumiko Tanaka (gidayu shamisen), Motoharu Yoshizawa (electric vertical bass).

CONDUCTION® No. 94
Rialto Theater, Atlanta, Georgia, March 22, 1998

Tokyo Skyscraper®: Tomomi Acachi (vocals), Kizan Daiyoshi (shakuhachi), Remi Fujimoto (sho), Hisami Hanaki (wa-daiko), Miki Maruta (koto), Sachika Nagata (percussion), Kenichi Takeda (taishokoto), Yumiko Tanaka (gidayu shamisen), Motoharu Yoshizawa (electric vertical bass).

CONDUCTION® No. 93/2
Walker Arts Center, Minneapolis, Minnesota, March 14, 1998

Tokyo Skyscraper® and Imp Ork: Jane Anfinson (violin), Eric Peterson (viola), Brad Bellows (trombone), John Devine (sax), Elaine Klaassen (piano), Charlie Braden (guitar), Chris Bates (bass), Sachika Nagata, Marc Anderson (percussion), Tomomi Acachi (vocals), Kizan Daiyoshi (shakuhachi), Remi Fujimoto (sho), Hisami Hanaki (wa-daiko), Miki Maruta (koto), Kenichi Takeda (taisho koto), Yumiko Tanaka (gidayu shamisen), Motoharu Yoshizawa (electric vertical bass).

CONDUCTION® No. 93/1
Walker Arts Center, Minneapolis, Minnesota, March 14, 1998

Tokyo Skyscraper®: Tomomi Acachi (vocals), Kizan Daiyoshi (shakuhachi), Remi Fujimoto (sho), Hisami Hanaki (wa-daiko), Miki Maruta (koto), Sachika Nagata (percussion), Kenichi Takeda (taisho koto), Yumiko Tanaka (gidayu shamisen), Motoharu Yoshizawa (electric vertical bass).

THE ART OF CONDUCTION 8

CONDUCTION® No. 92 Metronome Taller de Músics, Barcelona, Spain, January 24, 1998	
	Big Ensemble: Chefa Alonso (soprano sax), Barbara Meyer, Lito Iglesias, Michael Babinchak (cello), Benet Palet, Mark Cunningham (trumpet), Christiaan De Jong (flute), Agusti Fernandez (piano), John Leaman (double bass), Wade Matthews (bass clarinet, flute, alto sax), Marc Miralta (vibes), Steve Noble (drums, percussion), Javier Olondo (guitar), Joan Saura (sampler), Liba Villacheccia (tenor, soprano sax).
CONDUCTION® No. 91 Walker Arts Center, Minneapolis, Minnesota, March 14, 1998	
	Imp Ork: Jane Anfinson (violin), Eric Peterson (viola), Brad Bellows (trombone), John Devine (sax), Elaine Klaassen (piano), Charlie Braden (guitar), Chris Bates (bass), Marc Anderson (percussion).
CONDUCTION® No. 90 November Music Festival, Muziekcentrum Frits Philips, Eindhoven, Netherlands, November 13, 1997	
	Aquarius Ensemble and Big Band: Jacobien Rozemond, Matthijs Berger (violin), Dominique Eyckmans (viola), Wikkie Schlosser (cello), Bert Palinckx (double bass), Jeroen Van Vliet (piano), Tom Wauters (percussion), Philipe Wouters (guitar), Lia Koolmees (flute), Willem Van de Kar (oboe), Rick Huls (clarinet), Dirk Noyen (bassoon), Bart Maris (trumpet), Hans Sparia (trombone), Nick Roseeuw, Edward Capel (saxes).
CONDUCTION® No. 89 Vooruit, Ghent, Belgium, November 14, 1997	
	Aquarius Ensemble and Big Band: Jacobien Rozemond, Matthijs Berger (violin), Dominique Eyckmans (viola), Wikkie Schlosser (cello), Bert Palinckx (double bass), Jeroen Van Vliet (piano), Tom Wauters (percussion), Philipe Wouters (guitar), Lia Koolmees (flute), Willem Van de Kar (oboe), Rick Huls (clarinet), Dirk Noyen (bassoon), Bart Maris (trumpet), Hans Sparia (trombone), Nick Roseeuw, Edward Capel (sax).
CONDUCTION® No. 88 November Music Festival, Muziekcentrum De Toonzaal, s-HertogenBosh, Netherlands, November 15, 1997	
	Aquarius Ensemble and Big Band: Jacobien Rozemond, Matthijs Berger (violin), Dominique Eyckmans (viola), Wikkie Schlosser (cello), Bert Palinckx (double bass), Jeroen Van Vliet (piano), Tom Wauters (percussion), Philipe Wouters (guitar), Lia Koolmees (flute), Willem Van de Kar (oboe), Rick Huls (clarinet), Dirk Noyen (bassoon), Bart Maris (trumpet), Hans Sparia (trombone), Nick Roseeuw, Edward Capel (sax).
CONDUCTION® No. 87 Queen Elizabeth Hall, Southbank Centre, London, England, November 7, 1997	
	London Skyscraper®: Steve Beresford (piano), John Bisset (acoustic guitar), Gail Brand (trombone), John Butcher (soprano sax), Rhondri Davies (harp), Phil Durrant, Philipp Wachsmann, Aleks Kolkowski (violin), Simon H. Fell (double bass), Robin Hayward (tuba), Roger Heaton (bass clarinet), Zoe Marlew (cello), Kaffe Matthews (sampler), Evan Parker (tenor sax), Orphy Robinson (vibes), Keith Rowe (electric guitar), Nancy Ruffer (flute), Ansuman Biswas, Mark Sanders (percussion), Byron Wallen, Ian Smith (trumpet), Pat Thomas (electric keyboard), Alex Ward (clarinet).
CONDUCTION® No. 86 Arnolfini, Bristol, England, November 7, 1997	
	London Skyscraper®: Steve Beresford (piano), John Bisset (acoustic guitar), Gail Brand (trombone), John Butcher (soprano sax), Rhondri Davies (harp), Aleks Kolkowski, Philipp Wachsmann, Phil Durrant (violin), Simon H. Fell (double bass), Robin Hayward (tuba), Roger Heaton (bass clarinet), Zoe Marlew (cello), Kaffe Matthews (sampler), Evan Parker (tenor sax), Orphy Robinson (vibes), Keith Rowe (electric guitar), Nancy Ruffer (flute), Ansuman Biswas, Mark Sanders (percussion), Byron Wallen, Ian Smith (trumpet), Pat Thomas (electric keyboard), Alex Ward (clarinet).
CONDUCTION® No. 85 Royal Northern College, Manchester, England, November 4, 1997	
	London Skyscraper®: Steve Beresford (piano), John Bisset (acoustic guitar), Gail Brand (trombone), John Butcher (soprano sax), Rhondri Davies (harp), Aleks Kolkowski, Philipp Wachsmann, Phil Durrant (violin), Simon H. Fell (double bass), Robin Hayward (tuba), Roger Heaton (bass clarinet), Zoe Marlew (cello), Kaffe Matthews (sampler), Evan Parker (tenor sax), Orphy Robinson (vibes), Keith Rowe (electric guitar), Nancy Ruffer (flute), Ansuman Biswas, Mark Sanders (percussion), Byron Wallen, Ian Smith (trumpet), Pat Thomas (electric keyboard), Alex Ward (clarinet).
CONDUCTION® No. 84 St Barnabas Church, Oxford, England, November 2, 1997	
	London Skyscraper®: Steve Beresford (piano), John Bisset (acoustic guitar), Gail Brand (trombone), John Butcher (soprano sax), Rhondri Davies (harp), Aleks Kolkowski, Philipp Wachsmann, Phil Durrant (violin), Simon H. Fell (double bass), Robin Hayward (tuba), Roger Heaton (bass clarinet), Zoe Marlew (cello), Kaffe Matthews (sampler), Evan Parker (tenor sax), Orphy Robinson (vibes), Keith Rowe (electric guitar), Nancy Ruffer (flute), Ansuman Biswas, Mark Sanders (percussion), Byron Wallen, Ian Smith (trumpet), Pat Thomas (electric keyboard), Alex Ward (clarinet).

8 Conduction Chronology

CONDUCTION® No. 83 Adrian Boult Hall, Birmingham Conservatoire, England, November 1, 1997	
	London Skyscraper®: Steve Beresford (piano), John Bisset (acoustic guitar), Gail Brand (trombone), John Butcher (soprano sax), Rhondri Davies (harp), Aleks Kolkowski, Philipp Wachsmann, Phil Durrant (violin), Simon H. Fell (double bass), Robin Hayward (tuba), Roger Heaton (bass clarinet), Zoe Marlew (cello), Kaffe Matthews (sampler), Evan Parker (tenor sax), Orphy Robinson (vibes), Keith Rowe (electric guitar), Nancy Ruffer (flute), Ansuman Biswas, Mark Sanders (percussion), Pat Thomas (electric keyboard), Ian Smith, Byron Wallen (trumpet), Alex Ward (clarinet).
CONDUCTION® No. 82 Bluecoat, Liverpool, England, October 31, 1997	
	London Skyscraper®: Steve Beresford (piano), John Bisset (acoustic guitar), Gail Brand (trombone), John Butcher (soprano sax), Rhondri Davies (harp), Aleks Kolkowski, Philipp Wachsmann, Phil Durrant (violin), Simon H. Fell (double bass), Robin Hayward (tuba), Roger Heaton (bass clarinet), Zoe Marlew (cello), Kaffe Matthews (sampler), Evan Parker (tenor sax), Orphy Robinson (vibes), Keith Rowe (electric guitar), Nancy Ruffer (flute), Ansuman Biswas, Mark Sanders (percussion), Byron Wallen, Ian Smith (trumpet), Pat Thomas (electric keyboard), Alex Ward (clarinet).
CONDUCTION® No. 81 Bluecoat, Liverpool, England, October 30, 1997	
	London Skyscraper®: Steve Beresford (piano), John Bisset (acoustic guitar), Gail Brand (trombone), John Butcher (soprano sax), Rhondri Davies (harp), Aleks Kolkowski, Philipp Wachsmann, Phil Durrant (violin), Simon H. Fell (double bass), Robin Hayward (tuba), Roger Heaton (bass clarinet), Zoe Marlew (cello), Kaffe Matthews (sampler), Evan Parker (tenor sax), Orphy Robinson (vibes), Keith Rowe (electric guitar), Nancy Ruffer (flute), Ansuman Biswas, Mark Sanders (percussion), Byron Wallen, Ian Smith (trumpet), Pat Thomas (electric keyboard), Alex Ward (clarinet).
CONDUCTION® No. 80 Harbiye Askeri Müze ve Kültür Sitesi, Istanbul, Turkey, October 25, 1997	
	Double Skyscraper® (Istanbul & Berlin): Axel Dorner, Michael Gross (trumpet), Gregor Hotz (soprano, alto sax), Johannes Bauer (trombone), Aleks Kolkowski (violin), Dietrich Petzold (violin, viola), Nicholas Bussmann (cello), Matthias Bauer, David de Bernardi (double bass), Kirsten Reese (flute), Johanne Braun (oboe), Elisabeth Böhm-Christl (bassoon), Wolfgang Fuchs (bass clarinet), Olaf Rupp (guitar) Tatjana Schütz (harp), Tobias Dutschke (vibes), Michael Griener, Stephan Mathieu (percussion), Suleyman Erguner (ney), Ihsan Ozgen, Neva Ozgen (kermence), Orhun Ucar (ud), Mirsa Basara (tar), Hakan Gungor (kanun).
CONDUCTION® No. 79 Harbiye Askeri Müze ve Kültür Sitesi, Istanbul, Turkey, October 25, 1997	
	Istanbul Skyscraper®: Suleyman Erguner (ney), Ihsan Ozgen, Neva Ozgen (kemence), Orhun Ucar (ud), Mirsa Basaran (tar), Hakan Gungor (kanun).
CONDUCTION® No. 78 Harbiye Askeri Müze ve Kültür Sitesi, Istanbul, Turkey, October 24, 1997	
	Double Skyscraper® (Istanbul & Berlin): Axel Dorner, Michael Gross (trumpet), Gregor Hotz (soprano, alto sax), Johannes Bauer (trombone), Aleks Kolkowski (violin), Dietrich Petzold (violin, viola), Nicholas Bussmann (cello), Matthias Bauer, David de Bernardi (double bass), Kirsten Reese (flute), Johanne Braun (oboe), Elisabeth Böhm-Christl (bassoon), Wolfgang Fuchs (bass clarinet), Olaf Rupp (guitar) Tatjana Schütz (harp), Tobias Dutschke (vibes), Michael Griener, Stephan Mathieu (percussion), Suleyman Erguner (ney), Ihsan Ozgen, Neva Ozgen (kermence), Orhun Ucar (ud), Mirsa Basara (tar), Hakan Gungor (kanun).
CONDUCTION® No. 77 Harbiye Askeri Müze ve Kültür Sitesi , Istanbul, Turkey, October 24, 1997	
	Berlin Skyscraper®: Axel Dorner, Michael Gross (trumpet), Gregor Hotz (soprano, alto sax), Johannes Bauer (trombone), Aleks Kolkowski (violin), Dietrich Petzold (violin, viola), Nicholas Bussmann (cello), Matthias Bauer, David de Bernardi (double bass), Kirsten Reese (flute), Johanne Braun (oboe), Elisabeth Böhm-Christl (bassoon), Wolfgang Fuchs (bass clarinet), Olaf Rupp (guitar), Tatjana Schütz (harp), Tobias Dutschke (vibes), Michael Griener, Stephan Mathieu (percussion).
CONDUCTION® No. 76 Context, New York, NY, April 19, 1997	
	New York Skyscraper®: Gregor Huebner, Marlene Rice (violin), Maryann Blacksher, Ina Latera (viola), Monica Wilson (cello), Chris Higgins (double bass), Yuko Fujiyama (piano), Elizabeth Panzer (harp), Joe Giardullo (flute), Todd Brunel (clarinet), Avram Seffer (bass clarinet), Ron Gozzo (soprano sax), Marco Eneidi (alto sax), Karen Borca (bassoon), Natasha Henke (trumpet), Suzie Ibarra (drums).
CONDUCTION® No. 75 Context, New York, NY, April 18, 1997	
	New York Skyscraper®: Gregor Huebner, Marlene Rice (violin), Maryann Blacksher, Ina Latera (viola), Matt Goeke, Monica Wilson (cello), Chris Higgins, Matt Hughes (double bass), Yuko Fujiyama (piano), Elizabeth Panzer (harp), Joe Giardullo (flute), Todd Brunel (clarinet), Avram Seffer (bass clarinet), Ron Gozzo (soprano sax), Marco Eneidi (alto sax), Karen Borca (bassoon), Natasha Henke (trumpet), Britta Langsjoen (trombone), Suzie Ibarra (drums).

THE ART OF CONDUCTION 8

CONDUCTION® No. 74 Context, New York, NY, April 17, 1997	
	New York Skyscraper®: Marlene Rice (violin), Amy McNamara (viola), Matt Goeke, Monica Wilson (cello), Michael Bitz, Chris Higgins (double bass), Yuko Fujiyama (piano), Joe Giardullo (flute), Todd Brunel (clarinet), Avram Seffer (bass clarinet), Ron Gozzo (soprano sax), Marco Eneidi (alto sax), Karen Borca (bassoon), Natasha Henke (trumpet), Britta Langsjoen (trombone), Suzie Ibarra (drums).
CONDUCTION® No. 73 Context, New York, NY, April 6, 1997	
	New York Skyscraper®: Gregor Huebner, Marlene Rice (violin), Maryann Blacksher, Ina Latera, Amy McNamara (viola), Matt Goeke, Monica Wilson (cello), Michael Bitz, Chris Higgins, Matt Hughes (double bass), Yuko Fujiyama (piano), Joe Giardullo (flute), Todd Brunel (clarinet), Avram Seffer (bass clarinet), Ron Gozzo (soprano sax), Marco Eneidi (alto sax), Karen Borca (bassoon), Natasha Henke (trumpet), Britta Langsjoen (trombone), Suzie Ibarra (drums).
CONDUCTION® No. 72, Hospital for Sinners Visions Festival, New York, NY, June 1, 1997	
	Vision Festival Ensemble: Karen Borca (bassoon), Rob Brown (flute), Joseph Daley (tuba), Chris Jonas (soprano sax), Marco Eneidi (alto sax), Assif Tsahar (tenor sax), Masahiko Kono (trombone), Sabir Mateen (clarinet), Denman Maroney (piano), Chris Lightcap (double bass), Suzie Ibarra (drums).
CONDUCTION® No. 71 Paradiso, Amsterdam, Netherlands, November 26, 1996	
	The Nieuw Ensemble: Harrie Starreveld (flute), Ernest Rombout (oboe), Arjan Kappers (clarinet), Hans Wesseling (mandolin), Helenus de Rijke (guitar), Ernestine Stoop (harp), John Snijders (piano), Angel Gimeno (violin), Frank Brakkee (viola), Larissa Groeneveld (cello), Sjeng Schupp (bass), Herman Halewijn (percussion), Ab Baars (clarinet), Wilbert de Joode (bass), Martin von Duynhoven (drums).
CONDUCTION® No. 70, Tit for Tat Fabrikjazz, Zurich, Switzerland, September 29, 1996	
	Ensemble: Andy Guhl, Nicolas Sordet, Norbert Möslang (live electronics), Doro Schürch, Daniel Mouthon (vocals), Martin Schütz (electric cello), Hans Koch, Pete Ehrnrooth (reeds), Stephan Wittwer (electric guitar), Günter Müller (percussion, electronics), Edgar Laubscher (electric viola), Fredy Studer (drums), Marie Schwab (violin), B. Buster (turntables), Jim O'Rourke (guitar).
CONDUCTION® No. 69 Podewil, Berlin, Germany, October 20, 1996	
	Berlin Skyscraper®: Johannes Bauer (trombone), Matthias Bauer, David de Bernardi (bass), Elisabeth Böhm-Christl (bassoon), Johanne Braun (oboe), Nicholas Bussmann, Boris Rayskin (cello), Axel Dorner, Michael Gross (trumpet), Tobias Dutschke (vibes), Wolfgang Fuchs (bass clarinet), Michael Griener, Stephan Mathieu (percussion), Martin High de Prime (piano), Gregor Hotz (soprano, alto sax), Dietrich Petzold (violin, viola), Kirsten Reese (flute), Olaf Rupp (guitar).
CONDUCTION® No. 68 Podewil, Berlin, Germany, October 19, 1996	
	Berlin Skyscraper®: Johannes Bauer (trombone), Matthias Bauer, David de Bernardi (bass), Elisabeth Böhm-Christl (bassoon), Johanne Braun (oboe), Nicholas Bussmann, Boris Rayskin (cello), Axel Dorner, Michael Gross (trumpet), Tobias Dutschke (vibes), Wolfgang Fuchs (bass clarinet), Michael Griener, Stephan Mathieu (percussion), Martin High de Prime (piano), Gregor Hotz (soprano, alto sax), Aleks Kolkowski (violin), Dietrich Petzold (violin, viola), Kirsten Reese (flute), Olaf Rupp (guitar).
CONDUCTION® No. 67 Podewil, Berlin, Germany, October 18, 1996	
	Berlin Skyscraper®: Johannes Bauer (trombone), Matthias Bauer, David de Bernardi (bass), Elisabeth Böhm-Christl (bassoon), Johanne Braun (oboe), Nicholas Bussmann, Boris Rayskin (cello), Axel Dorner, Michael Gross (trumpet), Tobias Dutschke (vibes), Wolfgang Fuchs (bass clarinet), Michael Griener, Stephan Mathieu (percussion), Martin High de Prime (piano), Gregor Hotz (soprano, alto sax), Aleks Kolkowski (violin), Dietrich Petzold (violin, viola), Kirsten Reese (flute), Olaf Rupp (guitar).
CONDUCTION® No. 66, Only the Matter Projections Sonores Festival, Biel-Bienne, Switzerland, September 28, 1996	
	Ensemble: Andy Guhl, Nicolas Sordet, Norbert Moslang (live electronics), Doro Schurch, Daniel Mouthon (vocals), Martin Schütz (electric cello), Hans Koch, Pete Ehrnrooth (reeds), Jim O'Rourke (guitar), Stephan Wittwer (electric guitar), Günter Müller (percussion, electronics), Edgar Laubscher (viola), Fredy Studer (drums), Marie Schwab (violin), B. Buster (turntables).
CONDUCTION® No. 65, Four Images of Time Metro Pictures Gallery, New York, NY, September 7, 1996	
	A Chorus of Poets: Sheila Alson, Carmen Bardeguez-Brown, Harold Bowser, Martha Cinader, Samantha Coerbell, Carol Diehl, Pamela Grossman, Mia Hansford, Indigo, Sarah Jones, Angela Lukacin, Bobby Miller, Tracie Morris, Ra, Clara Sala, Susan Scutti, Edwin Torres, Gloria Williams, Yictove (voice).

8 Conduction Chronology

CONDUCTION® No. 64 Sjuhuis, Utrecht, the Netherlands, October 5, 1996	
	Maarten Altena Ensemble: Maarten Altena (bass), Erik van Deuren (clarinet), Wiek Hijmans (guitar), Alison Isadora (viola), Hans van der Meer (percussion), Jannie Pranger (vocals), Michel Scheen (piano), Wolter Wierbos (trombone).
CONDUCTION® No. 63 Paradox Jazz Club, Tilburg, Netherlands, October 4, 1996	
	Maarten Altena Ensemble: Maarten Altena (bass), Michael Barker (flute, electronics), Erik van Deuren (clarinet), Wiek Hijmans (guitar), Alison Isadora (viola), Hans van der Meer (percussion), Jannie Pranger (vocals), Michel Scheen (piano), Wolter Wierbos (trombone).
CONDUCTION® No. 62 Bimhuis, Amsterdam, Netherlands, October 3, 1996	
	Maarten Altena Ensemble: Maarten Altena (bass), Michael Barker (flute, electronics), Erik van Deuren (clarinet), Wiek Hijmans (guitar), Alison Isadora (viola), Hans van der Meer (percussion), Jannie Pranger (vocals), Michel Scheen (piano), Wolter Wierbos (trombone).
CONDUCTION® No. 61 Podewil, Berlin, Germany, September 20, 1996	
	Ensemble Eva Kant: Margareth Kammerer (vocals), Olivia Bignardi (clarinet, bass clarinet), Daniela Cattivelli (alto sax), Edoardo Marraffa (tenor sax), Riccardo Pittau (trumpet), Ferdinando D'Andria (violin, trumpet), Giorgio Simbola (trombone, banjo), Salvatore Panu (trombone, piano, accordion), Silvia Fanti (accordion), Filomena Forleo (piano), Tiziano Popoli (keyboards, piano), Paolo Angeli (acoustic, electric guitar, bass tuba), Domenico Caliri (acoustic and electric guitar, mandolin), Massimo Simonini (records, CDs, recorded tapes, objects), Marianna Finarelli (cello), Agostino Ciraci (double bass, trumpet), Pierangelo Galantino (violin, bass), Vincenzo Vasi (electric bass, vocals, vibes), Lelio Giannetto, Giovanni Maier, Luigi Mosso (bass), Andrea Martignoni, Mario Martignoni, Pino Urso (percussion), Stefano De Bonis, Fabrizio Publisi (piano), Francesco Cusa (percussion), Alberto Capelli (electric guitar).
CONDUCTION® No. 60, The Ploughing Season Konfrontationen, Nickelsdorf, Austria, July 21, 1996	
	Ensemble: Joelle Leandre, Matthias Bauer (bass), John Russell, Stephan Wittwer, Keith Rowe (guitar), Martin Schütz, Tom Cora (cello), Carlos Zingaro, Phil Durrant (violin), Otomo Yoshihide (turntables), Helge Hinteregger (electronics), Oren Marshall (tuba), Hans Koch, Ernesto Molinari (bass clarinet), Luc Ex (electric bass).
CONDUCTION® No. 59, Holy Sea, *(The) Devil's Music* Chiesa di San Domenico, Pistoia, Italy, February 10, 1996	
	Orchestra della Toscana: Andrea Tacchi, Giorgio Ballini, Paolo Gaiani, Maria Elena Runza (violin), Riccardo Masi, Alessandro Franconi, Dimitri Mattu (viola), Giovanni Bacchelli, Filippo Burchietti (cello), Raffaello Majoni, Gianpietro Zampella (contrabass), Michele Marasco (flute), Umberto Codeca (bassoon), Gianfranco Dini (French horn), Donato De Sena, Claudio Quintavalla (trumpet), Renzo Brocculi (trombone), Riccardo Tarlini (tuba), Morgan M. Torelli (timpani), Jonathan Faralli (percussion), Cinzia Conte (harp), J.A. Deane (live sampling, drum machine, trombone, electronics), Otomo Yoshihide (turntables, sampling, electronics), Riccardo Fassi (piano).
CONDUCTION® No. 58, Holy Sea, *Marble Dust* Teatro degli Animosi, Carrara, Italy, February 9, 1996	
	Orchestra della Toscana: Andrea Tacchi, Giorgio Ballini, Paolo Gaiani, Maria Elena Runza (violin), Riccardo Masi, Alessandro Franconi, Dimitri Mattu (viola), Giovanni Bacchelli, Filippo Burchietti (cello), Raffaello Majoni, Gianpietro Zampella (contrabass), Michele Marasco (flute), Umberto Codeca (bassoon), Gianfranco Dini (French horn), Donato De Sena, Claudio Quintavalla (trumpet), Renzo Brocculi (trombone), Riccardo Tarlini (tuba), Morgan M.Torelli (timpani), Jonathan Faralli (percussion), Cinzia Conte (harp), J.A. Deane (live sampling, drum machine, trombone, electronics), Otomo Yoshihide (turntables, sampling, electronics), Riccardo Fassi (piano).
CONDUCTION® No. 57, Holy Sea, *Shopping* Teatro Puccini, Florence, Italy, February 8, 1996	
	Orchestra della Toscana: Andrea Tacchi, Giorgio Ballini, Paolo Gaiani, Maria Elena Runza (violin), Riccardo Masi, Alessandro Franconi, Dimitri Mattu (viola), Giovanni Bacchelli, Filippo Burchietti (cello), Raffaello Majoni, Gianpietro Zampella (contrabass), Michele Marasco (flute), Umberto Codeca (bassoon), Gianfranco Dini (French horn), Donato De Sena, Claudio Quintavalla (trumpet), Renzo Brocculi (trombone), Riccardo Tarlini (tuba), Morgan M. Torelli (timpani), Jonathan Faralli (percussion), Cinzia Conte (harp), J.A. Deane (live sampling, drum machine, trombone, electronics), Otomo Yoshihide (turntables, sampling, electronics), Riccardo Fassi (piano).
CONDUCTION® No. 56, Beauty Sketch Total Music Meeting, Podewil, Berlin, Germany, November 5, 1995	
	Berlin Skyscraper®: Axel Dörner (trumpet), Gregor Hotz (soprano, alto sax), Marc Stutz-Boukouya (trombone), Aleks Kolkowski (violin), Dietrich Petzold (violin, viola), Nicholas Bussmann (cello), Davide De Bernardi (double bass), Kirsten Reese (flute), Johanne Braun (oboe), Elizabeth Böhm-Christl (bassoon), Wolfgang Fuchs (bass clarinet), Bernard Arndt (piano), Olaf Rupp (guitar), Tatjana Schütz (harp), Albrecht Reirmeier (vibes), Stephan Mathieu, Michael Griener (percussion).

THE ART OF CONDUCTION 8

CONDUCTION® No. 55, Distant Occident Total Music Meeting, Podewil, Berlin, Germany, November 4, 1995	
	Berlin Skyscraper®: Axel Dörner (trumpet), Gregor Hotz (soprano, alto sax), Marc Stutz-Boukouya (trombone), Aleks Kolkowski (violin), Dietrich Petzold (violin, viola), Nicholas Bussmann (cello), Davide De Bernardi (double bass), Kirsten Reese (flute), Johanne Braun (oboe), Elizabeth Böhm-Christl (bassoon), Wolfgang Fuchs (bass clarinet), Bernard Arndt (piano), Olaf Rupp (guitar), Tatjana Schütz (harp), Albrecht Reirmeier (vibes), Stephan Mathieu, Michael Griener (percussion).
CONDUCTION® No. 54 Total Music Meeting, Podewil, Berlin, Germany, November 3, 1995	
	Berlin Skyscraper®: Axel Dörner (trumpet), Gregor Hotz (soprano, alto sax), Marc Stutz-Boukouya (trombone), Aleks Kolkowski (violin), Dietrich Petzold (violin, viola), Nicholas Bussmann (cello), Davide De Bernardi (double bass), Kirsten Reese (flute), Johanne Braun (oboe), Elizabeth Böhm-Christl (bassoon), Wolfgang Fuchs (bass clarinet), Bernard Arndt (piano), Olaf Rupp (guitar), Tatjana Schütz (harp), Albrecht Reirmeier (vibes), Stephan Mathieu, Michael Griener (percussion).
CONDUCTION® No. 52, Dark Secret Total Music Meeting, Podewil, Berlin, Germany, November 2, 1995	
	Berlin Skyscraper®: Axel Dörner (trumpet), Gregor Hotz (soprano, alto sax), Marc Stutz-Boukouya (trombone), Aleks Kolkowski (violin), Dietrich Petzold (violin, viola), Nicholas Bussmann (cello), Davide De Bernardi (double bass), Kirsten Reese (flute), Johanne Braun (oboe), Elizabeth Böhm-Christl (bassoon), Wolfgang Fuchs (bass clarinet), Bernard Arndt (piano), Olaf Rupp (guitar), Tatjana Schütz (harp), Albrecht Reirmeier (vibes), Stephan Mathieu, Michael Griener (percussion).
CONDUCTION® No. 51, Berlin Basic Total Music Meeting, Podewil, Berlin, Germany, November 1, 1995	
	Berlin Skyscraper®: Axel Dörner (trumpet), Gregor Hotz (soprano, alto sax), Marc Stutz-Boukouya (trombone), Aleks Kolkowski (violin), Dietrich Petzold (violin, viola), Nicholas Bussmann (cello), Davide De Bernardi (double bass), Kirsten Reese (flute), Johanne Braun (oboe), Elizabeth Böhm-Christl (bassoon), Wolfgang Fuchs (bass clarinet), Bernard Arndt (piano), Olaf Rupp (guitar), Tatjana Schütz (harp), Albrecht Reirmeier (vibes), Stephan Mathieu, Michael Griener (percussion).
CONDUCTION® No. 50 P3 Art and Environment, Tokyo, Japan, March 5, 1995	
	Ensemble: Shonosuke Okura (o-tuzumi), Michihiro Sato (tugaru syamisen), Ayuo Takahashi (zheng), Yumiko Tanaka (gidayuu), Hikaru Sawai (koto), Kim Dae Hwan (percussion), Yoshihide Otomo (turntables, CD player), Haruna Miyake (piano), Asuka Kaneko (electric violin), Tomomi Adachi (vocals), Keizo Mizoiri (bass), Motoharu Yoshizawa (electric bass).
CONDUCTION® No. 49 P3 Art and Environment, Tokyo, Japan, March 4, 1995	
	Ensemble: Shonosuke Okura (o-tuzumi), Yukihiro Isso (nokan), Michihiro Sato (tugaru syamisen), Yumiko Tanaka (gidayu), Hikaru Sawai (koto), Kim Dae Hwan (percussion), Yoshihide Otomo (turntables), Haruna Miyake (piano), Asuka Kaneko (electric violin), Tomomi Adachi (voice), Keizo Mizoiri (bass), Motoharu Yoshizawa (electric bass).
CONDUCTION® No. 48, Art Tower Art Tower Mito, Ibaraki, Japan, February 26, 1995	
	Orchestra: Sachiko Nagato (percussion), Mamoru Fujieda (computer), Kenichi Takeda (taisyou koto), Kizan Daiyoshi (syakuhachi), Masaki Shimizu (bass), Tomomi Adachi (vocals), Yoshinori Kotaka, Minako Oya, Shiho Nagoya, Aki Satho (violin), Shinya Otsuka, Hironobu Kotaka (viola), Koichi Fukada, Yoshihiro Okada, Kazue Shimada, Kazuyo Miyoshi (voices), Taeko Osato, Ken Takahashi (flute), Kiyoshi Onishi, Kiyoshi Ouchi (horn), Yutaka Fukuchi, Masashi Iwasawa (trumpet), Nobutaka Konashi, Junzi Sakurai (trombone), Yuko Fukasaku, Marie Abe (percussion), Yoko Yagisawa (piano), Hitoshi Sakamoto, Ryu Jun Ando, Ryo Tofukuji (bass).
CONDUCTION® No. 47, Wuppertal Testament Wuppertal, Germany, January 26, 1995	
	Wuppertal Art Orchestra: Saviya Yannator, Caerina De Re, Judith Amber (vocals), Roderich Stumm (drums), Janek Klaus, Gunther Pitscheider, Andreas J. Leep, Andre Issel (bass), Stefan Kerne (soprano sax), Barbara Meyer, Yngo Stanelle (alto sax), Andre Linnepe, Robin Scheffel (guitar), Justin Sebastian (trumpet), Karola Pasquay, Angelika Flacke (flute), Katrin Scholl, Gunda Gottschalk, Christophe Yrmer, Marco Cristofolini (violin), Jam Keller (contrabass), Mathias Beck (cello), Axel Kottsieper (clarinet).
CONDUCTION® No. 46, Verona Skyscraper® Verona Jazz, Teatro Romano, Verona, Italy, June 27, 1995	
	Verona Skyscraper®: J.A. Deane (trombone, electronics), Stefano Benini (flute), Marco Pasetto (clarinet), Rizzardo Piazzi (alto sax), Francesco Bearzatti (bass clarinet), Zeena Parkins (harp), Myra Melford, Riccardo Massari (piano), Bill Horvitz (electric guitar), Carlo "Bobo" Facchinetti (drums), Le Quan Ninh (percussion).

8 Conduction Chronology

CONDUCTION® No. 45, Le Chaux de Fonds
Conservatoire de Musique de la Chaux-de-Fonds/Le Locle, La Chaux-de-Fonds, Switzerland, September 3, 1994

> **Ensemble:** Gwenaelle Cuquel, Martina Albiseti (violin), Manon Gertsch, Daniele Pintandi (piano), Yan Greub (bassoon), Oliver Olgieti, Carlos Baumann (trumpet), Manuel Van Sturler, Francois Callin, Yonn Bourquin, Jean-Jaques Pedretti, Priska Walls (trombone), Dorothea Schürch (vocals), Robert Dick (flute), Christy Doran (guitar), Olivier Magnenat (bass), Lucas N. Niggli (percussion), Alexandre Nussbaum (vibes), Martin Schütz (cello).

CONDUCTION® No. 44, Ornithology (A Dedication to Charlie Parker)
Tompkins Square Park, New York, NY, August 28, 1994

> **Ensemble:** Terry Adkins, Kitty Brazelton, Marty Ehrlich, Daniel Carter, Rolando N. Briceno, Margaret Lancaster, Elise Wood, William Connell, Sabir Mateen, Bruce Gremo, Kahil Henry, Jemeel Moondoc, Sarah Andrew, Laurie Hockman (flute), Christian Marclay (turntables), Arthur Blythe (alto sax).

CONDUCTION® No. 43, The Cloth
Verona Jazz, Teatro Romano, Verona, Italy, June 26, 1994

> **Verona Skyscraper®:** Riccardo Fassi, Myra Melford (piano), Zeena Parkins (harp), Mario Arcari (oboe), Stephano Montaldo (viola), J.A. Deane (trombone, electronics), Brandon Ross (guitar), Bryan Carrot (vibes), Martin Schütz, Martine Altenburger (cello), Le Quan Ninh (percussion).

CONDUCTION® No. 42, Lust/Sucht/Lust
Deutsches Schauspielhaus, Hamburg, Germany, May 21, 1994

> **Ensemble:** Nicola Kruse, Ulli Bartel (violins), Mike Rutledge, Jürgen Gross (viola), Claudius Molter (flute, alto flute), Wolfgang Schubert (oboe), Henning Stoll (bassoon), Jonas Mo (guitar), Thomas Breckheimer (harp), Jorn Brandenburg (piano), Claudio von Hassel (vibes), Martin Schütz (cello), J.A. Deane (sampling), Monica Bleibtreu, Martin Horn, Andre Jung, Albi Klieber, Martin Pawlowsky, Ozlem Soydan, Anne Weber, Inka Friedrich (voices).

CONDUCTION® No. 41, New World, New World
Opperman Music Hall, Florida State University School of Music, Tallahassee, Florida, February 4, 1994

> **New World Ensemble:** Jesse Canterbury, Mimi Patterson (clarinet), Gregor Harvey (guitar), Philip Gelb (shakuhachi), Ethan Schaffner (electric guitar), Elisabeth King (vocals), Daniel Raney, David Tatro (trombone), Scott Deeter (sax), Michael Titlebaum (alto sax).

CONDUCTION® No. 40, Threadwaxing
Threadwaxing Space, New York, NY, November 12, 1993

> **Ensemble:** Christian Marclay (turntables), Elliott Sharp (dobro), Chris Cunningham (guitar), Dana Friedli, Jason Kao Hwang (violin), Myra Melford (piano), Damon Ra Choice (vibes, percussion, snare drum), Reggie Nicholson (vibes, tom-tom), Michelle Kinney (cello), Elizabeth Panzer (harp), William Parker, Mark Helias (bass).

CONDUCTION® No. 39, Threadwaxing
Threadwaxing Space, New York, NY, November 11, 1993

> **Ensemble:** Christian Marclay (turntables), Elliott Sharp (guitar, dobro), Chris Cunningham (guitar), Gregor Kitzis, Dana Friedli, Jason Kao Hwang (violin), Myra Melford (piano), Damon Ra Choice (vibes, percussion, snare drum), Reggie Nicholson (vibes, tom-tom), Michelle Kinney, Diedre L. Murray (cello), Elizabeth Panzer (harp), William Parker, Mark Helias, Fred Hopkins (bass).

CONDUCTION® No. 38, In Freud's Garden
Muffathalle, Munich, Germany, December 11, 1993

> **Ensemble:** Myra Melford (piano), Zeena Parkins (harp), Brian Carrott (vibes), Brandon Ross (guitar), J.A. Deane (trombone, electronics, live sampling), Motoharu Yoshizawa (electric bass), Le Quan Ninh (percussion), Martin Schütz, Tristan Honsinger, Martine Altenburger (cello), Edgar Laubscher (electric viola), Hans Kock (soprano, tenor, bass, contrabass clarinet).

CONDUCTION® No. 37, American Connection 4
Muziekcentrum Vredenburg, Utrecht, Netherlands May 28,1993

> **Maarten Altena Ensemble:** Maarten Altena (bass), Michael Barker (recorder, blockflutes), Peter van Bergen (contrabass clarinet, sax), Wiek Hijams (guitar), Alison Isadora (violin), Jannie Pranger (vocals), Michel Vatcher (drums, percussion), Wolter Wierbos (trombone), Michiel Scheen (piano).

CONDUCTION® No. 36, American Connection 4
Bimhuis, Amsterdam, Netherlands, May 27, 1993

> **Maarten Altena Ensemble:** Maarten Altena (bass), Michael Barker (recorder, blockflutes), Peter van Bergen (contrabass clarinet, sax), Wiek Hijams (guitar), Alison Isadora (violin), Jannie Pranger (vocals), Michel Vatcher (drums, percussion), Wolter Wierbos (trombone), Michiel Scheen (piano).

CONDUCTION® No. 35, American Connection 4
deSingel, Antwerp, Belgium, May 26, 1993

> **Maarten Altena Ensemble:** Maarten Altena (bass), Michael Barker (recorder, blockflutes), Peter van Bergen (contrabass clarinet, sax), Wiek Hijams (guitar), Alison Isadora (violin), Jannie Pranger (vocals), Michel Vatcher (drums, percussion), Wolter Wierbos (trombone), Michiel Scheen (piano).

THE ART OF CONDUCTION 8

CONDUCTION® No. 34, American Connection 4 Korzo, Den Haag, Netherlands, May 23, 1993	
	The Maarten Altena Ensemble: Maarten Altena (bass), Michael Barker (recorder, blockflutes), Peter van Bergen (contrabass clarinet, sax), Wiek Hijams (guitar), Alison Isadora (violin), Jannie Pranger (vocals), Michel Vatcher (drums, percussion), Wolter Wierbos (trombone), Michiel Scheen (piano).
CONDUCTION® No. 33, American Connection 4 Theater Ann De Molenlaan, Bussum, Netherlands, May 21, 1993	
	Maarten Altena Ensemble: Maarten Altena (bass), Michael Barker (recorder, blockflutes), Peter van Bergen (contrabass clarinet, sax), Wiek Hijams (guitar), Alison Isadora (violin), Jannie Pranger (vocals), Michel Vatcher (drums, percussion), Wolter Wierbos (trombone), Michiel Scheen (piano).
CONDUCTION® No. 32, Eva Kant Dance AngelicA Festival Internazionale di Musica, Bologna, Italy, May 18, 1993	
	Eva Kant: Paolo Angeli (guitar, bass, tuba), Olivia Bignardi (clarinet, alto sax), Daniela Cattivelli (alto sax), Marco Dalpane (keyboards), Ferdinando D'Andria (violin, trumpet), Silvia Fanti (accordion), Filomena Forleo (piano), Pierangelo Galantino, Lelio Giannetto (double bass), Magareth Kammerer (vocals), Claudio Lanteri (electric guitar), Andrea Martignoni, Pino Urso (percussion), Mario Martignoni (drums, percussion), Salvatore Panu (trombone), Giorgio Simbola (euphonium), Massimo Simonini (records, CDs, live sampling, objects), Nicola Zonca (marimba), Stefano Zorzanello (flute, soprano sax, piccolo).
CONDUCTION® No. 31, AngelicA AngelicA Festival Internazionale di Musica, Bologna, Italy, May 16, 1993	
	Ensemble: Dietmar Diesner (soprano sax), Peter Kowald (bass), Wolter Wierbos (trombone), Steve Beresford (piano), Hans Reichel (guitar, sax), Tom Cora (cello), Catherine Jauniaux (vocals), Ikue Mori (drum machine, percussion), Han Bennink (drums).
CONDUCTION® No. 30, Just for Fun Nissan Power Station, Shinjuku (Tokyo), Japan, March 23, 1993	
	Tokyo Ska-Paradise Orchestra: Asa-Chang (percussion), Cleanhead Gimura, Toru Terashi (guitar), Kimiyoshi Nagoya (trumpet), Masahiko Kitahara (trombone), Tatsuyuki Hiyamuta (alto sax), Gamou (tenor sax), Atsushi Yanaka (baritone sax), Yuichi Oki (keyboards), Tsuyoshi Kawakami, Motoharu Yoshizawa (bass), Tatsuyuki Aoiki (drums), Yosuke Yamashita (piano), Keizo Inoue (bass clarinet).
CONDUCTION® No. 29, Man Made Island Xebec Hall, Kobe, Japan, April 11, 1993	
	Ensemble: Asami Mitsuto (alto sax), Matubara Nozomu, Kawabata Minoru, Sugai Kasumi, Sakamoto Etsuko, Asakura Mari (sax), Shouji Masaharu (sax, shakuhachi), Inoue Keizou (sax, clarinet), Masuda Tomoyuki (drums), Fikuda Haruhiko (synthesizer), Iuchi Kengo (electric guitar, vocals), Matsuyama Hiroshi (electric junk), Nimura Makoto (piano), Igarashi Yuuichi (dance), Yoshizawa Motoharu (electric bass).
CONDUCTION® No. 28, Cherry Blossom P3 Art and Environment, Tokyo, Japan, March 28, 1993	
	Ensemble: Yukihiro Isso (nokan), Shonosuke Okura (tutzumi), Makiko Sakurai (shomyo, music box), Michihiro Sato (tugaru syamisen), Kizan Daiyoshi (shakuhachi), Yuji Katsui (violin), Haruna Miyake (piano), Syuichi Chino (computer), Asuka Kaneko, Koihi Makigami (vocals), Otomo Yoshihide (turntables), Kazutoki Umezu (bass clarinet), Sachiko Nagata (percussion), Motoharu Yoshizawa (electric bass), Kazuo Oono, Koichi Tamano (Butoh dance).
CONDUCTION® No. 27, A Chorus of Poets Whitney Museum of American Art at Philip Morris, New York, NY, December 31, 1992	
	A Chorus of Poets: Sheila Alson, Carmen Bardeguez, Kymberly Brown, Dana Bryant, Devon, Carol Diehl, Evert Eden, Mia Hansford, Bob Holman, Indigo, Lee Klein, Patricia Landrum, Tracie Morris, Carolyn Peyser, Susan Scutti, Edwin Torres, Emily XYZ, Yictove, David Henderson (voice), J.A. Deane (musician, sound sculptor).
CONDUCTION® No. 26, Akbank II Cemal Reşit Rey Konser Salonu, Istanbul, Turkey, October 17, 1992	
	The Suleyman Erguner Ensemble: Hasan Esen (kemence), Mehmet Emin Bitmez (ud), Goksel Baktagir (kanun), Suleyman Erguner (ney), Le Quan Ninh (percussion), Bryan Carrott (vibes), Elizabeth Panzer (harp), J.A. Deane (trombone, electronics, drum machine, live sampling), Brandon Ross (guitar), Steve Colson (piano), Hugh Ragin (pocket trumpet).
CONDUCTION® No. 25, Akbank Conduction Cemal Reşit Rey Konser Salonu, Istanbul, Turkey, October 16, 1992	
	The Suleyman Erguner Ensemble: Hasan Esen (kemence), Mehmet Emin Bitmer (ud), Goksel Baktagir (kanun), Suleyman Erguner (ney), Le Quan Ninh (percussion), Bryan Carrott (vibes), Elizabeth Panzer (harp), J.A. Deane (trombone, electronics, drum machine, live sampling), Brandon Ross (guitar), Steve Colson (piano), Hugh Ragin (pocket trumpet).

8 Conduction Chronology

CONDUCTION® No. 24, Conduction and Retrospective Virginia Museum of Fine Arts, Richmond, Virginia, February 16, 1992	
	Ensemble: Karen Borca (bassoon), Bryan Carrott (vibes), J.A. Deane (trombone, electronics), James Gates Jr. (sax), Bob Hoffnar (pedal steel), Cecil Hooker (violin), Taylor McLean (percussion), Myra Melford (piano), Zeena Parkins (harp), Brandon Ross (guitar).
CONDUCTION® No. 23, Quinzaine de Montreal The Spectrum, Montreal, Quebec, Canada, April 11, 1992	
	Ensemble: Tristan Honsinger, Martin Schütz (cello), Ken Butler, Michelle Kinney (broom cello), Eric Longsworth (cello, vibes), Helmut Lipsky (violin), J.A. Deane (trombone, electronics, live sampling), Guillaume Dostaler (piano), Mike Milligan (bass), Pierre Dube (percussion).
CONDUCTION® No. 22, Documenta: Gloves and Mitts Documenta 9, Kassel, Germany, June 14, 1992	
	Ensemble: Martin Schütz (cello), Christian Marclay (turntables), Le Quan Ninh (percussion), J.A. Deane (trombone, electronics, live sampling), Günter Müller (drums, percussion, electronics), Lawrence D. "Butch" Morris (cornet, conductor).
CONDUCTION® No. 21, The Painted Bride The Painted Bride, Philadelphia, Pennsylvania, March 21, 1992	
	The Painted Bride Workshop Ensemble: Eric Jorgenson (cello), Gloria Galante (harp), Stanley Schumacher (trombone), Bobby Zankel (alto sax), Phil Black (contrabass clarinet), Umar Hakim (tenor sax), Damon Umholtz (electric guitar), Tony Miceli (vibes), Derek van der Tak (piano), Richard Maskowitz (percussion), Lenny Seidman (electronics, percussion).
CONDUCTION® No. 20 The Knitting Factory, New York, NY, June 28, 1991	
	Ensemble: The Soldier String Quartet, Myra Melford (piano), Elliott Sharp (guitar), Elizabeth Panzer (harp).
CONDUCTION® No. 19, The Klangbrücke Conduction Kunstmuseum Bern, Switzerland, June 15, 1990	
	Ensemble: Andres Bosshard (taped sound, switchboard), Dorothea Schurch, Daniel Mouthon (vocals), Phil Wachsman (violin), David Gattiker (cello), Hans Anliker, Conrad Bauer, Hannes Bauer (trombone), Jacques Widmer (drums, percussion), Günter Müller (drums, electronic percussion).
CONDUCTION® No. 18, Paintings and Drawings The Alternative Museum, New York, NY, May 24, 1990	
	Ensemble: Marion Brandis (flute), Vincent Chancey (French horn), Janet Grice (bassoon), Shelly Hirsch (vocals), Bill Horvitz (guitar, electronics), Jason Kao Hwang (violin), Michelle Kinney (cello), Taylor McLean (percussion), Zeena Parkins (harp), Motoharu Yoshizawa (bass).
CONDUCTION® No. 17, Grote Poel No. 2 Cultuurcentrum Berchem, Antwerp, Belgium, August 6, 1989	
	Ensemble: Derek Bailey (guitar), Heinz Becker, Eric Boeren (trumpet), Dietmar Diesner (soprano, alto sax), Klaus Koch (bass), Yves Robert (trombone), Louis Sclavis (bass clarinet, soprano, alto sax), Julie Tippetts (vocals), Sabu Toyozumi (drums), Benoit Viredaz (tuba).
CONDUCTION® No. 16, Rendez-Vous Zurich – New York Rote Fabrik, Zürich, Switzerland, July 1, 1989	
	Ensemble: Andreas Bossard (electronics), Christian Marclay (turntables), Wayne Horvitz (keyboards), Shelley Hearst (vocals), Günter Müller, Bobby Previte (percussion), Hans Koch (reeds), Martin Schütz (cello), Stephan Wittwer (guitar).
CONDUCTION® No. 15, Where Music Goes II Whitney Museum of American Art at Philip Morris, New York, NY, November 15 & 16, 1989	
	Ensemble: Arthur Blythe (alto sax), Marion Brandis (flute, piccolo), Vincent Chancey (French horn), Curtis Clark (piano), J.A. Deane (trombone, live sampling, electronics), Janet Grice (bassoon), Brandon Ross (guitar), Bill Horvitz (electric guitar), Jason Kao Hwang (violin), Thurman Barker, (vibes, percussion) Taylor McLean (percussion), Jemeel Moondoc (flute), Zeena Parkins (harp).
CONDUCTION® No. 14 Chapelle Historique du Bon-Pasteur, Montreal, Quebec, Canada, March 3, 1989	
	Ensemble: Tim Brady (guitar), Helmut Lipsky (violin), Allan Laforest (flute), Jean Beaudet (piano), Michel Ratté (drums), Bernard Brien (trumpet), Jean Vanasse (vibes), Charles Papasoff (soprano sax), Ruffus Cappadocia (cello), Normand Guilbault (bass), Vincent Dionne (percussion).

THE ART OF CONDUCTION 8

CONDUCTION® No. 13
Maison de la culture du Plateau-Mont-Royal, Montreal, Quebec, Canada, March 2, 1989

> **Ensemble**: Tim Brady (guitar), Helmut Lipsky (violin), Allan Laforest (flute), Jean Beaudet (piano), Michel Ratté (drums), Bernard Brien (trumpet), Jean Vanasse (vibes), Charles Papasoff (soprano sax), Ruffus Cappadocia (cello), Normand Guilbault (bass), Vincent Dionne (percussion).

CONDUCTION® No. 12
Maison de la culture Côte-des-Neiges, Montreal, Quebec, Canada, February 26, 1989

> **Ensemble**: Tim Brady (guitar), Helmut Lipsky (violin), Allan Laforest (flute), Jean Beaudet (piano), Michel Ratté (drums), Bernard Brien (trumpet), Jean Vanasse (vibes), Charles Papasoff (soprano sax), Ruffus Cappadocia (cello), Normand Guilbault (bass), Vincent Dionne (percussion).

CONDUCTION® No. 11, Where Music Goes
The Great American Music Hall, San Francisco, California, December 18, 1988

> **Rova PreEchoes Ensemble**: Bruce Ackley (soprano sax), Dave Barrett (alto sax), Jon Raskin (alto, baritone sax), Larry Ochs (sax), Chris Brown (piano, synthesizer, electric percussion), J.A. Deane (trombone, electronics, live sampling), Jon English (bass), Jon Jang (piano), Bill Horvitz (electric guitar, black lion, guitar, syntheiszer), Adrian Michael Plott (guitar), Kash Killion (cello), Kaila Flexer, Hal Hughes (violin), William Winant (percussion).

CONDUCTION® No. 10
Institute of Contemporary Art, London, England, November 9, 1988

> **Ensemble**: A. R. Penck (piano), Louis Moholo, Dennis Charles (drums), Coon Alberts, Fiddi Fiedler, Frank Wollny (guitar), Heinz Wollny (electric bass), Peter Kowald (bass), Frank Wright (tenor sax), Terry Atkins (alto sax), Conrad Bauer (trombone), Jeanne Lee, Phil Minton, Angela Liberg (vocals), Helge Liberg (trumpet).

CONDUCTION® No. 9
Institute of Contemporary Art, London, England, November 8, 1988

> **Ensemble**: A. R. Penck (piano), Louis Moholo, Dennis Charles (drums), Coon Alberts, Fiddi Fiedler, Frank Wollny (guitar), Heinz Wollny (electric bass), Peter Kowald (bass), Frank Wright (tenor sax), Terry Atkins (alto sax), Conrad Bauer (trombone), Jeanne Lee, Phil Minton, Angela Liberg (vocals), Helge Liberg (trumpet).

CONDUCTION® No. 8, Fall Conduction
Club Theolonious, Rotterdam, The Netherlands, October 20, 1987

> **Ensemble**: Herb Robertson, Leo Smith (trumpet), Konrad Bauer, George Lewis (trombone), Evan Parker (soprano sax), Ab Baars (clarinet), Fred von Hove (piano), Maartje ten Hoorn (violin), Maurice Horsthuis (viola), Tristan Honsinger (cello), Jean-Jacques Avenel (bass), Christian Marclay (turntables), Hans Hasebos (vibes), Han Bennink, Louis Moholo (drums).

CONDUCTION® No. 7, The Fall Conduction
October Meeting, Bimhuis Jazz, Amsterdam, Netherlands, October 21, 1987

> **Ensemble**: Herb Robertson, Leo Smith (trumpet), Konrad Bauer, George Lewis (trombone), Evan Parker (soprano sax), Ab Baars (clarinet), Fred von Hove (piano), Maartje ten Hoorn (violin), Maurice Horsthuis (viola), Tristan Honsinger (cello), Jean-Jacques Avenel (bass), Christian Marclay (turntables), Hans Hasebos (vibes), Han Bennink, Louis Moholo (drums).

CONDUCTION® No. 6, The Relâche Conduction
The New School for Social Research, New York, NY, February 16, 1987

> **Relâche Ensemble for Contemporary Music**: Laurel Wyckoff (flute), Wes Hall (clarinet), Steve Marucci (soprano sax), Marshall Taylor (alto sax), John Dulik (DX5), Guy Klucevsek (accordion), Barbara Noska (mezzo-soprano vocals), Chuck Holdeman (bassoon), Flossie Ierardi (vibes, tom-toms, snare drum, triangle, woodblocks), Bill Horvitz (guitar, electronics), Jason Kao Hwang (violin), Wilber Morris (bass), Tom Cora (cello), Wayne Horvitz (piano), Zeena Parkins, Carol Emmanual (harp).

CONDUCTION® No. 5, Escape from Purgatory
C.U.A.N.D.O., New York, NY, February 27, 1986
A Plexus Art Co-Opera by Willem Brugman, Sandro Dernini and "Butch" Morris, with 220 actors, dancers, visual artists and the 14-piece Systems Orchestra with 5 part voice chorus, which included:

> **Systems Orchestra**: Jason Kao Hwang (violin), Frank Lowe (sax), Eli Fountain (vibes, percussion), Alex LoDico (trombone), Marion Brandis (flute), James Zoller (trumpet), Vincent Chancey (French horn), Myra Melford (string board), William Parker, Wilber Morris (bass), Michael J. Zwicky (drums), Willem Brugman, Alva Rogers, Karen Yager (voice).

CONDUCTION® No. 3, Goya Time
C.U.A.N.D.O., New York, NY, June 13, 1985
An Art Co-opera by Greta Saferty, Sandro Dernini and "Butch" Morris, with 14 performers, 22 visual and multi-media artists and 5 dancers.

> **Ensemble**: Eli Fountain (vibes, percussion), Marion Brandis (flute), Myra Melford (piano), Wilber Morris (bass), Bill Horvitz (guitar, electronics), Alex LoDico (trombone), Vincent Chancey (French horn), Steven Haynes (trumpet), Somalia, Jason Kao Hwang (violin), Ellen Christy, Marve-Helen Bey, Lisa Sokolov (vocals), J.A. Deane (trombone, electronics).

8 Conduction Chronology

CONDUCTION® No. 2, The Image of None The Performing Garage, New York, NY, March 27, 1985 A Music-Theatre Work for Ensemble and Voice
Ensemble: Alex LoDico (trombone), Jason Kao Hwang (violin), Frank Lowe (sax), Bill Horvitz (guitar), Myra Melford (string board), Marion Brandis (flute), Eli Fountain (vibes), Wilber Morris (bass), Rod Williams (synthesizer), Alva Rogers, Willem Brugman, Karen Yeager (voices).
CONDUCTION® No. 1, Current Trends in Racism in Modern America (A Work In Progress) The Kitchen, New York, NY, February 1, 1985
Ensemble: Frank Lowe (sax), John Zorn (alto sax, voice (game calls)), Christian Marclay (turntables), Thurman Barker (marimba, tambourine, snare drum), Curtis Clark (piano), Brandon Ross (guitar), Zeena Parkins (harp), Eli Fountain (vibes), Tom Cora (cello), Yasunao Tone (vocals).

Conduction® Discography

2014	
	Possible Universe (Conduction® No.192)
	Nu Bop Records (Italy) – CD, limited edition, NBR/SA Jazz 014 Recorded: Sant'Anna Arresi Jazz Festival XXV, Ai Confini tra Sardegna e Jazz, Sardinia, Italy, August 29, 2010
2011	
	Verona – The Cloth (Conduction® No.43) / Verona Skyscraper® (Conduction® No.46)
	Nu Bop Records (Italy) – CD, CD 09 Recorded: Verona Jazz, Teatro Romano, Verona, Italy, June 26, 1994 (No.43); Teatro Romano, Verona, Italy, June 27, 1995 (No.46)
2010	
	Nublu Orchestra conducted by Butch Morris – Live At Saalfelden Jazz Festival
	Nublu Records (US) – CD, NUB00022 Recorded: Jazz Festival Saalfelden, Austria, August 25, 2007
2007	
	Conduction® / Induction – Sheng Skyscraper (Conduction® No.135) / EMYOUESEYESEE.IT (Induction No.2/1)
	Rai Trade (Italy) – CD, RTPJ 0009 Recorded: Biennale Musica di Venezia, 47. Festival Internazionale di Musica Contemporanea *ReMix, Structures and Improvisations*, Teatro alle Tese, Venezia, Italy, September 21, 2003 (No.135); AngelicA, Festival Internazionale di Musica, sedicesimo anno *Momento Maggio*, Teatro San Leonardo, Bologna, Italy, May 14, 2006 (No.2/1)
2007	
	Butch Morris – Ensemble Laboratorio Novamusica (Conduction® 143/1 - 143/2)
	Galatina Records (Italy) – CD, CD 0701 Recorded: Teatrino Groggia, Venice, Italy, November 2, 2004 (No.143/1); Total Music Meeting, Berlinische Galerie, Berlin, Germany, November 5, 2004 (No.143/2)
2003	
	The Jump Arts Orchestra – Conducted By Lawrence "Butch" Morris (Conduction® No.117)
	Jump Arts Records (US) – CDR, limited edition, JA002 Recorded: The Brecht Forum, New York, NY, April 13, 2001
2000	
	INTERFLIGHT (Conduction® No.113)
	CDR, Limited edition, in collaboration with David Hammons. Recorded: Global Fax Festival, Palacio de Cristal del Retiro, Madrid, Spain, October 1, 2000
1999	
	Lawrence D. "Butch" Morris – ORT: Orchestra della Toscana – Holy Sea (Conduction® No.57, No.58, No.59)
	Splasc(h) Records (Italy) – CD, CDH 802-803.2 Recorded: Teatro Puccini, Firenze, February 8, 1996 (No.57: *Shopping*), Teatro degli Animosi, Carrara, Italy, February 9, 1996 (No.58: *Marble Dust*), Chiesa di San Domenico, Pistoia, Italy, February 10, 1996 (No.59: *The Devil's Music*)
1998	
	Butch Morris Conducts Berlin Skyscraper (Conduction® No.51, No.52, No.55, No.56)
	FMP Records (Germany) – CD, FMP CD 92 / 93 Recorded: Total Music Meeting, Podewil, Berlin, Germany, November 1-5, 1995
1998	
	Tit For Tat (Conduction® No.70)
	For 4 Ears Records (Switzerland) – CD, CD 927 Recorded: Fabrikjazz Zürich, Switzerland, September 29, 1996

8 Conduction Discography

1998	
Aquarius Ensemble – Live at November Music 1997 (Conduction® No.88, No.89, No.90)	
	November Music (Netherlands) – CD. Recorded: November Music Festival, Eindhoven, November 13, 1997 (No.88); Ghent, November 14, 1997 (No.89); Hertogenbosch, November 15, 1997 (No.90)

1995	
Testament: A Conduction Collection	
	New World Records (US) – CD, 80478 – 10-CD box set
(Conduction® No.50)	
	New World Records (US) – CD, 80488-2 Recorded: P3 Art and Environment, Tokyo, Japan, March 5, 1995
New World, New World (Conduction® No..41)	
	New World Records (US) – CD, 80487-2 Recorded: Opperman Music Hall, Florida State University College (not School) of Music, Florida, February 4, 1994
In Freud's Garden (Conduction® No.38) / Thread Waxing Space (Conduction® No.39) / Thread Waxing Space (Conduction® No.40)	
	New World Records (US) – CD, 80486-2 Recorded: Muffathalle, Germany, December 11, 1993 (No.38); New York, NY, November 11, 1993 (No.39); New York, NY, November 12, 1993 (No.40)
AngelicA Festival Internazionale di Musica (Conduction® No.31) / American Connection 4 (Conduction® No.35) / American Connection 4 (Conduction® No.36)	
	New World Records (US) – CD, 80485-2 Recorded: AngelicA Festival Internazionale di Musica, 3rd edition, Teatro San Leonardo, Bologna, Italy, May 16, 1993 (No.31); Antwerp, Belgium, May 26, 1993 (No.35); Amsterdam, Holland, May 27, 1993
Cherry Blossom (Conduction® No.28) / AngelicA Festival Internazionale di Musica (Conduction® No.31)	
	New World Records (US) – CD, 80484-2 Recorded: P3 Art and Environment, Tokyo, Japan, March 28, 1993 (No.28); AngelicA Festival Internazionale di Musica, 3rd edition, Teatro San Leonardo, Bologna, Italy, May 16, 1993 (No.31)
Akbank (Conduction® No.25) / Akbank II (Conduction® No.26)	
	New World Records (US) – CD, 80483-2 Recorded: Istanbul, Turkey, October 16, 1992 (No.25); October 17, 1992 (No.26)
Quinzaine De Montreal (Conduction® No..23)	
	New World Records (US) – CD, 80481-2 Recorded: The Spectrum, Montreal, Quebec, Canada, April 11, 1992
Documenta: Gloves & Mitts (Conduction® No.22)	
	New World Records (US) – CD, 80481-2 Recorded: Documenta 9, Kassel, Germany, June 14, 1992
Where Music Goes II (Conduction® No.15)	
	New World Records (US) – CD, 80480-2 Recorded: Whitney Museum of American Art at Philip Morris, New York, NY, November 15-16, 1989

1992	
Selected Soundscape No.1: Klangbrücke Bern – A Sonic Architecture (Conduction® No.19)	
	For 4 Ears Records (Switzerland) – CD, CD 305 Recorded: Kunstmuseum, Bern, Switzerland, June 13-15, 1990
1985	
Butch Morris - Current Trends In Racism in Modern America (A Work in Progress) (Conduction® No.1)	
	Sound Aspects Records (Germany) – LP, SAS 4010 (CD, SAS CD 4010 1986) Recorded: The Kitchen, New York, NY, February 1, 1985

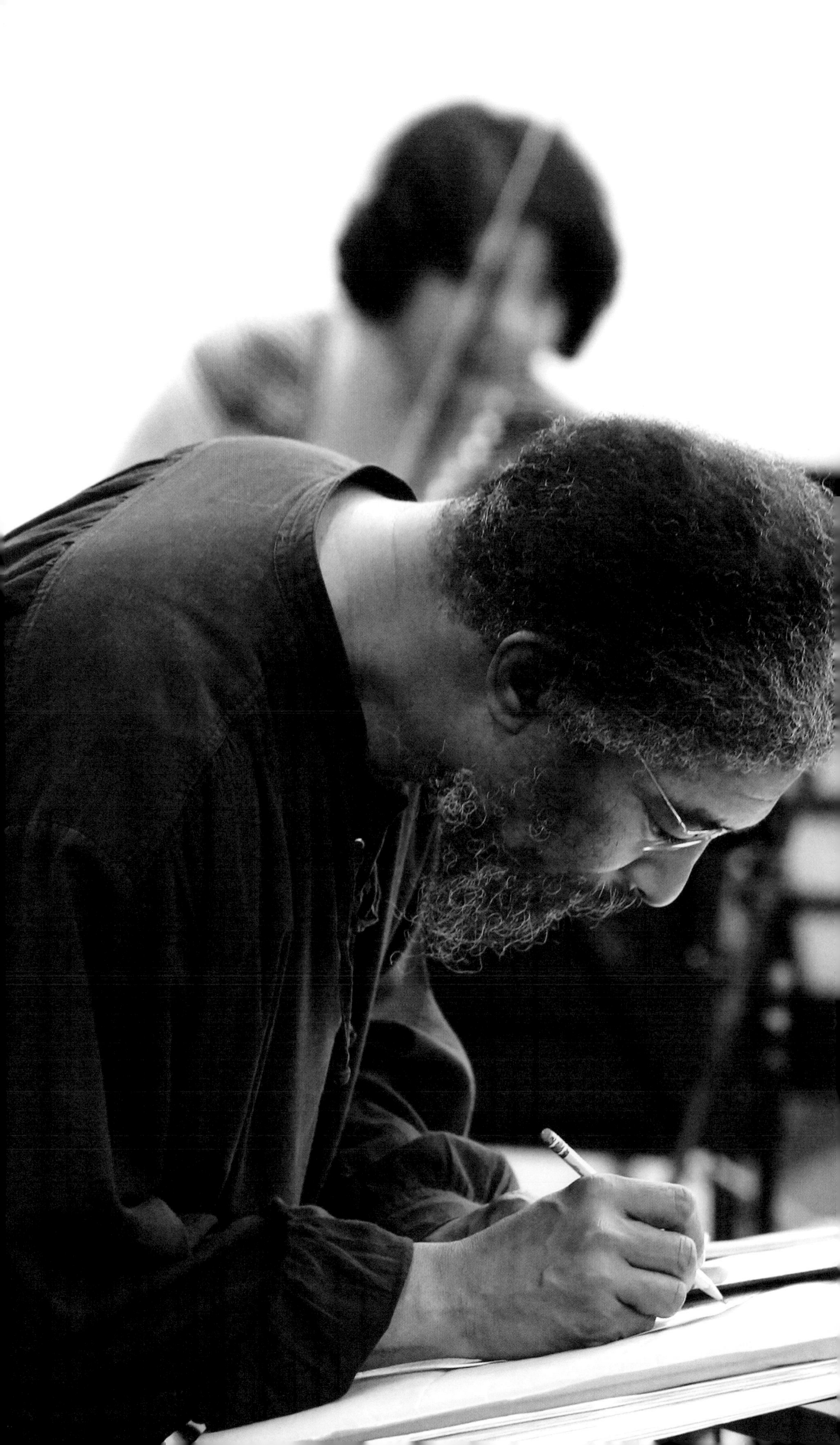

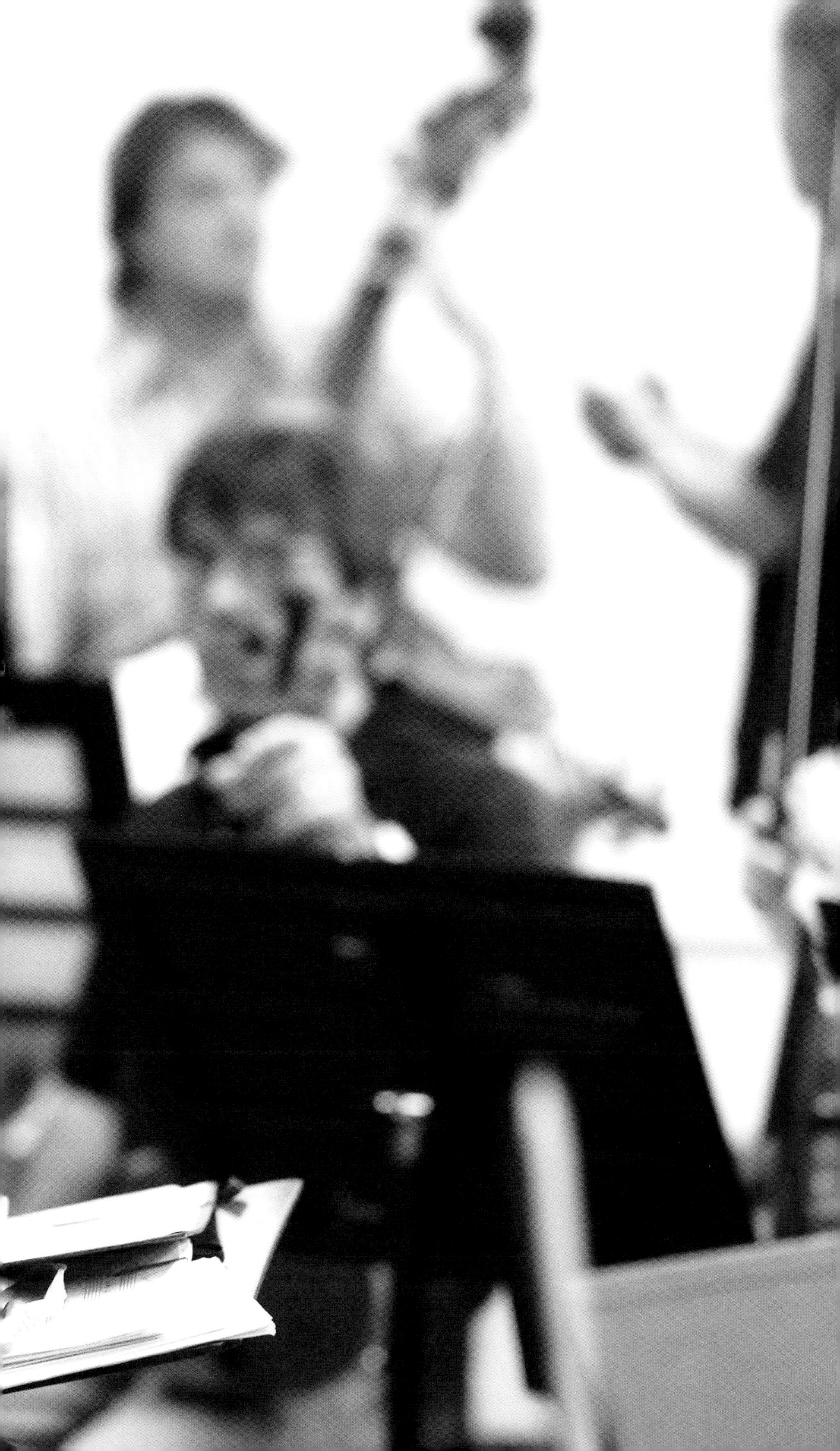

Contributors

J.A. Deane

is a multi-instrumentalist, sound designer and conductor. In the early 1980s, as trombonist in Indoor Life, a popular art/punk band from San Francisco, he pioneered the use of live-electronics, soon afterward touring the world as an electro-acoustic live-sampling percussionist with Jon Hassell. During that same period Deane became a close collaborator in Morris's Conductions, and in 1995 co-produced Morris's epic 10-CD box set *Testament* (New World Records). Deane coined the term "live-sampling," that is, recording members of an ensemble while in performance, manipulating the sound and playing back the recorded audio as part of the piece, all in real time. He is considered a master in this field.

With a career spanning four decades, Deane has an extensive background in composition for modern dance (in collaboration with his partner, the dancer/choreographer Colleen Mulvihill). He has a similarly rich history creating sound designs for the theater, working with writers/directors as diverse as Sam Shepard, Julie Hébert, Christoph Marthaler, and John Flax of Theater Grottesco. As a conductor, over the past eighteen years he has explored and applied Morris's Conduction Lexicon in performance and workshops at music festivals and conservatories all over the world. Visit jadeane.com.

Allan Graubard

is a poet, playwright, and critic who publishes internationally. He met Morris in the mid-1970s in San Francisco/Oakland, and began collaborating with him in New York in 1981 (*Music for Poets*, Newfoundland Theater). Their major works together include the book that accompanies the 10-CD set *Testament;* the opera they created together, Modette, and the evolution of a new form of performance with text and music in *Folding Space* and *Erotic Eulogy,* both performed in New York and Europe between 1983 and 2010, with Morris conducting.

Graubard's recent books include *Targets* (Anon Edition, NY, 2013), *And tell tulip the summer* (Quattro Books, Toronto, 2011) and *Invisible Heads: Surrealists in North America – An Untold Story* (Anon Edition, NY, 2011).

Contributors

Howard Mandel

is an award-winning music journalist, author of *Future Jazz* (Oxford University Press, Oxford, 1999) and *Miles Ornette Cecil – Jazz Beyond Jazz* (Routledge, New York, 2008), arts reporter for National Public Radio, and former adjunct professor at New York University. He attended Morris's Conduction no. 1, and many other of Morris's conductions, writing of what he saw and heard for *DownBeat*, the *Village Voice*, *The Wire* (UK), and other publications. Mandel is also president of the Jazz Journalists Association, and blogs at artsjournal.com/jazzbeyondjazz.

Daniela Veronesi

is assistant professor of linguistics at the Free University of Bozen-Bolzano, Italy. Her main interests include the study of social interaction, particularly in higher education and musical settings, with a specific focus on the interplay between verbal and visible semiotic resources. She has also worked on multilingualism, language biographies, metaphors, languages for special purposes, and foreign language acquisition, as documented in a number of publications in Italian, English, German, and French.

In the last decade she has collaborated with Morris as translator and interpreter, and assisted him at a number of Conduction workshops held in Italy between 2008 and 2011. Over the years, she has developed a specific interest in Conduction® and the lexicon of gestural instructions it is based on; since 2011 she has been working on a research project dedicated to the analysis of Conduction workshops (www.unibz.it).

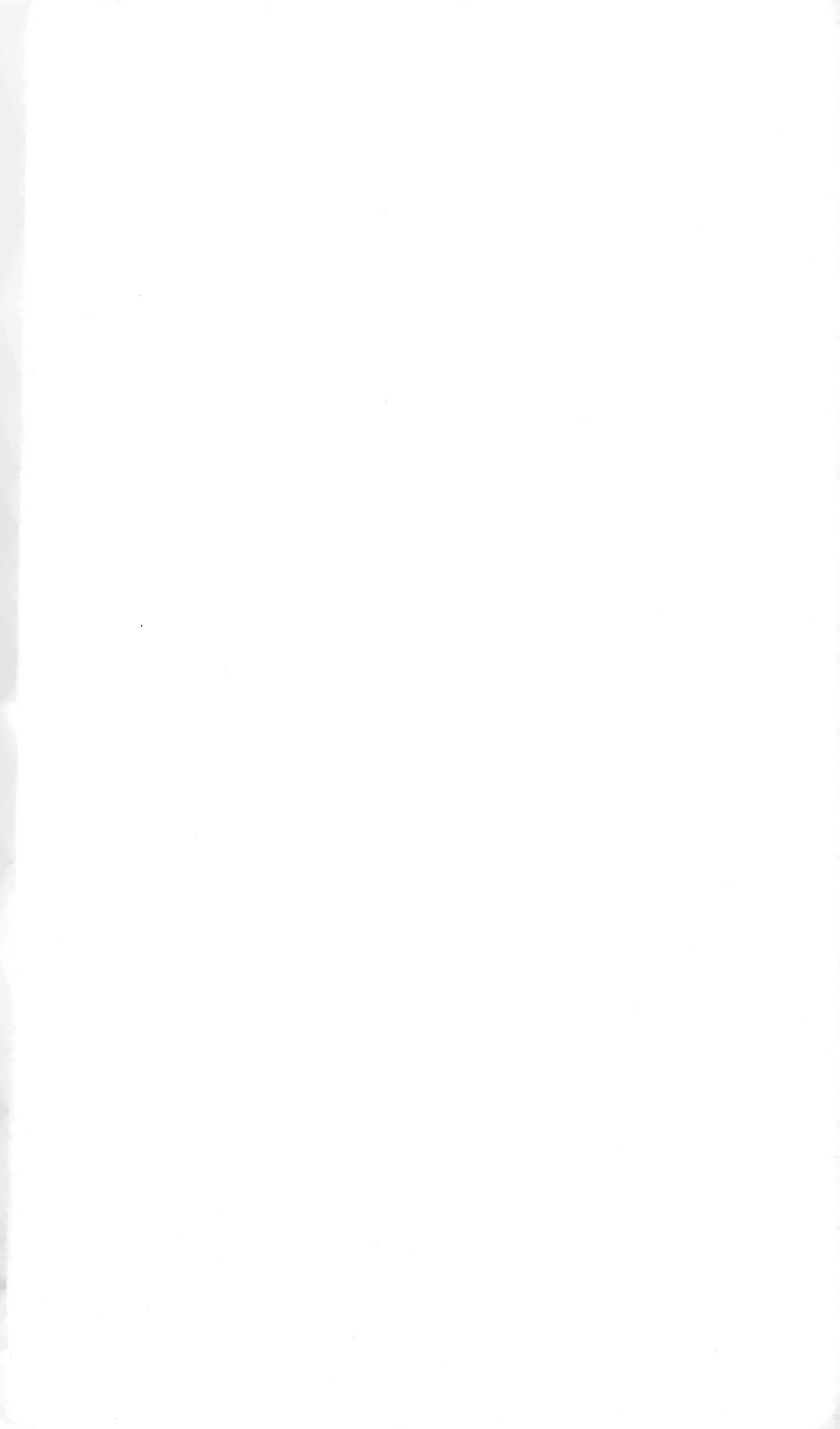

Lawrence D. "Butch" Morris

The Art of Conduction
A Conduction® Workbook

edited by **Daniela Veronesi**

Karma
with
Tilton Gallery
and
Pozitif

All rights reserved. No part of this publication may be reproduced,
stored in a retrieval system, or transmitted, in any form or by any means,
electronic, mechanical, photocopying, recording, or otherwise,
without the prior written permission of the publisher and the copyright holders.

General Editor
Daniela Veronesi

Project Coordinator
Alessandro Cassin

Editors
Daniela Veronesi and Allan Graubard (Chapters 2 and 3)
Daniela Veronesi and J.A. Deane (Chapters 4 and 5)

Book Design
Concetta Nasone and Massimo Golfieri

Drawings (Chapter 4)
Massimo Golfieri

Cover Art
David Hammons, "Concerto in Black and Blue," 2002, video still by Linda Bryant, Ace Gallery, New York.

Photographs
Luciano Rossetti: pp. 10, 37, 55, 60, 64, 70, 78, 84, 94, 102, 110, 122, 138, 150, 158, 182, 216
Massimo Golfieri: pp. 32, 40, 48, 174, 190

Materials provided courtesy of the Estate of Lawrence "Butch" Morris. Special thanks to Alexandre Morris.

Printed in Italy, C.T.S. Grafica S.r.l., Città di Castello (PG)

Published by
Karma, New York

This book was made possible through the generous support of

pozitif   TILTON GALLERY

ISBN 978-1-942607-42-7

Copyright © 2017 "Lawrence Butch Morris Legacy Project"

Except for
Foreword: © Howard Mandel
Photographs by Luciano Rossetti: Luciano Rossetti © Phocus Agency